Prepare the Way

How to Overcome Obstacles to God,
the Gospel, and the Church

Karlo Broussard

Prepare the Way

How to Overcome Obstacles to God,
the Gospel, and the Church

Catholic
Answers
Press

Published by Catholic Answers, Inc.
2020 Gillespie Way
El Cajon, California 92020
1-888-291-8000 orders
619-387-0042 fax
catholic.com

Printed in the United States of America

Cover design by eBookLaunch.com
Interior design by RussellGraphicDesign.com

978-1-68357-074-5
978-1-68357-075-2 Kindle
978-1-68357-076-9ePub

For my wife and children:
Jacqueline, Dominic, Savannah, Elijah, Catherine,
and Nathaniel

Contents

PART III

Prepare the Way for Jesus

PART IV

Prepare the Way for Christianity

PART V

Prepare the Way for the Church

Acknowledgements

I am grateful to Catholic Answers staff apologists Jimmy Akin, Tim Staples, Trent Horn, Fr. Hugh Barbour, Peggy Frye, and Michelle Arnold for all the apologetical formation that they've provided me, which went into writing this book. I am also grateful to the work of Dr. Edward Feser, from whom I derived much insight for the strategies in this book that deal with philosophical issues. I am *most* grateful to Todd Aglialoro, Catholic Answers Press director and editor, for investing so much time and effort into helping me achieve the goals that I set out to achieve with this book. If this book has any success, much will be due to his insights and suggestions.

Introduction

> A voice cries: "In the wilderness prepare the way of the
> LORD, make straight in the desert a highway for our
> God. Every valley shall be lifted up, and every moun-
> tain and hill be made low; the uneven ground shall be-
> come level, and the rough places a plain. And the glory
> of the LORD shall be revealed, and all flesh shall see it
> together, for the mouth of the LORD has spoken."
> —Isaiah 40:3–5

It was John the Baptist who prepared the way for the Lord, making straight a highway for God by preaching a message of repentance. He filled the valleys and lowered the mountains to make
an even ground for Jesus to make his appearance in history. Recognizing the importance of this ministry, Jesus said, "Truly, I
say to you, among those born of women there has risen no one
greater than John the Baptist" (Matt. 11:11).

Jesus didn't need John the Baptist. He could have done everything himself. But yet he chose to bestow upon John the
great dignity of cooperating with him in preparing a path for
his coming. And he gives *us* the same opportunity to cooperate
with him when we proclaim and defend the Faith. For, like hills
and valleys, many people face intellectual obstacles that prevent
them from encountering Jesus and the Church.

Any Catholic who does apologetics with Protestants, for instance, can point to obstacles that keep them from seriously considering the Church. For example, Protestants often get hung
up on Catholic teachings about Mary, or the Eucharist, or the
papacy. Before a positive presentation of Catholicism can begin,
it's necessary to clear away such roadblocks.

Obstacles to God

Obstacles abound for *unbelievers* as well. "How can I believe in God," they may object, "when there is so much evil in the world?"[1] No matter how many good arguments you present, they won't be open to God's existence until you deal with this first.

Others think that science is an obstacle to belief in God—that in order to be intellectually responsible they must reject God and embrace science. According to a 2011 study, this obstacle ranked third in a list of reasons why fifty-nine percent of young adult Christians disconnected themselves from church life after the age fifteen.[2]

Obstacles to Jesus

People who don't consider themselves atheists but are skeptical about Jesus face their own roadblocks to faith. For example, many can't get past the suspicion that Jesus wasn't a real historical person. Or that if he did exist, we don't know much about him because the Gospels aren't trustworthy sources of information about his life.

In the words of the late Christopher Hitchens and H.L. Mencken, "The New Testament is itself a highly dubious source,"[3] and "a helter-skelter accumulation of more or less discordant documents."[4] Why believe in Jesus if we cannot be certain that he ever claimed to be God, or that he rose from the dead to vindicate those claims?

Obstacles to Christianity

Unbelievers also have a problem with Christianity in general. They presume that Christian faith is *blind* faith—belief without reasonable evidence—and that's enough for them to discount it completely. Atheist Richard Dawkins writes, "Faith, being belief that isn't based on evidence, is the principal vice of any religion."[5]

Unbelievers are also repulsed by the idea that many Christians are hypocrites, or that religion does nothing but cause violence.

Obstacles to the Catholic Church

Unbelievers have their own beefs with the Catholic Church, different from those of Protestants (though sometimes they overlap). They may be turned off by the Church's opposition to abortion and so-called same-sex marriage. "How can the Catholic Church be Christian," so the argument goes, "when it doesn't even respect the fundamental right of women to choose or of people to marry whom they love?"[6]

Others can't look past what they perceive as superstition in Catholic piety, or Church rules, rituals, scandals, and wealth. For some people, many or all of these obstacles are present, adding up to a mountain so big that no way to the Lord can be seen over it.

Obstacles to truth

Sometimes people face an obstacle even more fundamental: the very reality of objective truth. They may say, "How can I believe in truth when so many people believe different things?" or "How can I believe in truth when it's intolerant to tell someone he's wrong?" A 2017 study identified this doubt in objective truth as a major reason why Millennials are abandoning God and Christianity.[7]

As Allan Bloom, in his influential work *The Closing of the American Mind,* observed, "There is one thing a professor can be absolutely certain of: almost every student entering the university believes, or says he believes, that truth is relative."[8]

Some unbelievers go so far as even to doubt the trustworthiness of their senses, and thus doubt whether we can know that truth exists. (As one of my college classmates once asked me, "How do you know we're not in the Matrix?" Not having any philosophical training at the time, I could only respond, "You'd know if I punched you in the mouth right now.")

Even if a person does acknowledge the existence of truth, often it is only what he considers *scientific* truth to the exclusion of *religious* truth. Like Dawkins, he believes that religious truth is purely subjective and "a betrayal of the intellect."[9] He will probably not be very receptive to the gospel unless you prepare the way of truth first.

The purpose of this book

Sometimes an obstacle is like the mountains and hills that Isaiah speaks of in the prophecy—that is to say, it's the *presence* of something that blocks the way. For example, the existence of evil blocks the way of belief in God. Sometimes the obstacle is the *absence* of something, as in the case of an atheist who has never met a genuine believer or heard a good argument for God's existence. This is analogous to the valleys in Isaiah's prophecy, where there is a great chasm separating the unbeliever from Jesus.

Jesus bestows upon us the great dignity of being his co-workers in leveling the mountains and filling the valleys. The purpose of this book is to give you strategies for carrying out that work effectively—with your friends and family members, with the stranger whom God puts in your path, and even perhaps in your own heart.

It is divided into five parts, each dealing with a particular topic: Truth, God, Jesus, Christianity, and the Catholic Church. Each short chapter addresses a particular obstacle relative to the topic and offers strategies to overcome that obstacle. An essential component of each strategy is *asking questions*: to stimulate thoughts, draw out ideas, and highlight the underlying presumptions barring the way to truth.

I hope you will find this book helpful, and I pray that you will be empowered by the Holy Spirit to be a faithful voice in the wilderness of our culture and to make straight the Lord's path.

PART I

PREPARE THE WAY FOR TRUTH

1

How can I believe in absolute truth when there is no such thing?

If you haven't seen "College Kids Say the Darndest Things," a video released by the Family Policy Institute of Washington (FPIW), check it out.[10] You will either laugh or weep.

Joseph Backholm, the executive director of FPIW, interviewed eight students from the University of Washington about so-called gender identity. Backholm, a white male of average height, asked the students what they would say if he told them he was a female. Every student was quick to say it would be okay.

Backholm then asked the students a series of questions that led to him identifying as a *six-foot-five Chinese* woman. Although a few of the students were a bit hesitant to affirm this assertion, they concluded it would be within his right to identify as he pleases.

You may be saying, "This is insane! How in the world did we get here?" The answer is, our culture has embraced *relativism*: the idea that there is no truth independent of what anyone happens to think. Something is "true," says relativism, only if it coheres with an individual or group's set of beliefs. Reality is something we *determine* rather than discover. The students in this video manifest relativism in all its glory!

Relativism is the first and biggest obstacle to belief in objective truth. It's a valley with the relativist standing on one side and the Lord standing on the other, with no way to cross

How do we bridge the gap and prepare a way for the Lord?

STRATEGY 1

Show that relativism is self-refuting.

In your first approach you want to show that relativism is self-referentially incoherent—which is just a fancy way of saying that it refutes itself. If you prove that relativism is false, then you automatically prove that objective truth exists. Consider this dialogue:

> *Q:* "You believe that there is no absolute truth, right?"

If your friend answers "yes," point out to him that there must be at least *one* absolute truth, then: the statement that there is no absolute truth. But this contradiction undermines relativism.

> *Q:* "How can something be absolutely true and
> not absolutely true at the same time and in the same
> respect?"

This belief violates the *principle of non-contradiction*, a first principle of reason. (See appendix A for a defense of the principle.) If your friend retorts that his claim is only relatively true, point out that he still is making an absolute claim—because the verb *is* always makes a statement about what is objectively real. He's saying it's absolutely true that his claim is only relatively true.

And this is the same thing as saying, "It's absolutely true that there is no absolute truth," which, as we saw, is a contradiction.

STRATEGY 2

Show that relativism makes all beliefs trivial, including the belief that relativism is true.

> *Q:* "When you say that the statement, 'There is no
> absolute truth' is relatively true, do you mean that it's
> true for you but may not be for others?"

If the relativist responds, "Yeah, that's right—it's true for me but not for others," then you can say, "Okay, so what? That doesn't tell me anything I don't already know." Since we already know that some people don't think relativism is true, the relativist's position is trivial and uninteresting.[11] Moreover, if relativism itself is just one belief among a set of personal beliefs for the relativist, then it is nothing more than a personal taste or preference.

> Q: "If relativism is just your personal taste, like your flavor preference for ice cream, then why should we be concerned with your claim that truth is relative?"

Personal tastes or preferences have no bearing on reality. They are just reports about what a person happens to like or dislike. And there is nothing more that we can say to that than, "Thanks for sharing."

STRATEGY 3

Show that relativism leads to absurdities.

In the aforementioned video, the interviewer takes the logic of relativism to areas where its absurdity can be made manifest: height, ethnicity, and sex. For some, these categories will be sufficient. If not we keep moving on and apply the logic to other categories.

> Q: "What if someone says he is a cat? Does that make him a cat? Or what if a person identifies as being disabled when he is able-bodied? Does that make it true for him?"

Lest your friend think you're off your rocker and that such things would never happen, consider the story of twenty-year-old Nano from Oslo, Norway, a young woman who claimed to be a cat trapped in a human body.[12] This phenomenon is a real psychological disorder called *species dysphoria* or *species dysmorphia*. It manifests itself in either a person thinking of himself as an actual animal or excessive concern that his body is of the wrong species.

Or take Chloe Jennings-White, a Ph.D. with degrees from Cambridge and Stanford, who desires to be a paraplegic and identifies as "disabled."[13]

> Q: "If it's true that a man is a woman because he says that he is, then why can't a woman be a cat, or a healthy person be a paraplegic, for the same reason?"

If we have to accept that someone who looks like a five-foot-nine white male *is* a six-foot-five Chinese woman because he claims to be, since truth is relative, we likewise must say that Nano *is* a cat—whether she has fur and claws or not—and Chloe *is* a paraplegic, even though her legs work fine.

Relativism can't differentiate between a man rejecting his genetic makeup for the sake of redefining his gender and a woman rejecting her genetic makeup for the sake of redefining her species or a woman rejecting her healthy physical condition for the sake of being disabled. If the logic of relativism demands we accept transgenderism, then it also demands we accept transpeciesism, transableism, and whatever other transism comes our way.

A final point to make is that relativism makes morality an illusion, and thus makes the accusation of wrongdoing impossible.

> Q: "If there are no moral beliefs or opinions that we can say are absolutely true, then how can there be any such thing as morality? Wouldn't it be the case that all moral beliefs and opinions are reduced to just that—beliefs and opinions?"

In the mental framework of relativism, there can be no moral belief that is a *true* belief. Morality is reduced to mere personal codes or preferences. No one can claim that there are any behaviors that are always right or wrong for everyone.

Q: "If right and wrong were a matter of personal definition, then how could you say that murder is wrong? If the murderer believes his actions are good for him, who are you to say otherwise?"

As philosopher Peter Kreeft put it:

He [moral absolutist] alone can say to a Hitler, "You and your whole social order are wrong and wicked and deserve to be destroyed." The relativist could only say, "Different strokes for different folks, and I happen to hate your strokes and prefer mine, that's all."[14]

If your friend replies, "No, murder is wrong because it hurts someone else," then he has asserted a moral absolute and ceased to be a relativist. And perhaps he is ready to take a step forward in his thinking.

Q: "What choice will you make? Will you keep your relativism and give up saying that murder (or rape or racism) is wrong? Or will you give up relativism so that you can confidently identify good and evil when you see it?"

THE WAY PREPARED: Absolute truth does exist.

Once any theory of knowledge makes the claim to effectively block any access to time and place transcending objective truth, it immediately turns back upon itself and self-destructs, like a snake devouring its own tail.[15]
    —W. Norris Clarke (Catholic philosopher)

2

How can I believe in truth when people believe so many different things?

If there is one thing you learn when you travel and encounter other cultures—or even visit your local college campus—it is that people have different beliefs about reality. As philosopher Jesse Prinz puts it, "One group's good can be another group's evil."[16]

To demonstrate, Prinz lists a series of practices about which cultures differ in their moral evaluation, including blood sports, public torture and execution, body modification, and attitudes toward sex and marriage. He then argues that the explanation for such variation is that absolute truth doesn't exist—at least when it comes to morals. "If morality were objective," he writes, "shouldn't we see greater consensus?"[17]

Whether this *argument from differing beliefs* is used to undermine objective truth in general or moral truth in particular, it is an obstacle that blocks the way of the Lord.

STRATEGY 1

Show that the argument from differing beliefs is a *non sequitur*.

Your first approach shows how the conclusion, "There is no absolute truth," doesn't logically follow from the premise, "People differ in their beliefs." Philosophers have a term for this type of argument: *non sequitur*, which is Latin for "it does not follow."

If you can demonstrate the lack of logical connection between the two statements, then you can show how the argument from differing beliefs fails. You can do this by taking the logic embedded in the argument and applying it to other things people disagree on.

> *Q:* "If you and I disagree about the shape of the earth—you say it's flat and I say it's spherical—does that mean there is no shape to the earth?"

In order for your friend to be reasonable he has to answer no, since if the earth had no shape we wouldn't be here! But of course he wouldn't say such a thing.

Consider another example. Ask your friend to imagine that you are driving together down a long stretchy road in the Arizona desert, and you see what you think is water on the road up ahead. But your unbelieving friend says, "That's not water; it's just a mirage."

> *Q:* "Does the fact that we disagree about whether there is water up ahead on the road mean there is no objective truth about the matter?"

I think it's safe to say your friend will see that the answer is no. It's either water or not water; a mirage or not a mirage.

You are now in a position to connect the dots.

- Just as the conclusion "There is no absolute truth about the shape of the earth" doesn't follow from the premise "We disagree about the shape of the earth" . . . .

- . . . and the conclusion "There is no absolute truth about whether there is water on the road" doesn't follow from the premise "We disagree about whether there is water on the road" . . . .

- . . . so too the conclusion "There is no absolute truth" doesn't follow from the premise "People disagree in their beliefs."

Since there is no logical connection between the statements, "No absolute truth," and "People believe different things," the argument from differing beliefs fails to justify relativism.

STRATEGY 2

Show that the argument from differing beliefs begs the question.

Begging the question does not mean to raise or lead to a question; rather, it is a logical fallacy in which a conclusion is assumed true without evidence other than the conclusion itself. The current objection begs the question because it *assumes* that universal agreement is the criterion for truth when in fact that is the issue being debated.

> *Q:* "Okay, you're saying that there is no absolute truth because there is no universal agreement over what's true. Does this mean that universal agreement is necessary for there to be absolute truth?"

To stay true to his argument, your friend has to answer yes. This puts you in a position to begin exposing the fallacy. Notice that the belief that universal agreement is necessary for absolute truth implies that there is no objective truth independent of what people happen to think—for if objective truth existed, then it wouldn't matter if everyone agreed or not.

But to imply that there is no objective truth is the *essence of relativism*.

By making this argument, your friend assumes what he is trying to prove—namely, that truth is relative. The argument amounts to, "Truth is relative because truth is relative."

STRATEGY 3

Show that the argument, when it pertains to morality, falsely assumes that there is no substantial uniformity in moral principles and that where differences do occur it's in the moral principles themselves rather than factual judgments.

Prinz argues that there are no absolute moral truths because of the diverse moral practices that exist among cultures. The key to this strategy is pointing out that there actually is great uniformity in moral principles across times and cultures, and where there are differences it's usually due to judgments about the facts. With regard to cross-cultural agreement, Peter Kreeft and Ronald Tacelli write,

> [E]ven opinions about right and wrong are not wholly relative to cultures. No culture ever existed which taught a *totally* different set of values. For example, honesty, justice, courage, cooperation, wisdom, self-control and hope were never all thought to be evil, and lying, theft, murder, rape, cowardice, folly, addiction, despair and selfishness were never all thought to be good.[18]

To use an example from Francis Beckwith and Gregory Koukl's book *Relativism: Feet Firmly Planted in Mid-Air,* seventeenth-century Hudson Bay tribes believed it noble to have your children strangle you to death when you became old and incapable of supporting yourself by your own labor. The idea that dying for the sake of the welfare of the group is a noble act is something that all cultures share. Where cultures differ is in judging *what* actually counts as a noble death on behalf of the group.

Another example that Beckwith and Koukl use to illustrate this point is the belief in India that killing and eating cows is immoral. At first glance it would seem that we have conflicting moral principles (unless you think hamburgers are murder), but in reality it is merely a difference in what we think about cows. In India they don't eat cows because they consider cows sacred. In Western cultures we do not. So the moral principle is the same—respect what is sacred—but our understanding of the facts is different.

Once you show that there is great uniformity among cultures in moral principles, and that where differences appear it's usually due to factual judgments, then the obstacle of differing moral beliefs disappears. Differing beliefs may make it hard to arrive at a correct moral judgment, but it doesn't mean absolute moral truths don't exist.

THE WAY PREPARED: Differing beliefs make knowing the truth difficult, but they don't prove that no objective truth exists.

> *People seek in different ways to shape a "philosophy" of their own . . . . What inspires [this] is the desire to reach the certitude of truth and the certitude of its absolute value.*[19]
> —Pope St. John Paul II

How can I believe in truth when it's intolerant to say someone is wrong?

In *Revenge of the Sith,* Obi Wan Kenobi tells Anakin Skywalker, "Only a Sith deals in absolutes." Today's enemies of truth say the same thing: anyone who believes in absolute truth is a bad guy. "We should accept everyone's opinions as equally valid," say the relativists, "and since you absolutists don't, you're intolerant."

This idea has influenced the minds of college students. A young woman from the video mentioned in chapter one told the interviewer, "I feel like that's not my place, as like, another human, to say someone is wrong or to draw lines or boundaries."

The charge of intolerance is a major obstacle that stands in the way of accepting the reality of objective truth. No one wants to be on the Dark Side.

How do we lay low this mountain that blocks the path of Jesus?

STRATEGY 1

Show that the argument from tolerance is self-defeating for a relativist.

You can show that the argument from tolerance is self-defeating for a relativist in two ways. First, it implies an absolute truth.

Q: "Is it absolutely true that we should be tolerant?"

If your friend wants to stick with his argument, he has to answer yes. But notice this answer implies that there is at least one absolute truth—namely, everyone ought to be tolerant.

Point out to your friend that objective truths cannot exist within the mental framework of relativism.

> Q: "How can you believe that it's absolutely true that we should be tolerant when your relativistic worldview doesn't allow for absolutes?"

Once you get your friend in this position, you can challenge him to make a choice: either give up relativism for the sake of tolerance or reject the objective good of tolerance in order to keep relativism. But he can't have it both ways.

The second way this argument is self-defeating for the relativist is that it undermines tolerance itself.

> Q: "What if someone believes that intolerance is a good thing? What if he says that in his culture it's good to be intolerant of people who disagree? In that case isn't it right for him?"

Remind your friend that relativism holds that a belief is true if it corresponds to the set of beliefs of an individual or a society. In which case we would have to say that someone who believes that intolerance is a good thing is true for him shouldn't be criticized. Is your friend okay with that?

> Q: "How can relativism promote tolerance when its framework allows for the acceptance of an individual's belief that intolerance is a good thing?"

Notice how relativism doesn't promote tolerance—it actually works against it. The relativist thinks relativism is the guardian of tolerance, but it turns out relativism is tolerance's undertaker. A culture that embraces relativism is fertile soil for a tyrant to rear his ugly head. It is a green light for tyranny.

STRATEGY 2

Expose the relativist's misunderstanding of tolerance.

You can start your second strategy by getting your friend to express what *he* means by tolerance with a question like this:

> Q: "Are you saying that absolutists are intolerant for saying someone's belief is wrong, and that in order to be tolerant we must accept everyone's belief equally?"

Your friend has to answer yes if he is to hold to his argument. You are now in a position to point out that this is a misunderstanding of tolerance. One way to do this is to show the absurdity of identifying tolerance with believing everyone's belief to be true:

> Q: "What sense can be made out of saying that we 'tolerate' people who share our own views? Do you tolerate other people who embrace relativism as a worldview?"

When you put it like this, it becomes clear how it's meaningless to speak of tolerance when people agree on something. We don't tolerate people's beliefs that we agree with; we tolerate people's beliefs that we disagree with. But to disagree with someone's belief means to think he's *wrong*. Thinking someone is wrong, therefore, belongs to the meaning of tolerance. This shows the incoherence of your relativist friend's charge.

> Q: "How can absolutists be intolerant for saying someone is wrong when you can't be tolerant unless you first think someone is wrong?"

Your friend's argument from tolerance probably stems from an assumption that absolutists coerce people (physically, emotionally, or psychologically) into believing things their way. But assure him that it's not belief in absolute truth itself that leads to the violation of a person's freedom; rather, it is the misapprehension of the truth about the dignity of a human being. And most absolutists, especially those of the Christian stripe, believe it's *absolutely* wrong to coerce someone (physically, emotionally, or psychologically) to acknowledge a belief to be true.

STRATEGY 3

Show how the relativist is inconsistent in applying his understanding of tolerance.

Even if for argument's sake we grant tolerance to mean you can't say that someone else is wrong, your friend is not applying that principle to himself.

> Q: "Am I wrong for believing other people's beliefs are wrong?"

For your friend to be consistent with his argument, he has to answer yes. But in doing so he is saying *that you are wrong*—the very thing he said no one should do.

> Q: "Why is it that I can't say someone's belief is wrong, but you can?"

Point out to your friend that if he thinks intolerance means saying someone's belief is wrong, then he's intolerant for saying your belief in absolute truth is wrong. He ends up embracing the very thing he says he despises.

THE WAY PREPARED: To claim to know the truth doesn't make you an intolerant person, since tolerance necessarily involves judging a belief contrary to yours as wrong.

> *The proposition that we ought to tolerate the views of others, or that it is right not to interfere with others . . . bears all the marks of a non-relative account of moral rightness.*[20]
> —Tom L. Beauchamp (American philosopher)

4

How can I believe that we can know truth when we can't trust our senses?

Both Aristotle and St. Thomas Aquinas taught that our knowledge of the truth comes first from our senses.[21] This is something that seems true in our common human experience. We go about our everyday lives trusting that our senses give us reliable information.

But what if our senses were not reliable? After all, sometimes they deceive us. For example, at a distance a man looks shorter than he actually is. A stick in the water looks bent when it actually is not.

As the seventeenth-century French philosopher René Descartes argued, if our senses at times have deceived us, and it is never prudent to trust completely that which can deceive us, then we ought not to trust our senses.[22] If our senses have deceived us before, how do we know our senses are not deceiving us now?

Some skeptics, following the legacy of Descartes, attempt to undermine the trustworthiness of our senses by saying perhaps everything we perceive isn't real but is merely an illusion caused by a malignant being manipulating our sensory powers. Or perhaps, once again as Descartes argued, our experiences are merely dreams. Ask yourself the question, "How do I know I'm not dreaming right now?"

This lack of trust in the senses is like a dry-rotted rope bridge crossing a gaping valley. Our Lord, bearing the gift of truth, will not be able to cross it. How can we bolster the bridge?

STRATEGY 1

Show that the apparent deception is not in our sensory powers but in our judgments about the way things are.

Your first strategy can start with the example of the man who appears small at a distance and then big when close up.

> *Q:* "How can your senses be deceiving you when they are reporting exactly what they perceive—namely, the appearance of a small man and then the appearance of a tall man?"

Point out to your friend that this is not deception. The sense of sight relays the appearance of a small man at a distance, and then the appearance of a big man when seen close up—that's what you see. As the philosopher D.Q. McInerny writes, "This is the sense of sight functioning just as it should, in order to give me a proper knowledge of distance."[23] Error comes in only if your friend makes the judgment, "That man *is* small and then *becomes* big." Do you see how truth and falsity do not reside in sensory perception but in the act of judging that perception?

A second way that you can show that deception doesn't reside in our sensory powers themselves is to point out how often the apparent deception is only due to *one* sensory power. It's often the case that in order to test whether one sense is deceiving us, we must use another.

> *Q:* "When you see a crooked stick partially in the water, how do you determine if it really is crooked or not?"

Your friend should agree that he can make the correct judgment that the stick is straight by employing another sensory power: touch. And he must trust this sensory power in order to make the proper judgment. If he couldn't trust any sensory power, then he couldn't judge the stick to be straight even if he picked it up out of the water. He would have to conclude either that the stick changed shape when removed from the water, or that the stick has no shape at all because the stick is merely an illusion. But he's unlikely to think either of those things.

A similar line of reasoning applies to Descartes's example of the man appearing small at a distance and then large when up close. If your friend couldn't trust any sensory power, then he couldn't judge the man to be a normal size when he finally touches and sees him up close. The man either would have changed sizes as he approached your friend or his size would have been an illusion all together. But as in the stick's case, it's unlikely he's going to believe either of those things.

Furthermore, we only think that a man's apparent small stature when viewed at a distance is unusual because we trust our previous sensory experience of how tall the man actually is, or how tall men in general are. As Ralph McInerny notes, "[Descartes] must trust his senses in order to doubt them."[24]

So, apparent sensory deceptions are not good reasons to doubt the trustworthiness of our senses. We can trust them in our quest for truth.

STRATEGY 2

Show how it's unreasonable to think our waking is dreaming.

Your second strategy must address the objection raised from dreams. Taking their cue from Descartes, radical skeptics attempt to undermine trust in the senses by asking, "How do you know you're not dreaming right now?" I think we can respond in two ways.

First, since we experience ourselves being awake your friend must shoulder the burden of proof and give reasons why we should doubt that experience.

> Q: "Since I experience myself being awake and not dreaming, what good reasons can you give me to think otherwise? What evidence suggests that I am in a dream state?"

Don't let your friend just make an assertion. Demand that he give good reasons to believe we're not awake. Like Descartes, most skeptics cannot.

A second way we can respond to the "dream objection" is to show its incoherence. Consider that in order to determine if our current experience is a dream state we would have to be able to know what it *means* to be dreaming. We would have to be able to *identify* what a dream state is. But this causes a problem for the skeptic: we can't identify a dream state unless we're able to compare it to our waking consciousness.

> *Q:* "How could I know if I'm dreaming unless I know what it means to be awake? And how could I ever know what it means to be awake if my experience of being awake is a dream?"

Notice that it's incoherent to conjecture that waking is actually dreaming. If our waking were dreaming, there would be no possible way to even talk of dreaming because we would never know what dreaming or waking is—they both become unintelligible. As the philosopher Kenneth Gallagher explains,

> It would be literally nonsensical to ask: how do I know that waking is not what I ordinarily mean by dreaming, because if it were, I wouldn't know what I ordinarily mean by dreaming.[25]

Therefore, the thought experiment that considers our awakened state as a dream fails; it's certainly no good reason to doubt the trustworthiness of our senses as a source of truth.

STRATEGY 3

Show how the possibility of deception by a malignant being is not a good reason to doubt the trustworthiness of our senses.

Recall that some skeptics, following again in the footsteps of Descartes, argue that our senses are untrustworthy because our perceptions could be the product of some powerful and evil being manipulating us. Maybe we *are* in the Matrix after all! How do we respond to this?

First, just because it's *not logically impossible* that we are being deceived by a malignant power doesn't mean it's *plausible.* Plausibility requires good reasons for thinking something to be the case. Again, it's not enough to throw out this fantastic possibility; there has to be evidence for it.

> *Q:* "What good reasons can you give me to think my current experience is only an illusion being created by a malignant being?"

As with the dream objection, skeptics tend not to give good reasons to think our current experience of reality is other than what it is. Your friend probably won't, either.

A second way you can respond is to show how the only possible way to settle the question is to use the very sensory faculties that are being called into question.

> *Q:* "Tell me what powers you would use to reflect on whether your sensory powers are an illusion or not? Wouldn't you have to use the very powers your calling into question? For example, wouldn't you be using your sensory powers, like imagination and sense memory, to reflect upon whether the things that you've sensed in the past are real or not?"

As these questions show, it's impossible to reflect upon our sensory faculties apart from their activities. Referring to the broader category of our cognitive faculties, of which our sense powers are a part, philosopher Peter Coffey sums up the critique in this way:

> [C]ognitive faculties cannot be tested or examined in

themselves and abstracting from their activities: whatever
we know or can know about the nature of the mind and
its faculties we can know only through their activities:
there is no other channel of information open to us.[26]

Point out to your friend that if doubting our sensory faculties
presupposes their use, then there is no way to question their validity.
Finally, you can show how the objection is self-refuting.

> Q: "If it's possible that we're being deceived, then
> wouldn't it also be true that any evidence we have for
> this could be just another deception?"

Notice how the objection pulls the rug out from underneath
its feet. It allows for the possibility that we're being deceived in
everything, including the reasons that we might have for believing a malignant being is deceiving us. But if we can't even trust
the evidence that would lead us to this conclusion, then there
can be no trustworthy way to know it or demonstrate it. You
can't trust anything to be real if it's possible that *everything* is
an illusion. The malignant-being objection, therefore, gives no
good reason to doubt the trustworthiness of our senses, and thus
no good reason to doubt our ability to know the truth.

THE WAY PREPARED: Our senses are reliable in our pursuit
of objective truth.

> *Nothing is in the intellect that was not first in the senses.*[27]
> —St. Thomas Aquinas

5

How can I believe in religious truth when science is the only reliable source of truth?

In a 2013 Cambridge Union Society debate with Rowan Williams, the former archbishop of Canterbury, popular atheist Richard Dawkins claimed that religion is "a betrayal of the intellect."[28] He asserted that appealing to God to explain the universe is "a phony substitute for an explanation," and "peddles false explanations where real explanations could have been offered."[29] For Dawkins, *science*—repeatable and verifiable to our eyes—is the only thing that counts as a real explanation.

This belief is called *scientism*, and it is a serious obstacle to the Lord's gift of truth—a mountain, not a hill. How can an unbeliever be persuaded by a philosophical argument for God's existence if he doesn't think philosophy is a rational form of inquiry? The answer is he can't. So we must prepare the way.

STRATEGY 1

Show that scientism is self-refuting.

There are two ways to show that scientism is self-refuting. First, explain how the statement, "Scientific knowledge is the only legitimate form of knowledge," is itself not scientific knowledge—that is to say, we cannot determine the truth-value of this statement using the scientific method.

Q: "With what sense can we observe the truth of this

statement? Or what scientific tests can you perform to prove it?"

The absurdity of these questions shows that the truth-value of scientism is not empirically verifiable or quantifiably measurable, and thus not subject to scientific inquiry. We cannot know whether scientism is true or false using the scientific method. But this causes a serious problem for the believer in scientism: it means that scientism is not real knowledge.

> Q: "If science can't verify the truth of scientism, then
> how can scientism be real knowledge? And if it's not
> real knowledge, why would you believe it?"

A second way to show that scientism is self-refuting is by explaining how scientism undermines science as a rational form of inquiry. Consider that science *presupposes* various philosophical assumptions that are not subject to scientific verification—for example, that there is an external world outside the minds of scientists, that the world consists of cause-and-effect patterns, and the human intellect is capable of uncovering these patterns.

> Q: "In view of scientism, how can science be a
> legitimate form of rational inquiry if its presupposed
> assumptions are not the product of scientific inquiry?"

Those who profess scientism seek to exalt science, but it actually undermines science. Your friend has to make a choice: accept scientism and reject science, or reject scientism and keep science.

STRATEGY 2

Show that scientism confuses methodology with ontology.

The believer in scientism confuses methodology (the method we use to discover reality) with ontology (reality itself). Once the confusion is corrected, the obstacle shrinks.

You can begin by drawing out the principle that scientism assumes. People who think that science is the only rational form of inquiry do so because they assume that what science cannot detect doesn't exist. They view such things as mere superstition or imaginative constructs.[30] But this line of reasoning is fallacious.

Consider the following scenario.[31] Let's say we set out to find plastic cups on the beach, and to do so we are going to use a metal detector. We spend all day scanning the beach, and lo and behold we come up empty—we don't detect any plastic cups.

> Q: "Is it reasonable to conclude that plastic cups
> aren't real because the metal detector can't detect
> plastic cups?"

Of course your friend will see that the metal detector's failure to detect plastic cups says nothing about whether or not plastic cups exist. It's simply a result of the limitations of method.

Now you are in a position to make the application to God and science.

> Q: "If it's not reasonable to conclude that plastic
> cups don't exist because the metal detector can't
> detect plastic cups, then isn't it also unreasonable
> to conclude that God doesn't exist because science
> can't detect God?"

Hopefully your friend will see the flow of the logic and answer yes. If your friend doesn't see the connection, you might have to go through the example again.

Our inability to detect God using science says nothing about whether he exists, but merely reveals the limitations of science: it can only be used to discover those things empirically verifiable and quantifiably measurable. In order to arrive at knowledge of the things that science can't detect, such as God, we must use other methods, such as philosophy and/or divine revelation.

To say otherwise, to claim that whatever we can't know by science isn't real, is to let the method dictate what is real rather than letting reality dictate the proper method for studying it.

STRATEGY 3

Show that scientism undermines the reality of the human mind.

A third way of helping your friend overcome the obstacle of scientism comes from the philosopher Edward Feser, who argues that scientism is unsustainable because it leads to the denial of the human mind.[32] And without the human mind, there can be no argument for scientism.

Scientism says that anything that cannot be empirically verified or quantifiably measured is not real. But, Feser points out, the *mind is not subject to empirical verification and is non-quantifiable.* The mental activities that occur even in the practice of science, such as the formulation of hypotheses, the weighing of evidence, technical concepts, and the construction of cause and effect patterns cannot be described in the language of mathematics. There is no microscope or telescope that can show us the existence of mental *thoughts*, although some machines are able to detect the *effects* that thoughts can have on brain activity. Therefore, on the grounds of scientism, the mind cannot be real.

> Q: "How can you argue for scientism when such argumentation presupposes the very thing scientism logically denies: the mind?"

If your friend does not want to go that far, he must reject scientism. But if he chooses to follow the logic and reject the mind outright, perhaps viewing human thoughts as mere physical processes of the brain, you must press him to see the absurdity of the conclusion, and thus that scientism is unreasonable.

STRATEGY 4

Show that even though science is not the right tool for detecting God, it does give us some knowledge that would make belief in God reasonable.

Modern cosmology gives evidence that the universe is finely tuned to allow life to develop. And since chance fails as a reasonable explanation for such fine-tuning, so the argument goes, one is left with the hypothesis of a transcendent intelligence as the most plausible.

One example of this fine-tuning is the numerical values of the universal constants, which are those fixed numerical quantities used in the equations of physics and that control the laws of nature. For example, in the equation $E=MC^2$, C is the constant for the speed of light (approximately 186,000 miles per second).

The oddity of these constants is that they could have had *any* numerical quantity at the Big Bang, higher or lower, but they just so happened to have the exact value needed in order for our universe to house life—from the simplest to the most complex (you and me).

For example, if the values of the gravitational constant or the weak force constant varied higher or lower by one part in 10^{50} (.00000000000000000000000000000000000000000000000000 01), the universe would have either exploded in its initial expansion or collapsed into a black hole. Suffice to say that if this happened there would be no life.[33] This is just one among many examples that are too numerous to list here.[34]

The same type of fine-tuning exists for the initial conditions of the universe, such as the amount of matter and energy present at the Big Bang that is optimal for the evolution of life. One example is the level of entropy. *Entropy* is basically the measurement of disordered energy within a physical system. The more ordered a system is, the lower the entropy; the more disordered, the higher the entropy. The universe needs low entropy for life to develop.

According to the calculations of Oxford University emeritus professor Roger Penrose, the odds against the ordered energy (low entropy) at the beginning of the universe were $10^{10^{123}}$ to one.[35] That degree of improbability is virtually beyond our comprehension. If you wrote this number with a single exponent, it would be 10 with the exponent's number being a one with 123 zeroes behind it! That number is impossible to write out without an exponent; in fact, Penrose says, there would be more zeroes in it than there are particles in the entire universe.[36] That's a BIG number.

Compare it with the odds of getting dealt a royal flush fifty straight times in a poker game. The odds for *one* royal flush are around one in 650,000. But to make things simpler, let's suppose it's one in a million $(1/10^6)$. By this number, the odds of getting fifty straight royal flush hands by pure chance would be $1/10^{300}$. Despite how incredibly improbable this is, the odds of getting dealt fifty straight royal flushes *every day for the rest of your life* are still incalculably better than the probability of low entropy being present at the beginning of the universe.

How can we explain these finely tuned universal constants and initial conditions? Here's something to get your friend thinking:

> *Q:* "Would you believe me if I told you I was dealt fifty straight royal flush hands in a game of poker last night by pure chance?"

No one would believe this. You're now in a position to drive the point home:

> *Q:* "If you think it's unreasonable to believe the highly improbable event of being dealt fifty straight royal flush hands by pure chance, then wouldn't it also be unreasonable to believe that the vastly more

improbable event of the universal constants and initial
conditions having the values they needed to have for
life to develop happened by pure chance?"

Our experience of *intelligence* being the source of events that
are extremely improbable gives us reason to believe that the
improbability of the fine-tuning of the universe also has a de-
signing intelligence as its source. And since we're talking about
the beginning of the universe (the beginning of time and physical reality), such an intelligent designer would be beyond the
material world. This doesn't prove God as classically defined
(absolute being, omnipotent, omniscient, eternal, etc.), but it
does make belief in a transcendent god at least reasonable on
scientific grounds.

Your friend may attempt to explain the fine-tuning evidence
with an appeal to the *multiverse theory*, since positing more uni-
verses allows for a higher probability of getting a universe suited
for life. Yet if the multiverse theory were true, there couldn't
be an infinite number of tries to get the desired result. According to the 2003 Borde-Vilenkin-Guth theorem,[37] the multiverse
would have needed a beginning. That puts your friend in the
same predicament that he started out with: the need for an intelligent designer.

The multiverse explanation also just pushes the problem back
one step. All multiverse hypotheses require fine-tuning in their
initial conditions. Physicist Paul Davies explains: "[The multiverse cannot be] a complete and closed account of all physical
existence [because the] meta-laws that pervade the multiverse
and spawn specific bylaws on a universe-by universe basis . . .
remain unexplained."[38]

Q: "How can the multiverse ultimately explain the
problem of fine-tuning when its fine-tuning needs an
explanation as well?"

The multiverse theory, therefore, is insufficient for avoiding the designer hypothesis, and theism stands as a credible option even on scientific grounds.

THE WAY PREPARED: Scientific knowledge is not the only real form of knowledge.

> *Science can say something about everything, but in fact very little about most things as long as one thinks that the words "what," "why," "for what purpose," "morally good or bad" are not taken for mere words.*[39]
> —Stanley Jaki, O.S.B.

PART II

PREPARE THE WAY FOR GOD

6

How can I believe in God when there are no good arguments for his existence?

If you are a regular listener to the "Why Are You an Atheist?" edition of *Catholic Answers Live*, you know that the most common reason atheists and agnostics give to justify their unbelief is that they have not heard any good arguments for God.

But when they're prodded about which arguments they have considered, it becomes clear that most haven't seriously looked at *any*. And if they have, it's never the traditional arguments put forward by people of the likes of St. Thomas Aquinas. For those atheists and agnostics who have considered theistic arguments, it's often either the *ontological argument*[40] from St. Anselm or the *Kalam argument*[41] made popular by Christian apologist William Lane Craig.

An examination of these arguments goes beyond our scope here, but suffice to say that both have flaws that make them ultimately unsatisfying to many atheists.

For this reason, and because you might not have an opportunity to present more than one argument to your friend, let's limit ourselves to what some call the *existential argument* of Thomas Aquinas. Rather than following our common pattern of strategies for preparing the way, we'll consider the argument as a single strategy and divide it into several steps.

STEP 1

Establish that things we experience, like a tree, have an *act of being* that distinguishes them from nothing.

Our first step is to consider the existence of something mundane, such as a tree. Assuming we are not being manipulated by an evil being (see chapter four), when we look at the tree we notice it exists. There is something to the tree that distinguishes it from nothing.

> Q: "Assuming you agree with me that the tree exists,
> what do you think distinguishes it from nothing?"

Your friend probably will give you a blank stare, but that's okay. Just get him to agree that without something to distinguish the tree from nothing, it would be identical to nothing—for wherever there is no difference (nothing to distinguish one thing from another) there is identity. But we perceive that the tree *is* distinct from nothing. Therefore, it must have something that distinguishes it from nothing. Aquinas calls it *esse* (Latin, "to be"), the act of being—that by which a thing exists.[42]

STEP 2

Establish that things of our experience, like a tree, do not have the act of being by nature.

The tree's act of being (existence) is either going to be *identical to its nature* or not. If the tree's existence were identical to its nature, then it would belong to its nature to exist—just like it belongs to a triangle's nature to have three sides. Its existence (*that* it is) would be part of its essence (*what* it is). If the tree's existence were not identical to its nature, then its existence would be different from its essence.

Which is it? Does the tree exist by nature or not?

Consider this. If the tree's existence were identical to its nature, then there never could be a time when it didn't exist. But obviously there was a time when the tree did not exist, and there will be a time in the future when the tree will no longer exist.

Therefore, the tree's existence is not identical to its essence—

it doesn't belong to the tree's nature to exist. There is a difference between *what* it is and *that* it is.

STEP 3

Show that anything that doesn't have its existence by nature, like a tree, must receive its existence from a cause outside itself.

Since we know that the tree's existence does not belong to its nature, we must ask the question, "Where does it come from?" Perhaps the tree gave itself its own existence?

> *Q:* "Is it possible for the tree to have existence (in order to give it) and not have existence (since it's receiving it) at the same time and in the same respect?"

Assuming your friend accepts the principle of non-contradiction (see appendix A if he doesn't), he must answer no. So the tree didn't give existence to itself.

If your friend speculates that the tree's existence could have come from sheer nothingness, see appendix B for a full response.[43] Suffice to say for now, *ex nihilo, nihil fit*—"from nothing, nothing comes."

If the tree cannot give itself its own existence, and if its existence cannot come from sheer nothingness, then the only other option is that the tree's existence must come from something outside itself. (We have arrived at a very important metaphysical principle!) Such a cause is called an *existential cause.*

STEP 4

Formulate the argument with a syllogism.

PREMISE ONE: If everything was caused to exist by something else, then there would be an infinite series of existential caused causes.

PREMISE TWO: But there cannot be an infinite series of existential caused causes.

CONCLUSION: Therefore, not everything can be caused to exist by something else. There must exist at least one existential cause that doesn't have to receive its existence from something outside itself—an uncaused cause. Such a reality is what we call God.

STEP 5

Elaborate on the syllogism.

Let's take premise one. No legwork is needed to see that if everything were caused, then there would be an infinite series of caused causes. However, the *kind* of series this argument involves is often misunderstood.

Someone could read the argument and think of an existential causal series as, "Oh, I get it; I came from my dad, my dad came from his dad, and my grandfather came from his dad, and so on." But this is not the kind of causal series the above argument has in mind. This is called an *accidentally ordered series* as opposed to an *essentially ordered series.*

An accidentally ordered series is a series where the causal activity of the causes in the series is not essential but accidental, for the effect here and now. For example, I am able to exercise my generating powers independent of my father's. Sure, his generating power was necessary for me to receive mine, but I can exercise my generating power without my father exercising his. His power to generate is not essential to my power to generate.

In an *essentially ordered* series of causes, the causal activity of each cause in the series is necessary at every moment the effect exists. This type of series is like a series of interlinked train cars in which the motion of each car, no matter where it is in the series, is essential to the caboose's motion. Our syllogism likewise presents a series of existential causes in which every cause in the series is essential for the existence of the effect.

The reason for this is that whatever does not have existence by nature, like the tree, not only requires a cause to come into existence, but to *remain in existence*. Just like each train car needs the car in front of it in order keep its motion, at every moment the tree exists it needs an existential cause outside itself to remain in existence, since existence doesn't belong to its nature.

Now, if the cause of the tree's continued existence, Cause A, also does not have its existence by nature, then it too would need an existential cause to remain in existence: Cause B. Notice that in this series the tree's existence right here and right now would not only be dependent on the existential causal activity of Cause A, but also the existential causal activity of Cause B, since Cause A could not cause the existence of the tree without the simultaneous existential influence of Cause B. Cause A would be an instrument of Cause B This is what is meant by an essentially ordered series of existential causes.[44]

STEP 6

Show why there can't be an infinite series of existential causes ordered in an essential way, and thus there must exist at least one uncaused existential cause, which is what we call God.

The question now becomes, "Can there be an infinite series of existential caused causes ordered essentially?" In other words, is it possible for the tree's existence to be caused here and now by a series of causes where every cause derives its existence from something else? This brings us to premise two in the above argument: "There cannot be an infinite series of existential caused causes ordered in an essential way."

To help your friend grasp this, ask him to imagine the caboose of our train passing by.

Q: "What car is the caboose receiving its motion from?"

He will be inclined to say, "The moving car in front of it." But then you would ask, "What is that car receiving its motion from?" and he would say, "The car in front of it."

Though your friend would be correct, ultimately the caboose is receiving its motion from the engine car *through* the intermediate cars. No intermediate car is the proper cause (the cause ultimately responsible for the effect) of the caboose's motion but is only an *instrumental* cause, deriving its causal power ultimately from the engine car.

In other words, the intermediate cars cause the caboose to move only because the engine car is imparting motion to them.

> Q: "What would happen if the engine car stopped working or ceased to exist?"

The obvious answer is that no intermediate car—an instrumental cause—would have the power to cause motion, and thus the caboose would not move.

You are now in a position to apply this line of thinking to a series of existential causes. If there were no first cause outside the series of existential causes with derived existence, a cause that doesn't derive its existence but has existence "built-in" as it were (where essence and existence are identical), then no instrumental existential cause in the series (Cause A, Cause B, etc.) would have existence to impart to the tree. A series of instrumental existential causes where there is no first cause for them to be instruments of couldn't cause the tree to exist any more than the above series of instrumental train cars could cause movement in a caboose if they were not instruments of an engine car.

But the tree does exist. Therefore, in order to explain why the tree exists here and now, at least one existential cause that is not caused must exist. Unlike the existential caused causes in the series, such a cause does not have to derive its existence from something outside itself because its nature (essence) and act of being (existence) are identical. Its nature *is to be*. It is what Aquinas called *ipsum esse subsistens*—subsistent being itself,[45] or what we call God.

Is such a reality worthy of being called God? Let's take a look.

STEP 7

Show that an uncaused existential cause is God.

What is this uncaused cause like?

We know that an uncaused cause would have to be *unlimited* in its being—that is to say, infinite. Every finite being must have a cause, because it must have a sufficient explanation for why it is what it is—say, a frog—and not something else (a butterfly). But an uncaused cause cannot have a cause. Therefore, an uncaused cause must be infinite, or unlimited and unrestricted, in being.

We also know that an uncaused cause would have to be *absolutely simple*. What this means is that it could not be composed of any parts whatsoever, physical or metaphysical. We've already seen in our reasoning above how an uncaused cause would be metaphysically simple in that its nature (essence) would have to be identical to its act of being (existence).

A further reason, however, that precludes any sort of composition altogether is that anything that is composed of parts needs a composer—a cause that puts the parts together.[46] But the uncaused cause cannot be caused. Therefore, the uncaused cause can't have any parts, which means it's absolutely simple.

From absolute simplicity follows *immateriality* (not being made of matter). Every material thing is composed of parts. An uncaused cause can't be composed of parts. Therefore, an uncaused cause can't be material.

From absolute simplicity also follows absolute *uniqueness*. If there were more than one uncaused cause, there would have to be a differentiating factor—something to distinguish one from the other. But if there were a differentiating factor, then the one with the differentiating factor would be a composite of existence *plus* the differentiating factor. But an uncaused cause can't be a composite being, since a composite being requires a composer. Therefore, there can be only one uncaused cause whose essence is existence.

Furthermore, the uncaused cause must be *immutable* (unable to change). Wherever there is change, there is an actualized potency—a movement from potency to act. But no potency can be actualized without something already actual—that is to say, a cause. Since the uncaused cause can't be caused, it follows that it can't change.

Eternality follows from immutability. Everything that is bound by time changes. The uncaused cause can't change. Therefore, the uncaused cause is not bound by time.

The uncaused cause must also be *personal*. As pure infinite being, it must have all actuality and perfections. But intelligence and will are perfections. Therefore, the first cause must have both intelligence and will.

We can also see how the uncaused cause that is responsible for *this* tree's existence is the continuous cause of existence for *everything* else that exists (*that other* tree, you, and me). Recall that everything whose essence is distinct from its existence is dependent right here and right now on an essentially ordered series of existential causes that terminates in an uncaused cause. But there can only be *one* uncaused cause. Therefore, it follows that *everything* that exists besides the uncaused cause (all trees, you, and me) is continuously sustained in existence at every moment it exists by *that* one uncaused cause. Without the one uncaused cause, the tree, you, and I, would lapse into nothingness.

Finally, since anything that has existence must be caused to exist by the one uncaused cause, the causal power of the one uncaused cause extends to all things that have existed, are existing, and will exist, and even things that could possibly exist. This means the one uncaused cause is *omnipotent* (all-powerful). From this it follows that the uncaused cause would be *omniscient* (all-knowing) as well, since he would know all the modes of being that his power does and could extend to.

Note that the premises in the above syllogisms we used to reason to each of the attributes would need to be defended, a project that goes beyond the scope of this chapter and book.[47] But at least your friend can see why we consider ourselves justified in not only calling the uncaused cause God, but also asserting that it *is* God.

THE WAY PREPARED: The argument for God's existence from existential causality arrives at a conclusion that is necessarily true, the denial of which leads to an absurdity.

> *The same holy mother Church holds and teaches that God, the source and end of all things, can be known with certainty from the consideration of created things, by the natural power of human reason.*[48]
> —First Vatican Council

7

How can I believe in God when evil exists in the world?

The problem of evil is perhaps the greatest obstacle anyone faces when considering the question of God's existence. In his *Summa Theologiae*, St. Thomas lists it as one of the two strongest objections.[49]

The objection from evil usually takes on one of two forms: the intellectual problem and the emotional problem. The intellectual problem involves the question of whether it's reasonable to think God and evil can coexist. The emotional problem arises when a person struggles with angry feelings toward God, and is repulsed at the idea that God would allow terrible things to happen to him or to others. This person is not interested in philosophical arguments; he just wants the pain to go away or to find some meaning and purpose in it.

It is important to distinguish between these two problems because the answers for the intellectual problem will seem dry and uncaring to a person who is struggling with the emotional problem. On the other hand, to a person for whom evil is an intellectual puzzle the answers to the emotional problem will seem uninteresting and weak.

In this chapter and the next we will look at strategies for tackling the intellectual problem. The emotional problem will be covered a little later.

The intellectual problem has two versions. For some atheists, the existence of evil and the existence of God are logically contradictory. They think it's *impossible* for God and evil to coexist.

If an all-good and all-powerful God exists, so atheists argue, evil cannot exist. Since evil does exist, they conclude, God doesn't. This is referred to as the *logical* version.

Other atheists think evil only makes God's existence highly unlikely, thus justifying their atheism as a rational position. They reason that although the existence of God and the existence of evil are not logically contradictory, there is so much *gratuitous* evil in the world that God probably doesn't exist. This is called the *evidential* version.

Among atheists that argue from the logical version, some identify the problem in God being the creator of all things. They argue that if everything comes from God, and evil exists, then God must create evil. But if God creates evil then he can't be all-good, in which case he doesn't exist—since God's omnibenevolence belongs to the classical definition of God.

Others see the problem in an all-good God *permitting* evil and not eliminating it. They reason that even though God might not create or cause evil, it would still be contrary to God's all-good nature to allow evil when he has the power to stop it.

Here is a diagram that breaks down the problem of evil into its various forms:

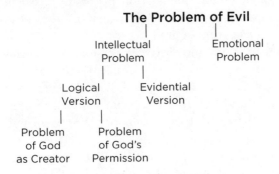

The Problem of Evil

- Intellectual Problem
  - Logical Version
    - Problem of God as Creator
  - Evidential Version
    - Problem of God's Permission
- Emotional Problem

The problem of evil, in all its forms, may be the biggest mountain that blocks the way of our Lord. Bringing down such a mountain is not an easy task. Perhaps drilling a hole through the mountain is a better metaphor for our approach.

The three strategies below will address the *logical* version of the intellectual problem of evil. Strategies one and two deal with atheists who identify the problem in God as the creator of all things. Strategy three deals with atheists who see the logical problem in God permitting evil. We will save the *evidential* version of the intellectual problem of evil for the next chapter.

STRATEGY 1

Show that God cannot make evil as an existing thing given a proper understanding of evil.

There are two kinds of evil: moral and physical. Moral evil, or what philosopher Brian Davies calls "evil done,"[50] is evil caused by the abuse of human freedom—that is to say, sin. Physical evil, or "evil suffered,"[51] refers to any sort of suffering, decay, or corruption caused by nature, or sin.

Your first strategy involves showing how evil, whether physical or moral, is a *privation* of a due good—also a privation of being[52]—and thus is not *made to be* by God. This strategy addresses atheists who argue that evil and an all-good God are incompatible based on the alleged premise that God must create evil since he is the Creator of all things. Kreeft and Tacelli state the dilemma succinctly:

> If evil were a being, the problem of evil would be insolvable, for then either God made it—and thus he is not all-good—or else God did not make it—and thus he is not the all-powerful creator of all things.[53]

As always, you can begin the conversation with a question.

Q: "What is it about blindness that makes it *bad*?"

The answers you'll get will likely boil down to the same point— the eye *lacks* the sight that it ought to have, given its nature. You can flesh this idea out further with the simple example of a sock with a hole in it, which I'm sure your friend will agree is a bad sock in a certain sense.[54]

> Q: "What makes a sock with a hole in it bad? Isn't it bad because it is missing or lacking what ought to be there given its nature, namely fabric?"

Notice that in the examples above the badness (evil) is an absence or deprivation of a good that belongs to each thing given its nature. Blindness is the absence of sight for the eye; the hole is an absence of fabric for the sock. Both the eye and sock lack what is perfective of its nature. In other words, they both lack a due good.

The same line of reasoning can be applied to moral evil.

> Q: "What is it about murder that makes it *bad*?"

Your friend will probably say, "It takes the life of an innocent human being, which is an injustice." You can point out that injustice implies a deprivation of *justice*—of a failure to give another person his due. Taking the life of an innocent human being is also a failure to love our neighbor, which nature inclines us all to do. Whether we look at it from the perspective of a failure in justice or a failure in love of neighbor, there is a failure in achieving what is perfective of our human nature.

The takeaway from these reflections is that evil, whether moral or physical, is essentially a *gap* between what actually is and what should be. As Davies writes, when we call something bad or evil, "we are lamenting an absence of being, the fact that what could and should be there is not there."[55]

Now explain that if evil is a *lack* of being, then it's not actual, for all things are actual inasmuch as they have being.

> Q: "How can evil be a real existing thing if it doesn't have an act of being to distinguish it from nothing?"

Sure, the absence of being is real, since there actually is a hole in the sock, the defect in the eye actually is there, and the failure to choose the good actually occurred. But the lack of the due good is not a subsistent/actual thing in and of itself that has positive qualities and attributes.

With this background knowledge, you are now in a position to show how evil, whether physical or moral, cannot be something that God *creates*.

In the classical tradition of philosophical theology (the study of God by reason apart from divine revelation), "being" is the proper effect of God as the first cause.[56] He is the ultimate source of being for all real (actual) and really possible beings. Only that which is *real* can be attributed to God as a proper effect of his creative action.

So, if evil is the absence of being (what is not there), and God can only create being (what is there), then it follows that God cannot make evil to be. Davies puts it succinctly: "What is not there cannot be thought of as made to be by the source of the being of things."[57] Therefore, we conclude with him that "evil, including evil suffered, cannot intelligibly be thought of as something which God has made to be."[58]

Such a conclusion provides the relevant information needed to refute the atheist's argument. Recall that he argues that God and evil are logically incompatible *because* God must create evil, since he is the creator of all things. But as we've shown above, God doesn't create evil because evil is not an existing entity with being in itself. Therefore, the argument fails.

STRATEGY 2

Explain the different causal roles that God plays in cases of physical and moral evil.

Perhaps God doesn't make evil to be a subsistent thing, such as a human being. But evil still exists, and God causally interacts with things in the world in which evil is found. So, we need to spell out precisely what is, or is not, God's causal role in cases of moral and physical evil. Let's start with physical evil.

> Q: "Would you agree with me that in a material world things have the potential to corrupt?"

This question should not cause any controversy. Whatever is composed of parts has the potential to break down into its component parts, and material things are composed of parts; therefore, material things have the potential to break down into their component parts, which is another way of saying they can corrupt (see appendix D for more details).

Now, point out to your friend that in the material world such corruption (physical evil) is always due to the flourishing activity of something else, which is a good. You can illustrate this principle with various examples.

> Q: "Isn't it true that the animal in the forest fire suffers death due to the fire succeeding in giving off heat? Isn't it true that the gazelle becomes defective (physical evil) due to the flourishing activity of the lion (eating the gazelle)? Isn't it true that if I become sick and defective in my health (and thus suffer a form of corruption), it's due to the successful activity of germs?"

Notice how in all these examples the success of one thing in being the kind of thing it is (a good) causes the defect in another (a bad). The fire succeeds in being good fire, the lion succeeds in being a good lion, and the germs succeed in being good germs.

As these examples show, one material thing corrupts due to the flourishing activity of another, which is a good. Davies explains it this way:

We have evil suffered [physical evil] only when we have goodness curtailed by goodness. Or, to put it another way, there is always concomitant good when it comes to evil suffered, for evil suffered only occurs as something thrives at the expense of something else.[59]

The point here is that physical evil is part the material world (since the world has not achieved its perfection—see CCC 310). The good of one thing often curtails the good of another. And God is causally related to such physical evil inasmuch as he causes the flourishing of those things that cause defect in others. Aquinas puts it this way: "God, by causing in things the good of the order of the universe consequently . . . causes the corruptions of things."[60] This is what he means when he says, "[T]he evil which consists in the corruption of some things is reduced to God as the cause."[61]

At this point your friend might object, "I'll grant you that God only causes the good on which evil is parasitic. But inasmuch as God designed things to seek their good at the expense of something else, he is thereby still responsible for physical evil, and thus is still evil, or at least either stupid or disingenuous."

Some may respond to this objection by saying that God's original design for the material world didn't involve death and decay, and that such physical evil is a result of the fall of man. Although it's true that the fall brought death into "*human* history" (*Catechism of the Catholic Church* 400, emphasis added; cf. 376), it's not Catholic teaching that the fall brought death and decay (physical evil) to *all* material things (see CCC 310).

You can agree that God is responsible for physical evil inasmuch as he created material beings whose good could entail the destruction of other material beings. But it doesn't follow that God is evil, stupid, or disingenuous, because God's willing the corruption of some things as a consequence of something else flourishing belongs to the order of the universe. We're going to elaborate more on this point in strategy three below. We're also going to see here (as well as in chapter eight and appendix D) that it's not necessary for God to remove all evil, or create an evil-free world, in order to be wise and good.

So, inasmuch as God doesn't cause physical evil as an end in itself but only as a consequence of causing the flourishing activity of other things in the universe (for the sake of the "order of the universe"), the presence of physical evil is not logically incompatible with an all-good Creator.

This explanation holds even in those cases where God wills to bring about physical evil for the sake of some greater purpose in his providential plan. For example, he disciplines Paul by giving him what Paul describes as a "thorn in my flesh" (2 Cor. 12:7). In Numbers 12:9-14, God causes the *mycobacterium leprae* bacteria to flourish in Miriam's body and bring about leprosy for the sake of punishment.

For Aquinas, this is what God means when he says in Isaiah 45:7, "I create woe."[62] God doesn't create that which has no substance. But he does, at times, providentially cause some things to flourish in order to bring about physical evil in human beings for the sake of discipline or punishment.[63]

Explain to your friend that God's willing physical evil for the sake of discipline and punishment doesn't amount to moral evil. You can use this example.

> *Q:* "Is it contrary to the goodness of a father to give a little swat on his four-year-old son's bottom as a form of punishment? What about a father who grounds his seventeen-year-old son for ditching school?"

The father who swats his son causes a little physical and mental distress. Grounding a seventeen-year-old also causes a physical evil: privation of the pleasure that comes with the exercise of freedom.

In both scenarios, the fathers cause physical evil. But they don't will it *as an end in itself*. They will it as a part of their orderly plan to discipline their sons, which is a good thing.[64] Therefore, neither father is guilty of moral fault.

Similarly, when God wills physical evil as part of his providential plan to establish justice through punishment, and to develop the moral character of his children through discipline (see Heb. 12:5), he is not thereby guilty of moral fault.

Whether it's a physical evil that is willed as part of the material world in which God causes the good of one thing to curtail the good of another, or a physical evil that God wills for discipline and/or punishment, neither one is logically incompatible with an all-good Creator.

Let's now take a look at moral evil and see how God's causal role is essentially different from that with physical evil. Unlike physical evil, moral evil is purely the absence of a good, and God *in no way wills it* (neither directly or indirectly—see CCC 311). In other words, when the murderer fails to choose what is good, there is no concomitant good that God causes to cause the defect. The lack of good (the moral evil) in the action is attributable to the agent (the murderer) *alone*, not to God. Therefore, although God causes the existence of the murderer, and even sustains his power to act and choose, God in no way is the cause of the evil (the lack of good or disorder) in the act, so moral evil is not incompatible with the existence of an all-good God.

> Q: "Let's say I have a deformity in my leg that causes me to limp. When I limp, is it my power to move that is causing the limp, or is it the deformity in my leg?"

The deformity or infection is the obvious answer. Point out to your friend that although the limp is caused by the deformity or infection in your leg, the motion of the leg is caused by your power to move the limping leg. Here's how Aquinas articulates this argument:

> [Moral evil] is not reduced to God as its cause, but to the free will: even as the defect of limping is reduced to a crooked leg as its cause, but not to the motive power, which nevertheless causes whatever there is of movement in the limping. Accordingly God is the cause of *the act* of sin: and yet he is not the cause of sin, because he does not cause the act to have a defect.[65]

What Aquinas means here is that God causes the act of choosing (e.g., you causing the act of motion in the leg), not the defect in the choice—the failure to choose the good (e.g., you don't cause the limp). The evil in *moral* evil is attributable to the acting agent but not to God, who sustains the agent's power to act and choose.

So, physical evils arise due to the material nature of things, whereby one thing flourishes at the expense of the destruction of another. Moral evils arise because humans misuse their power of freedom and fail to direct it to their true good. Therefore, since God in no way causes moral evil, and doesn't cause physical evil as an end in and of itself, neither physical nor moral evil is evidence that God is a malevolent Creator.

STRATEGY 3

Explain how the logical problem of evil falsely assumes that an all-good and all-wise God must eliminate evil completely.

Your third strategy addresses atheists who object that an all-good and all-wise God would *permit* evil rather than eliminating it. You can begin the discussion by asking this question:

> *Q:* "Must a good person always eliminate evil as far as he can?"

Your atheist friend will probably answer yes.

> *Q:* "Does it count against a father's goodness if he chooses not to stop his wife from inflicting pain (physical evil) on his son as she washes out his son's dirty cut even though he has the power to stop her?"

No, the father is aware of a greater good that will be brought about from his allowance of the inflicted pain.

> *Q:* "Let's assume for argument's sake that contraception is immoral. Does it count against a

ruler's goodness if he chooses not to penalize couples that are using it?"

Although it would be within right reason for the ruler to prohibit the distribution of contraceptives, your friend should see that any regulation to stop couples from actually using contraceptives would preclude the good of privacy and violate the intimacy that belongs to the nature of the sexual act.

These examples show that it is not necessarily true that a good person must always eliminate evil as far as he can. When there is a greater good in view, or a great good that would be lost otherwise, it's possible for a person to permit an evil, even though he has the power to prevent it, and still be considered good.

Similarly, as Aquinas argues,[66] even though God has the power to eliminate evil, it doesn't count against his goodness that he doesn't since, given his infinite power, there is no good that he cannot bring about to outweigh the evil permitted. God will not permit an evil unless he intends to order it toward a greater good.

Christians are able to provide a perfect example of this: the grace of salvation that Jesus' death on the cross won for us. This was the rationale behind St. Paul's statement in Romans 5:20: "Where sin increased, grace abounded all the more." Pope St. Leo the Great echoed Paul when he wrote, "Christ's inexpressible grace gave us blessings better than those the demon's envy had taken away."[67]

Similarly, in view of Jesus's death on the cross that came as a result of Adam's sin, Aquinas writes, "There is nothing to prevent human nature's being raised up to something greater, even after sin; God permits evil in order to draw forth some greater good."[68]

God ordered the greatest evil—the crucifixion of the Son of God—to the greatest possible good: the redemption of the human race and the grace to live with him for an eternity in a state of supreme happiness. Therefore, we have good reason to conclude that evil is not logically incompatible with the existence of an all-good and all-powerful God.

Here's where your friend's objection from strategy two above comes into play, since he will probably be thinking, "So what if

God can bring about a greater good from a physical or moral evil? It still seems stupid and disingenuous that he designed things in a way that makes physical and moral evil even possible."

Start your response with this analogy.[69] Suppose a professor began drawing a circle on the chalkboard and stopped in the middle of drawing it, leaving it unfinished and looking like a "C." Considered in and of itself, it's a bad circle. And the professor is indirectly responsible for the privation inasmuch as he didn't put all the good into the circle that he could have.

> *Q:* (To use your friend's words) "Is the professor
> thereby stupid? Is he disingenuous?"

He would be only if he were looking out solely for the good of the circle. But as professor, his role is not solely to look out for the good of the circle. He must provide for the good of other things in his care, namely, his students. And their good involves a philosophical knowledge of the concept of evil as privation.

So, in order to teach his students the privation theory of evil, he refrains from completing the circle. The professor's choice not to complete the circle (a defect) thereby becomes part of an overall good: giving his students a philosophical knowledge of evil. For this reason he is not stupid or disingenuous for drawing an incomplete circle.

Similarly, God's role is not solely to look out for the good of some particular thing. As Aquinas says, he is the "universal provider of all being."[70] Therefore, Aquinas concludes, "it pertains to [God's] Providence to permit certain defects to be in some particular things [not willing all the good that he could have, like the professor not willing a full-drawn circle], lest the perfect good of the universe be obstructed [think of the overall situation of the students having philosophical knowledge], for if *all* evils were prevented [professor doesn't refrain from completing the circle], much good would be lacking to the universe [students would lack philosophical knowledge of evil]."[71]

Consider the category of physical evil, for example. Without death, the multiplication of living, material beings would soon create a state where the Earth would no longer be able to support its inhabitants (there would be a lack of food, water, space, etc.). In the words of philosopher George Hayward Joyce, "Death is thus an essential part of nature's provision for the benefit of the species."[72]

If it were not for the destructive activity of germ life, which makes inanimate bodies resolve back into their constituent parts, the planet would be a vast collection of corpses. Inasmuch as God freely chose to create a world with successive generations of living material beings, we can see how incidents of physical evil to these sorts of creatures can be permitted in order to contribute to an overall good situation.

"But," your friend might say, "if God is all-powerful, couldn't he perform a perpetual miracle and keep all material things from dying and provide them the food, water, and space that they need?" Sure he could. But for reasons why God might not do this, hold off until strategy three of the next chapter.

Even physical evils that humans experience, whether they are caused by other physical evils or moral evils, can be permitted for the sake of the good of the whole. For example, courage couldn't exist if there weren't any real dangers for us to face and overcome in the pursuit of the good.[73] Aquinas gives the example of the patience of martyrs: "[T]here would be no patience of martyrs if there were no tyrannical persecution."[74] Furthermore, there would be no compassion if there weren't any suffering, for compassion necessarily involves suffering alongside someone.

So, inasmuch as God is the universal provider who wills a material world with material beings, and a world where human beings can develop virtues like courage and compassion and grow in virtue through discipline and punishment, it is not contrary to his goodness or wisdom to will that physical and moral evil be possible, because their possibility belongs to the good of the whole.

And even if we can't clearly see how a particular instance of physical or moral evil fits in the order of the whole, like we can when it comes to gazelles and lions or real dangers and courage, we have good reason to think that it does, because we already have good reason to think, in light of the argument in chapter six, that God exists. And being the infinite Creator that he is, he is the all-wise and all-good universal provider. We should expect such ignorance, given his infinite nature and our finite minds.

THE WAY PREPARED: God's permission of evil while having the power to stop it doesn't count against his goodness, since in his infinite power he can always bring about a greater good.

> O truly necessary sin of Adam, destroyed completely by the Death of Christ! O happy fault that earned so great, so glorious a Redeemer![75]
> —The Exsultet: The Proclamation of Easter

8

How can I believe in God when there is so much useless suffering in the world?

In our last chapter we looked at the *logical* problem of evil. We went through strategies that show how the presence of physical and moral evil in the world doesn't disprove God's existence. We addressed atheists who see the problem in the alleged conclusion that God must *cause* evil. We also addressed atheists who identify the problem in God *permitting* evil when he has the power to eliminate it.

In this chapter, we are going to address atheists who recognize that God may permit some evil for a greater good, but since there exists so much *gratuitous* evil they conclude that it's unlikely God exists.

For example, in reference to the millions of years of animal suffering and the occasions of innocent children being crushed in earthquakes, atheist philosopher Stephen Law says, "I think these sorts of consideration do establish beyond any reasonable doubt that there is no all-powerful all-good God."[76]

In philosophy this argument is called the *evidential* version of the intellectual problem of evil. It takes the following form:

PREMISE ONE: If gratuitous evils exist, then it's reasonable to conclude God doesn't exist.

PREMISE TWO: Gratuitous evils exist.

CONCLUSION: Therefore, it's reasonable to conclude God doesn't exist.

The three strategies below will teach you how to refute this argument, and show how the evidential version of the problem of evil need not be an obstacle that blocks the way of the Lord.

STRATEGY 1

Show how the argument begs the question.

Recall that *begging the question* is a fallacy in which someone assumes as a conclusion what he is trying to prove. Such a fallacy is also called *circular reasoning*. You can begin the discussion by asking your friend this question:

> *Q:* "Why do you think some evils are gratuitous?"

Your friend will probably answer, "Because there is no possible greater good that can come from them."

> *Q:* "But why can't there be any greater good that can come from such evils?"

If your friend answers, "Because I can't see any greater good," then you can respond with the *non sequitur* response found in strategy two. But push that off for now, since there is a deeper problem at hand.

Point out to your friend that the *only way* no greater good could possibly come about is if God doesn't exist.

> *Q:* "Okay, so you say that there are some evils from which it's impossible for a greater good to come about. But wouldn't that be true only if God doesn't exist? Wouldn't it be true that if an infinite being with infinite power existed, then it could bring about a greater good, thus making an evil non-gratuitous? And if he were all-good, then he would bring about a greater good to outweigh the evil permitted?"

The point of these questions is to show that evils would be gratuitous only if God didn't exist. If God existed, and he was infinite in knowledge and power, there would be no good that he couldn't bring about. If he existed and were all-good, then he *would* bring about a greater good lest the evils permitted not be brought into the order of the good of the whole.

You are now in a position to show that your friend assumes what he is trying to prove.

> *Q:* "How can you use gratuitous evils to show the likelihood of God's non-existence when gratuitous evils presuppose God's non-existence?"

Hopefully your friend can see now that his attempt to show the likelihood that God doesn't exist actually begins by *assuming* that God doesn't exist. He is asking you to stipulate to his conclusion in order to support his premise. That's begging the question, and it's not kosher logic.

STRATEGY 2

Explain why the judgment that gratuitous evils exist is unwarranted.

Whereas strategy one challenged the argument as a whole in showing that it begs the question, your second strategy involves challenging premise two—that gratuitous evils exist. You can show that it is unreasonable on two counts.

First, if your friend thinks gratuitous evils exist because he can't see or think of a good that can come from some particular evil, then his reasoning is weak. Just because he personally can't see or think of a good, it doesn't follow there *is no* good.

> *Q:* "Before around 1920, scientists were uncertain whether protons existed.[77] Would they have been justified in concluding, based on lack of evidence, that protons didn't exist?"

The absence of evidence doesn't necessarily mean *evidence of absence*. Just because before 1920 scientists didn't have evidence to prove that protons existed, it didn't follow at the time that protons didn't exist. To say that a lack of evidence would have justified the claim that they *didn't* exist would have been to confuse an epistemological issue (*knowing* whether something exists) with a metaphysical issue (whether something exists). The same would hold true today if we were to assert that strings don't exist because we currently don't have any evidence for them, or that the multiverse doesn't exist because we don't have evidence for it.

You are now in a position to make the application to God and evil.

> *Q:* "If it would have been unreasonable for scientists to conclude that protons didn't exist because they didn't have evidence for them, or for us to conclude today that strings or the multiverse do not exist because we don't have evidence for them, wouldn't it also be unreasonable to conclude that no good can come from a particular evil just because you can't see or think of one?"

This first critique doesn't definitively undermine premise two, but it does show that one cannot judge that gratuitous evils exist for the reason mentioned above.

In order to show definitively that premise two is unwarranted, we need to show that it's impossible for your friend to prove that there is no good reason why God permits a horrific evil. If you can show this, then he would have no way of proving that gratuitous evils exist, and thus he would have to give up the argument.

> *Q:* "How could you, a finite being limited in intelligence, space, and time, possibly know that an infinitely intelligent and powerful God has no good reason for allowing a horrific evil? Isn't it possible that if he exists, he would already be doing something, or at least

intending to do something, to bring about a greater
good from some evil, and you just don't know it?"

Your friend has to admit that this is a possibility; otherwise
he would be failing to distinguish between infinite and finite
knowledge.

Point out to your friend that we simply are not in a position to
know that God doesn't have a good reason for permitting evil.
You can use an example from apologist Trent Horn to get this
point across:[78]

Q: "Would it be reasonable for us to conclude that
there are no elephants in the backyard right now?"

I think it's safe to say your friend will have no qualms with
answering yes. Explain that this answer is justified because you
are both in a position to make such a claim. Given the nature of
elephants with their size and smell, if one were standing nearby
in the backyard, both you and your friend would know about it.

Q: "Would it be reasonable for us to conclude that
there are no fleas in the backyard right now?"

When contrasted with the question about the elephant, it becomes clear the answer to this question is no. The reason is that
you and your friend are not in a position to know whether fleas
are present, given their small size and the vast amount of places
in the yard where they could be.

It is true, perhaps, that with some sort of high-tech equip-
ment and enough observers, you could be in a position to make
a reasonable conclusion that fleas are not present in your backyard. But this is not the case when it comes to God.

God is infinite, and we are finite. He is beyond space and
time, and we're not. Evil may appear gratuitous from our limited perspective, but from God's perspective of eternity, which
we don't have access to, the evil is not gratuitous.

Therefore, it is not only unlikely that we could know for sure that God has no good reason for permitting an evil—it's *impossible*. And if that's the case, then it's impossible to say for sure that gratuitous evils exist. As the late Norris Clarke put it, "Our ignorance cannot be a basis for blaming God for what he is already doing."[79]

STRATEGY 3

Show that there are good reasons why God would permit physical and moral evils.

Let's start with physical evils. In our previous chapter we gave one possible answer as to why God would permit physical evils: it belongs to the nature of material beings that the good of one thing curtails the goodness of another, and that defects in nature can contribute to the good of the whole.

> Q: "Why would it be contrary to God's goodness and wisdom to let material beings function in the way that he created them to function? Why would it be unwise for him to permit a being to be defective in some way for the general order of his work, 'that an inferior good should be sacrificed to a higher good'?"[80]

Since God willed that material things have such a nature, and since he has care of the whole order of the universe, it's not gratuitous for him to permit physical evils.

Another possible answer concerning physical evil is that in order for God to stop physical evil he would have to perform a perpetual miracle. But if God were to miraculously stop physical evils from occurring on a regular basis, then he would make it difficult for human beings to discern the supernatural charac- ter of the miraculous, which wouldn't be good since God uses miracles to lead human beings to believe in him.

Q: "If miracles were as common as rain, then wouldn't it be difficult to distinguish between the supernatural and the natural?"

It seems there would be such a difficulty, since we can only know the supernatural by contrast with the natural. Feser argues that such difficulty is not good because it could lead to one of two extremes.[81]

One extreme is an *occasionalist* view of the world, which holds that God does not cooperate with natural causes but causes everything directly. This would not be good for science, to say the least.

The other extreme is the view that there is no order to the universe at all. This wouldn't be good either, because if there were no order there would be no causal regularity. And if that were the case, it would be impossible to reason to God's existence, giving atheism stronger grounds to stand on.

There is also good reason to think that God wouldn't always perform miracles to stop moral evil. For example, if God always gave an extraordinary amount of grace to someone so that he couldn't do anything but choose the good, that person wouldn't have the great dignity of being a real cause (though secondary) of his own good moral character. This line of reasoning is implicit in Aquinas's treatment on the dignity of secondary causes:

> [T]here are certain intermediaries of God's providence; for he governs things inferior by superior, not on account of any defect in his power, but by reason of the abundance of his goodness; so that *the dignity of causality is imparted even to creatures.*[82]

Elsewhere in the *Summa*, Aquinas writes:

> It is not on account of any defect in God's power that he works by means of second causes, but it is for the perfection of the order of the universe, and the more manifold

outpouring of his goodness on things, through his be-
stowing on them not only the goodness which is proper
to them, *but also the faculty of causing goodness in others.*[83]

For Aquinas, God's providence consists of leading things
to their ends, including human beings.[84] But he wills to do so
through "intermediaries," or secondary causes. For humans, this
involves us choosing good over evil because such moral choices
constitute our good moral character, which belongs to our perfection. And as Aquinas says, that God has bestowed upon us the
faculty to cause good in things, including ourselves, is a "more
manifold outpouring of his goodness."[85]

So, if God were to miraculously fill us with the grace of
the Beatific Vision so we could never have the opportunity to
choose between good or evil, then we would never have the
dignity of being a cause of our own perfection. God's goodness
would be less manifest,[86] and we would lose the *glory* of meriting
our eternal reward of heaven.

> *Q:* "What constitutes a higher destiny: receiving a
> reward with or without effort?"

Surely, it's a higher destiny "to receive our final beatitude as
the fruit of our labors, and as the recompense of a hard-won victory . . . than to receive it without any effort on our part."[87] (For
more, see appendix C.)

"Okay," your friend might say, "Maybe God doesn't have to
perform that kind of miracle. Perhaps he could do something
like change a bullet into butter every time a murderer fires a
gun."

Here's how you can answer: if God were to do this, he would
be devaluing our capacity to choose good or bad.

> *Q:* "How could there be any real value in man's ability
> to do good or evil if God never allowed the choices of
> man to have bad effects?"

It doesn't take much thought to see that if no bad effects could result from my choice to do evil, there would be no point in even having such a capacity. The alternative of a bad choice would never be a real alternative. How could it be if it never could bring about bad effects?

You are now in a position to formulate an argument:

PREMISE ONE: If no bad effects were possible from man's choice to do evil, then there would be no value in man's power to choose good or evil.

PREMISE TWO: But God values man's power to choose good or evil.

CONCLUSION: Therefore, there must be bad effects that arise from man's choice to do evil.

It's reasonable to conclude, then, that God doesn't ordinarily perform miracles to stop the bad effects of evil acts, because he values man's power to choose good over evil.

THE WAY PREPARED: Just because we don't immediately see the good that God can bring about from suffering it doesn't mean there is no good that he will bring about.

> *We may not know the meaning of every event, but we know it is meaningful.*[88]
> —Peter Kreeft

9

How can I believe in God when he allows so many bad things to happen to me?

In our previous two chapters we dealt with the *intellectual* problem of evil. We gave reasons why it's not a logical contradiction to say that both evil and an all-good God exist, and why evil doesn't make God's non-existence more probable. In this chapter we will deal with the *emotional* problem of evil: when a person struggles with angry feelings toward God, and is repulsed at the idea that God would allow terrible things to happen to him.

The person who struggles emotionally with evil is not interested in philosophical arguments; he just wants the pain to go away, or at least to find meaning and purpose in it. He wants help in getting through the darkness of suffering and despair. For this obstacle we need to look beyond reason and logic for a successful strategy—we need to look to Christian revelation.

It is true that we haven't yet established the truth of Christianity, but it's necessary that we explain here to our unbelieving friend the view of suffering that Christianity has to offer. Such a view has the potential to shed some light on the darkness, and provide those who suffer the courage to find meaning and purpose in it. A glimpse, if not exactly a proof, of the light that Christianity has to offer can be sufficient to prepare the way of the Lord.

STRATEGY 1

Explain how Christianity teaches that for those who believe in Jesus, all suffering will eventually end,

and they will be compensated with great rewards in the eternal life of heaven.

Begin your first strategy by sharing these Bible passages that reveal the promise of eternal life:

- *Matthew 5:4*: "Happy are those who mourn, for they shall be consoled."

- *Romans 8:18*: "I consider that our present sufferings are not worthy comparing with the glory that will be revealed in us."

- *Romans 8:28*: "And we know that in all things God works for the good [eternal life] of those who love him."

- *1 Peter 5:10*: "And after you have suffered for a little while, the God of all grace, who has called you to his eternal glory in Christ, will himself restore, support, strengthen, and establish you."

- *Revelation 21:1, 4*: "Then I saw a new heaven and a new earth . . . . He [God] will wipe every tear from their eyes. Death will be no more; mourning and crying and pain will be no more."

With the promise of eternal life now established, give your friend a sense of what this eternal life will be like. Share the *Catechism's* teaching that heaven is "the ultimate end and fulfillment of the deepest human longings, the state of supreme definitive happiness" (CCC 1024). This means that there will be no human desire that is left unfulfilled, and thus there will be *complete* satisfaction.

Another point you want to explain to your friend is that heaven is a happiness that is bodily, not just spiritual. Point out that an essential part of Christian teaching is that the righteous will rise to live a life with a new and glorified body. Use this passage from St. Paul to explain:

> So is it with the resurrection of the dead. What is sown is perishable, what is raised is imperishable. It is sown in

dishonor, it is raised in glory. It is sown in weakness, it is raised in power. It is sown a physical body, it is raised a spiritual body. If there is a physical body, there is also a spiritual body (1 Cor. 15:42–43).

Highlight the characteristics of the glorified body. For example, the new body will be "imperishable"—that is to say, it will not be subject to decay. It will be raised in "glory," which refers to the radiant brightness with which the righteous will shine (Matt. 13:43). The glorified body will also have "power" far beyond what we can imagine.

Finally, it will be a "spiritual body," which means it will share in the powers of spirit, such as not being confined to space and the boundaries of matter. This is why Jesus was able to appear in the upper room while the doors were locked (John 20:19), and disappear from the apostles' sight when he ascended into heaven (Acts 1:9).

The Christian teaching of heaven and the bodily resurrection, which is modeled after Jesus' bodily resurrection (1 Cor. 15:49), can give your suffering friend hope.

> *Q:* "Suppose I were to tell you that if you sat still and quiet for five minutes, I'd give you a million dollars. Wouldn't you agree that the reward would be more than worth the trivial effort?"

The same principle applies to our present sufferings when compared to heaven. The supreme happiness and satisfaction of heaven makes the effort of getting there worthwhile, and when we experience that glory, the present sufferings of this life will seem trivial.

The Christian teaching on heaven shows that your friend's desire for a life without suffering is not futile. It's a desire that Christianity says can be fulfilled. Such knowledge can inspire hope, which in turn gives us the strength to persevere in suffering.

Explain to your friend that from a Christian perspective, his sufferings do not have to be *ultimately* tragic. If he believes in

Jesus, and perseveres in that belief until death, then at the end of time he will receive recompense in his glorified body and experience a definitive and supreme state of happiness that is glorious enough to offset the tragedies of this life.

STRATEGY 2

Explain how Christianity teaches that suffering, when offered to God out of love through Jesus Christ, can be a means of obtaining eternal life.

Share with your friend Paul's promise in Romans 8:17: "If only we suffer with him so that we may also be glorified with him."

Now explain *how* suffering can help us obtain eternal life. It does so in several ways.

First, it can *preserve* us from certain things that can keep us out of heaven, such as self-centeredness. This is one of the many benefits that Paul saw in his own suffering: "Therefore, in order to keep me from becoming conceited, I was given a thorn in my flesh" (2 Cor. 12:7). Paul recognized that his physical ailment, whatever it may have been, kept him aware that he needs the help of others, and the help of God.

Thomas Aquinas held a similar view. In his commentary on Paul's letter to the Thessalonians, he writes,

> As water extinguishes a burning fire, so tribulations extinguish the force of concupiscent desires, so that human beings do not follow them at will.[89]

By *concupiscent desires* Aquinas means our tendency to seek physical pleasures, material goods, and achievements contrary to reason (see CCC 377).

Aquinas understands that suffering can limit our pursuit of these things, and as such, can keep us from indulging in them inordinately. Therefore, suffering acts first as a preventative against sin.

A second way suffering can help us attain eternal life is that it can produce within us a character that is fitting for heaven. Here are two Bible passages that make this point:

- *Romans 5:3–5*: "[W]e rejoice in our sufferings, knowing that suffering produces endurance, and endurance produces character, and character produces hope, and hope does not disappoint us, because God's love has been poured into our hearts through the Holy Spirit who has been given to us."

- *James 1:2–4*: "Count it all joy, my brethren, when you meet various trials, for you know that the testing of your faith produces steadfastness. And let steadfastness have its full effect, that you may be perfect and complete, lacking in nothing."

A third way suffering can be ordered toward the good of obtaining eternal life is that it can widen our capacity for love.

> Q: "Isn't it true that suffering creates needs within us? And when we have needs it creates an opportunity for others to come to our aid?"

Suffering puts us in a position to receive love from others, and that can prepare us for heaven, because heaven is the perfect exchange of love with God and everyone else there. Perhaps this is what Paul means when he writes in 2 Corinthians 4:17: "For this slight momentary affliction is *preparing* for us an eternal weight of glory beyond all comparison."

A fourth way suffering can contribute to our obtaining eternal life is if we make it a sacrificial offering to God through Jesus Christ. This is what Paul tells the Christians to do in Romans 12:1: "I urge you, brothers and sisters . . . to offer your bodies as a living sacrifice, holy and pleasing to God—this is your true and proper worship."

Emphasize for your friend that Christianity makes it possible for suffering not to go to waste. Instead, when done through

Jesus it can actually be transformed into an act of *worship*, and thus an act of love for God, which in turn will be rewarded with eternal life in heaven.

Finally, when animated by love for God and others, suffering has the potential to conform us to Christ and make us more like him. Share with your friend these Bible passages:

- *1 Peter 2:21*: "For to this you have been called, because Christ also suffered for you, leaving you an example, that you should follow in his steps."

- *Luke 9:23*: "Whoever wants to be my disciple must deny themselves and take up their cross daily and follow me. For whoever wants to save their life will lose it, but whoever loses their life for me will save it."

Explain that by uniting our suffering to Christ and offering it to God in self-sacrificial love we become like Christ who offered his suffering in self-sacrificial love, and as a result receive the reward of eternal life.

STRATEGY 3

Explain how Christianity teaches that suffering, when offered to God out of love through Jesus Christ, can help others obtain eternal life.

This third strategy highlights the role suffering can play in helping other people obtain salvation—similar to how Christ offered his own life in sacrifice for the salvation of the world.

> *Q:* "Is it heroic for soldiers to sacrifice themselves in battle for the freedom of others?"

Most would say yes.

Q: "Wouldn't it be great if you could be a hero and make a sacrifice for others to have freedom?"

It's common among people to have a desire to sacrifice themselves for a noble cause—to make a positive difference outside of oneself. Your friend should at least gravitate toward this idea to some degree:

Q: "When you're lying on your deathbed and are asked, 'What difference did you make in your life?' would you want the answer to be 'None'?"[90]

You can point out that Christianity says he can make a difference and be a hero who wins freedom for others, not only through his good works and positive contributions to the world around him, but also by uniting his suffering to Christ and offering it as a form of intercessory prayer for others along the path to heaven. Here are two Bible passages that speak to this point:

- *2 Corinthians 1:6*: "If we are afflicted, it is for your comfort and salvation."

- *Colossians 1:24*: "Now I rejoice in my sufferings for your sake, and in my flesh I complete what is lacking in Christ's afflictions for the sake of his body, that is, the church."

In both passages Paul sees his own suffering as a way of helping others obtain eternal life. Although exactly *how* this works is a great mystery, he knows that somehow his suffering, when united to Christ and offered to God, is a prayer that can merit graces for other people.

To contribute to the eternal destiny of another human being is a big deal. Only Christianity finds in suffering the potential for such meaning and purpose.

THE WAY PREPARED: No suffering in this life is ultimately tragic, because Jesus promised to redeem all suffering in heaven, offering us a way to make our suffering a means to attaining final salvation.

> *Apart from the cross there is no other ladder by which we may get to heaven.*[91]
> —St. Rose of Lima

10

How can I believe in God when he never shows himself to me?

If there is one thing that atheists and theists can agree on, it's the problem of God's hiddenness. At one point or another we have cried out, "Where are you God?" But the difference is that atheists think this is a reason to reject belief in God; theists don't.

The problem of *divine hiddenness* can take on one of two forms. The first goes as follows: if an all-knowing and all-loving God existed, and if he desired a relationship with me, then he would at least convince me that he exists, providing me with absolute evidence that removes all doubt. God knows I would follow such evidence if he provided it, but since he hasn't, it's reasonable to conclude that he doesn't exist.

The second version doesn't merely demand that God make his *existence* known, but that he manifest himself in a way that would ensure a *relationship* with him. In other words, if God existed and desired a relationship with me, he would manifest himself to me in a way that leads me to love him. But since he hasn't done this, it's reasonable to conclude that he doesn't exist. This second version demands God to manifest his *essence*, which precludes the ability to reject him, since the will cannot do anything but love the ultimate good.

Since most atheists do not hold to version two, the strategies below for preparing the way only apply to version one. For a response to version two, see appendix C.

STRATEGY 1

Explain how God is not bound to give absolute indubitable evidence, but only intellectual indubitable evidence—evidence that excludes prudent doubt.[92]

You can start strategy one by asking these questions:

> *Q:* "Isn't it reasonable for a man to marry his fiancée even though he doesn't have evidence that excludes all possible doubt of whether she loves him? How could he have such evidence, since anything she does could be meant to deceive him into thinking that she loves him?"

If absolute indubitable evidence were needed for a reasonable decision to marry, then everyone who chooses to marry would have to be considered irrational. But that is absurd.

A man should not refrain from marriage just because his fiancée can't provide evidence that excludes *all possible* doubt concerning her love for him. All he needs to make a reasonable decision is evidence that excludes prudent doubt.

Now, it's true that the analogy falls short when applied to God, since God *could* provide absolute indubitable evidence if he wanted to, whereas the fiancée could not. However, the analogy does show that absolute indubitable evidence for God's existence is not needed for your friend to *reasonably* direct his life toward him, just evidence that excludes prudent doubt. And thus the argument from divine hiddenness fails.

Even if, for argument's sake, we conceded your friend's demand for absolute indubitable evidence that God exists, the theist can argue that God *has* given such evidence. Sure, God hasn't immediately presented himself to your friend's intellect leaving nothing to be done on his part. However, a theist can argue that God has provided indubitable evidence on an objective level, and your atheist friend is simply failing to see the evidence, making the problem subjective (the atheist's intellectual deficiency or ill will) and not objective (the evidence itself).

For example, Thomas Aquinas's first cause argument (a variant put forward in chapter six) is a metaphysical demonstration, which means the conclusion is necessarily true because it follows from necessarily true premises. To deny the conclusion that God exists is to end in a contradiction—namely, the denial that *things* exist. Such a conclusion is as indubitable as self-evident truths, such as the principle of non-contradiction. Trying to deny them always ends in a contradiction.

The difference, however, is the *way* in which these truths are arrived at. Self-evident truths are arrived at *immediately*—the truth is known when the terms are understood. For example, *the whole is greater than its parts.* Or, *something cannot be and not be in the same respect at the same time.* Demonstrative truths, on the other hand, are arrived at *mediately* through what is called a middle term, such as "man" in the following syllogism: "All *men* are mortal; Socrates is a *man*; therefore Socrates is mortal."

So, your friend's failure to be convinced that God has provided evidence for his existence is not necessarily due to the evidence itself. It could be due to his own deficiencies, whether intellectual or moral.

At this point your friend may counter, "Okay, but couldn't God make up for my deficiencies, and enhance my intellectual capabilities to where I could see the truth of the evidence? Or maybe he could just present himself directly to my intellect, and bypass the proofs altogether?"

The answer is yes. God could do both. But that raises the question for your friend, "Why doesn't he?" Strategies two and three below give the answer.

STRATEGY 2

Explain how rational inquiry belongs to man's nature, and since God relates to man in accord with his nature, it befits God's goodness to allow man to rationally inquire about his existence.[93]

Q: "Do you think rational inquiry is a good thing?"

I think it's safe to assume that your friend will answer yes, since he is inquiring about how to reconcile God's existence with his lack of belief in God.

Explain to your friend that rational inquiry is a distinct *mode of knowledge* that God has bestowed upon human beings. It belongs to the nature of man to acquire knowledge through experience with material things, and from that experience to abstract and engage in rational inference.

For example, we experience Socrates, and then we abstract from Socrates the nature or essence of man, which is a rational being that is a body-soul composite. From this we are able to conclude that such a being is subject to death, since what is composed of parts can break apart. But we can also reason that man's rational soul is not dependent on the body for its existence, and thus can continue to exist after death. By going through such a process, we arrive at various truths about the nature of a human being: humans are both corporeal and incorporeal, subject to death, but yet immortal in spirit.

Although this mode of acquiring knowledge is inferior to that of receiving knowledge immediately, as the angels do, it is nevertheless a good mode, and imitates in its own distinct way the infinite perfection of God.

Q: "Wouldn't it belong to God's goodness and wisdom to will that we discover truth, especially the truth about his own existence, according to our mode of knowledge, which is rational inquiry?"

It's reasonable to conclude that God would relate to us in accord with the nature that he gave us, allowing us to discover the truth about him instead of forcing it on us. It *doesn't* seem reasonable that God would create us with this capacity and not allow us to use it to know him. The bottom line is that there is something *human* about the quest for truth.

Thomas Aquinas argued along these same lines in response to the objection that angels should communicate to us through visible apparitions:

> To the sixth objection it is to be said that such visible apparitions of the angels, which are above the course of nature, inspire a certain stupor, and in a certain way incite consent violently: in which perishes some good of man with regard to the condition of nature, which is rational inquiry. Whence such apparitions do not appear to all; but they were made to some for the confirmation of faith in the many, just as miracles were done.[94]

You could summarize the argument this way:

PREMISE ONE: God wills whatever is good for man.
PREMISE TWO: Rational inquiry is good for man.
CONCLUSION: Therefore, God wills rational inquiry.

And inasmuch as rational inquiry includes the possibility of falling short of the truth, it is no surprise that some people fall short of seeing the truth that God exists.

STRATEGY 3

Explain how rational inquiry into God's existence could be the condition for seeing the indubitableness of the evidence, making one's knowledge of his existence more rewarding.

Your third strategy follows from the second in that it gives another reason why it befits God's goodness to will that rational inquiry be a means by which we can arrive at knowledge of his existence.

Start the conversation by getting your friend to recall his days in math class.

> *Q:* "Why do you think your math teacher always said,
> 'Show your work'? Wasn't it because you learned
> better by going through the steps instead of just
> looking up the answer in the book?"

Your friend should see that working through a problem in order to arrive at the answer is better than merely looking it up. Working through the *steps* that lead to the answer shows the reasons why the answer is true, thus removing doubt.

If the answer were merely given, the student's knowledge that it's true would rely on the testimony of the teacher or the author of the book. There's nothing wrong with relying on the authority of the one who testifies, but it does leave room for doubt. By working through the steps, the student no longer has to *believe* that the answer is true. He can *know* for himself that it is. The rational process gives the student certain knowledge.

Explain to your friend that a similar line of reasoning can be applied to God's choice not to make his existence known immediately to our intellect. Rational inquiry into God's existence, both through philosophical and historical investigation,[95] can lead to a firmer belief in it.

Furthermore, it's possible that our knowledge of him would be more appreciated.

> *Q:* "What is nobler and more rewarding, to be the
> number-one seed in a sports tournament because
> your team is the only team in the league, or to be the
> number-one seed because your team is the best?"

Your friend shouldn't have a hard time seeing that the more rewarding experience lies in the latter scenario. Similarly, it's possible that God allows the search so that when we do come to know that he exists, our knowledge of his existence will be a more rewarding experience. The effort contributes to the satisfaction of the reward.

At this point your friend may ask, "But what if I never get to that point?"

You can reply that if your friend's lack of assent to God's existence is due to honest intellectual deficiencies, and he is seeking truth in the ways he knows how, God will not hold him accountable for his unbelief.

> *Q:* "If God is perfectly just, then wouldn't it be true that he could not unjustly punish you? And if he can't unjustly punish you, then wouldn't it also be true that he couldn't condemn you for not believing in him if you were doing your best to pursue truth, and if your lack of conviction were through no fault of your own?"

Explain to your friend that God will not punish someone for lack of explicit belief in him, on condition that the person has an upright will, is honestly seeking the truth in ways that he knows how, and honestly does not see the arguments for God's existence as convincing. The Second Vatican Council teaches as much in its Dogmatic Constitution on the Church *Lumen Gentium*:

> Those also can attain to salvation who through no fault of their own do not know the Gospel of Christ or his Church, yet sincerely seek God and moved by grace strive by their deeds to do his will as it is known to them through the dictates of conscience...Nor does divine providence deny the helps necessary for salvation to those who, without blame on their part, have not yet arrived at an explicit knowledge of God and with his grace strive to live a good life (16).[96]

Confirm for your friend that he has no reason to fear, and encourage him to continue sincerely seeking God in the quest for truth. If he can come to have this type of disposition, God's hiddenness should no longer be an obstacle to belief in God.

THE WAY PREPARED: God is not entirely hidden, and he wills that we seek him in a way that befits our nature as human beings.

> *To men and women there falls the task of exploring truth with their reason, and in this their nobility consists.*[97]
> —Pope St. John Paul II

11

Why should I believe in God when I can be a good person without him?

In 2011, the Freedom from Religion Foundation sponsored a billboard in Columbus, Ohio featuring an atheist and the caption, "I can be good without God."

This billboard expresses a major obstacle atheists and agnostics face when it comes to acknowledging God's existence. They think that because they can be good without God, God is not necessary for morality. And if God is not necessary for morality, they argue, then it's likely he doesn't exist. Even if he did, he wouldn't be the God of traditional theism.

This false perception of God's irrelevance to morality is like a valley, a *lack* of something—namely, insight into the connection between God and morality.

So let's fill the valley and prepare a way for the Lord.

STRATEGY 1

Agree with the atheist that he can be good in some sense without acknowledging God.

There's a kernel of truth in the argument: it's not necessary to acknowledge God's existence in order to do what is good—at least in some respects.

When we speak of good and bad behavior, we refer to the kinds of acts that either achieve or frustrate the ends toward which our nature directs us (self-preservation, propagation of the species, knowledge, love, harmonious living in society, etc.). And these can be identified without appeal to God.

For example, an atheist can know that killing an innocent human being is bad because it unjustly thwart's another's self-preservation and freedom—both of which are ends toward which our nature directs us. An atheist can also know that lying to a person is bad because it frustrates his achievement of truth, which is another natural human end.

These precepts, among others, make up what is known in the Catholic tradition as the *natural moral law*—a law built into the nature of man and known by the light of human reason. The American legal scholar Charles Rice defines the natural moral law as "a set of manufacturer's directions written into our nature so that we can discover through reason how we ought to act."[98]

St. Paul describes this law in Romans 2:14–15, when he reflects on the Gentiles' ability to know God's law without having the benefit of Judeo-Christian revelation:

> When Gentiles who have not the law do by nature what
> the law requires, they are a law to themselves, even
> though they do not have the law. They show that what
> the law requires is written on their heart.

Since this law is inscribed in human nature, and is accessible by the natural light of human reason, then we must conclude that atheists and agnostics can know and follow it—at least *some* aspects of it.

Atheist Dan Barker, the president of the Freedom from Religion Foundation, seems to hold to this system of morality in seed form:

> There is an objective basis for morality . . . It's human
> nature and pain. We evolved to require water, for ex-
> ample. What if we had evolved to require something
> else like arsenic? . . . [B]ut relative to our human nature
> to what helps us, and what either enhances our life or

what causes harm for our life, we can say relative to our human nature, this is something that's good.[99]

Barker expresses what many atheists mean when they say they can be good without God. This is something that Catholics can agree with to a point.

But this doesn't mean God is irrelevant to morality. In the next two strategies, we'll show why.

STRATEGY 2

Show that the natural law also involves our duty to God, and thus our duty to God constitutes our good.

> *Q:* "If God, by definition, is the creator and sustainer of our existence—the one to which we owe every ounce of our being—then wouldn't it be true that he has an absolute right to our worship and adoration?"

Ask your friend to consider this further point:

> *Q:* "If God, by definition, is pure truth and goodness itself, and the desire to know the truth and choose the good is inscribed in our human nature, then wouldn't it belong to our human nature to orient our lives toward God as our ultimate end?"

The point is that if God exists, and we have shown he does, then the natural moral law would *necessarily* involve our duty to God. That is, worshipping him and orienting our lives toward him are part of being a good human being. For this reason, no account of morality is *complete* without God.

> *Q:* "If God exists, can someone really be considered a good person if he willfully rejects, with full knowledge, his natural ordination to God as his ultimate end?"

This brings up an important point. What if an atheist honestly seeks the truth, and simply has not been convinced of the evidence? Can he still be considered good? Would salvation be possible for him? We briefly answered this question in our last chapter, but let's look at it again here with a few more considerations.

The *Catechism* identifies atheism as a sin against the virtue of religion, but also states "the imputability of this offense can be significantly diminished in virtue of the intentions and the circumstances" (2125). In other words, it's possible for someone to embrace atheism (grave matter), and only be venially culpable for it (1862).

One scenario could involve an atheist who is not responsible for his own ignorance of the truth concerning God's existence (perhaps he had bad teachers) and is trying to live according to the truth that he can grasp by the natural light of human reason. He would still be considered good, since inasmuch as he is honestly seeking truth he is seeking God. God could even administer his saving grace to such an atheist apart from the sacrament of baptism (CCC 1257), and on condition the atheist remain in that state of grace until death he would be saved.

Another scenario could involve an atheist who was baptized during his infancy and then later in life rejected God and the Christian faith, due to some bad experience (e.g., abuse from a pastor), or a false understanding of the nature of God (e.g., God is an old man in the sky always looking to punish you).

Although the repudiation of theism and Christianity is grave matter, it's possible that the gravity of the sin not have a mortal effect on the soul, and thus sanctifying grace would remain—provided such an individual has not committed some other mortal sin. And given that sanctifying grace remains in his soul, he would be considered good and would attain salvation on condition that he died in such a state.

Remember that God is truth itself. Inasmuch as someone honestly seeks truth, and has not hardened his heart through sin, he is seeking God even though he may not know it. Only God knows the inner secrets of the heart (Psalm 44:21).

Another point to consider for this strategy is that an atheist's claim that he can be completely good without God presupposes that God doesn't exist (otherwise God might have had something to do with his being good). Therefore, if an atheist uses his good character as a reason to justify his atheism, then he is begging the question—assuming what he's trying to prove: namely, that God doesn't exist.

In order to prove that he is being a good person in a *complete* sense, he would first have to prove that God doesn't exist. But this cannot be done, for reasons we have seen.

STRATEGY 3

Show that God is necessary for moral obligation in following the order of human nature.

Your third strategy involves showing why God is necessary for the order of human nature to be a moral *law*.

> Q: "If God doesn't exist, then what morally binds us to follow the order of human nature? Why should we follow the dictates of our human nature and behave in such a way that achieves the ends toward which our nature directs us?"

If your friend is sharp, he may reply, "Because it's the reasonable thing to do—we're rational animals, you know, naturally ordered to the good." He'd be partially correct.

As rational beings, we are directed toward the pursuit of what the intellect perceives as good. And what is good is the achievement of the various ends inherent in human nature. Therefore, being rational is the same as being good.

But still this doesn't give a sufficient explanation for the *obligation*—the imposed necessity on the will—to follow nature. We all intuitively recognize within ourselves the binding power of our conscience: a sense of duty to do what we know to be good and avoid what we know to be evil. So the question is, "From where does this imposed necessity come?"

Here you want to exhaust the options for your friend. Let's start with nature. There are two reasons why nature can't be the *ultimate*[100] explanation of the binding power of conscience.

First, if nature were the ultimate source, then the precept to do good and avoid evil would be an internal *necessity*, very much like how fire has an internal necessity to rise given its nature.

> *Q:* "But can any sense be made in saying that fire is bound to rise like we're bound to do good and avoid evil?"

It should be apparent to your friend that the internal necessity of fire is not the kind of necessity that we're talking about when we speak of moral obligation.

Of course, nature directs our wills to the good in general, so much so that we can only choose anything insofar as we perceive it under the aspect of some good.[101] But it does not direct us to choose *this* good or *that* good in accord with the hierarchy of goods (see appendix C for further explanation on this point). This is why we're considered *moral* beings, worthy of praise or blame.

Nature, therefore, can't be the ultimate source of the binding power of conscience (the imposed necessity to do good and avoid evil). It must have its source in some outside agent. This is why Aquinas concluded, "binding . . . has place only in things which are necessary with a necessity *imposed by something else*.[102]

It's important to note, however, that this imposed necessity to do good and avoid evil is not one of coercion, which is repugnant to free will.[103] Rather, it is like the *command* of a ruler or king imposing necessity on his subjects to do something to achieve some end. In our case, it's an imposed necessity to do *this* good or *that* good in order to achieve the end of human perfection.

There is another reason why nature can't be the ultimate source of the binding power of our conscience, at least according to atheism. Point out to your friend how atheists don't think the order of nature expresses the intelligence or will of any rational being superior to humans. Then ask,

> Q: "How could something that is the byproduct of random and chaotic non-rational processes morally bind anyone?"

Intuitively we see that this doesn't make sense. But we can do better than intuition. Thomas Aquinas defines a law as "an ordinance of *reason* for the common good, made by him who has care of the community"[104] and is "*imposed* on others by way of a rule and measure."[105] A law being an ordinance of *reason* that is *imposed* presupposes a being of intelligence and volition that can impose it. Therefore, if the order of human nature that determines what's good for us is to be a law that morally binds us, there *must* exist a being superior to humans that has intellect and will. Without such a *personal* being that has care of the human community as a whole, there could be no moral obligation.

These reasons why nature can't be the ultimate source of moral obligation also help us see why our own conscience doesn't suffice either. First, recall how we said above that the imposed necessity we experience must come from *something outside ourselves.*

Second, a person is not bound except through a superior. As St. Thomas writes, "one is under no obligation to an inferior as such,"[106] the implication being that one is obliged only to a superior. Elsewhere he teaches that one has authority over another only insofar as he has been invested with authority by a higher authority.[107] But your friend's conscience can't be superior to himself. For these reasons, conscience doesn't suffice as an explanation for moral obligation.

If the imposed necessity must come from an outside agent, perhaps it could be another human being. But if atheism is true, this doesn't work, either. Remember, only a superior can morally bind a person's will. But in the atheistic view there is no higher authority than human beings to invest one person with authority over others. Thomas Merton sums it up quite nicely:

> In the name of whom or what do you ask me to behave? Why should I go to the inconvenience of denying myself the satisfactions I desire in the name of some standard that exists only in your imagination?[108]

Merton recognized that without God, no human being could morally bind us to do good and avoid evil. All moral precepts would be simply expressions of personal wishes—"I would *like* for you to do that" or "I *wish* you would do this." There could be no commands to "*Do* this" or "*Do* that."

Francis Beckwith and Gregory Koukl describe the unreasonableness of the moral atheist's position:

> A moral atheist is like someone sitting down to dinner who doesn't believe in farmers, ranchers, fishermen, or cooks. She believes the food just appears, with no explanation and no sufficient cause. This is silly. Either her meal is an illusion or someone provided it. In the same way, if morals really exist . . . then some cause adequate to explain the effect must account for them. God is the most reasonable solution.[109]

Beckwith and Koukl understand that denying God's existence results in an insufficient explanation for moral obligation. How can the moral law be a *law* if there is no moral lawgiver behind it that surpasses human authority?

It can't.

There are many moral atheists and agnostics with whom we could lock arms in the pursuit of a just and peaceful society. However, only the theist would be consistent in saying that just and peaceful behaviors are morally *obligatory*. You can get away with personal moral codes without God, including following some aspects of the order of human nature, but not moral obligation.

Atheists have to make a choice: either give up atheism in order to keep moral obligation, or give up moral obligation in order to keep atheism. Let's hope your friend will choose the former.

If your friend decides to go with the latter option and give up moral obligation, then you're in the arena of moral relativism, which, as we saw in strategy three of chapter one, makes morality a mere illusion. If we're not obliged to do what is good for us as human beings, then there is no morality, since the first precept of the natural moral law is "good is to be done and pursued, and evil is to be avoided."[110]

Your friend may follow the logic and concede moral relativism. If he does, show the incoherence of his claim that he can be good without God:

> Q: "If you're willing to give up on morality inasmuch as you think there is no moral obligation, then how can you say that you can be 'good' without God? If there is no morality, there is no being good or bad."

Hopefully your friend will not willingly retreat to the corner of moral nihilism into which you've logically pushed him. If he does, all you can do is leave him there and assure him that when he's ready to come out you will be there for him.

THE WAY PREPARED: God is the ultimate explanation for our moral obligation to live in harmony with the order of goodness inscribed within our human nature.

> *The greatest deception, and the deepest source of unhappiness, is the illusion of finding life by excluding God.*[111]
> —Pope St. John Paul II

12

How can I believe in God when so many reasonable people don't?

If most intelligent people you know believed something, would you believe it?

For many people who don't believe God exists, this is one reason why: the smart people they know and respect, such as scientists and philosophers, are often atheists. For example, ninety-three percent of the members of the National Academy of Sciences (NAS), one of the most elite scientific organizations in the United States, deny God's existence.[112] One study found that seventy-three percent of professional philosophers are atheists.[113]

With such an overwhelming amount of smart people embracing atheism, it's no surprise that a person who wants to be intellectually responsible will be disinclined to acknowledge that God exists. Let's look at some strategies for how we can lower this mountain, and prepare a way for the Lord.

STRATEGY 1

Explain that just because someone is smart in one area of expertise doesn't make him competent when it comes to the question of God's existence.

Q: "Would you trust a mechanic's views on politics because he is a good mechanic?"

I think it's safe to say your friend will answer no. The training that a mechanic receives *as a mechanic* doesn't equip him with political knowledge or wisdom. Explain that the same principle applies to what natural scientists and philosophers who are not trained in philosophy of religion, for example, say about God's existence.

You can remind your friend that God is not subject to scientific inquiry. God is an immaterial being who transcends the boundaries of science's data source—namely, physical reality. This being the case, no amount of scientific training is going to equip a scientist to pursue the philosophical inquiry of God's existence.

> *Q:* "If you shouldn't trust a mechanic's views on politics just because he knows cars, then why should you trust a scientist's views about God because he knows chemistry?"

Since the question of God's existence is beyond a scientist's expertise, as a matter of authority his opinion on the matter is of equal value to that of any other educated non-scientist—just like his opinion on art, or history, or sports.

This same line of reasoning employed applies even to philosophers who have not trained in the philosophy of religion. Even if three-quarters of professional philosophers are atheists, that doesn't mean every one of those philosophers is competent when it comes to the question of God's existence, any more than a biologist is competent in questions of astrophysics. A philosopher can go through his whole career, whether in the philosophy of mind, science, history, etc., and never seriously consider the arguments for God's existence as a philosopher of religion would. Even a philosopher, then, is not necessarily more competent to weigh in on God's existence than an educated non-philosopher.

Many philosophers, accordingly, misunderstand the traditional arguments for God's existence (e.g., Aquinas' five ways), and spend their time refuting only a straw-man version of them. Atheist Daniel Dennett does this, for example, in his book *Breaking the Spell*:

The Cosmological Argument, which in its simplest form states that *since everything must have a cause* the universe must have a cause—namely God . . . [But then] what caused God?[114]

Dennett exposes his ignorance of the cosmological argument by thinking that its key premise is *everything must have a cause.* But our type of cosmological argument doesn't claim that. It starts with the principle that whatever *is caused* must be caused by something else, since it cannot be the cause of itself. It allows for the possibility that something might be uncaused.

When the arguments are worked out, as we saw in chapter six, we find that a series of caused causes (whether we're talking about motion, efficient causality, or necessity) cannot regress infinitely, requiring the existence of a first cause that is uncaused. That this uncaused cause stops the regress, therefore, is not the "entirely unwarranted assumption" that Richard Dawkins thinks it is.[115] Such a conclusion can't be unwarranted when logic demands it!

STRATEGY 2

Explain how the stats concerning the beliefs of scientists and philosophers actually favor theism.

Your second strategy is not meant to prove that theism is true, but simply to let your friend know that if he were to believe in God merely based on the testimony of others, it would be rational.

Concerning the beliefs of scientists, the NAS statistic above is misleading, because that academy only represents a small and select number of scientists, with only about 2,000 members.[116] (There are more than two million scientists employed in the United States.)[117] A better overview of the religious beliefs of scientists can be found in a 2009 study by the Pew Research Center:[118]

• Fifty-one percent believe that God or some higher power exists.

- Forty-one percent of scientists reject the concepts of God or a higher power.

- Seventeen percent of scientists actually identify themselves with the term *atheist*.

Likewise, you can tell your friend, the great majority of philosophers of religion are theists—seventy-two percent, in fact.[119] As atheist philosopher Quentin Smith remarks: "God is not 'dead' in academia; he returned to life in the late 1960s and is now alive and well in his last academic stronghold, philosophy departments."[120]

> *Q:* "If you're willing to embrace a belief on the basis of what smart and competent people think, then wouldn't it be reasonable for you to embrace theism— since the majority of scientists and philosophers competent on the question are theists?"

Whether your friend decides to believe in God or not, at least he will know that he cannot justify his atheism on the basis that most scientists and philosophers are atheists, too. And he need not fear that belief in God puts him in an anti-intellectual crowd.

STRATEGY 3

Name some smart people who were/are believers in God or some transcendent power.

Your friend doesn't merely have to trust polls that say many scientists and philosophers are believers. You can share with him the names and pro-God quotes of some of the greatest minds of history. Some of them laymen who were/are theists:

Nicolaus Copernicus (1473–1543), father of the heliocentric theory of the solar system:

> The universe has been wrought for us by a supremely good and orderly Creator.[121]

Max Planck (1858–1947), originator of the quantum theory:

Religion is the link that binds man to God—resulting from the respectful humility before a supernatural power, to which all human life is subject and which controls our weal and woe.[122]

Albert Einstein (1879–1955):

Certain it is that a conviction, akin to religious feeling, of the rationality and intelligibility of the world lies behind all scientific work of a higher order... This firm belief, a belief bound up with a deep feeling, in a superior mind that reveals itself in the world of experience, represents my conception of God.[123]

Hermann Weyl (1885–1955), one of the great mathematicians of the twentieth century, who also played a role in theoretical physics:

Many people think that modern science is far removed from God. I find on the contrary, that it is much more difficult today for the knowing person to approach God from history, from the spiritual side of the world, and from morals; for there we encounter the suffering and evil in the world, which it is difficult to bring into harmony with an all-merciful and all-mighty God. In this domain we have evidently not yet succeeded in raising the veil with which our human nature covers the essence of things. But in our knowledge of physical nature we have penetrated so far that we can obtain a vision of the flawless harmony which is in conformity with sublime reason.[124]

Fred Hoyle (1915–2001), British astronomer:

Would you not say to yourself, "Some super-calculating intellect must have designed the properties of the carbon atom, otherwise the chance of my finding such an atom through the blind forces of nature would be utterly miniscule?" Of course you would . . . . A commonsense interpretation of the facts suggests that a superintellect has monkeyed with physics, as well as with chemistry and biology, and that there are no blind forces worth speaking about in nature. The numbers one calculates from the facts seem to me so overwhelming as to put this conclusion almost beyond question.[125]

Robert Jastrow (1925–2008), founding director of NASA's Goddard Institute for Space Studies:

The scientist . . . has scaled the mountains of ignorance; he is about to conquer the highest peak; as he pulls himself over the final rock, he is greeted by a band of theologians who have been sitting there for centuries.[126]

Antony Flew (1923–2010), English philosopher who converted from atheism to theism:

I now believe that the universe was brought into existence by an infinite Intelligence. I believe that this universe's intricate laws manifest what scientists have called the Mind of God. I believe that life and reproduction originate in a divine Source. Why do I believe this, given that I expounded and defended atheism for more than half a century? The short answer is this: this is the world picture . . . that has emerged from modern science.[127]

Johannes Kepler (1571–1630), German mathematician and astronomer known for Kepler's Laws of planetary motion:

Praise and glorify with me the wisdom and greatness of the Creator, which I have revealed in a deeper explication of the form of the universe, in an investigation of the causes, and in my detection of the deceptiveness of sight.[128]

[May] God who is the most admirable in his works
. . . deign to grant us the grace to bring to light and illuminate the profundity of his wisdom in the visible (and
accordingly intelligible) creation of this world.[129]

Isaac Newton (1642–1726/27), English physicist and mathematician who is widely recognized as one of the most influential
scientists of all time:

> This most beautiful system of the sun, planets and com-
> ets could only proceed from the counsel and dominion
> of an intelligent and powerful Being. This Being gov-
> erns all things not as the soul of the world, but as Lord
> over all; and on account of his dominion he is wont
> to be called 'Lord God' . . . or 'Universal Ruler' . . .
> And from his true dominion it follows that the true God
> is a living, intelligent and powerful Being . . . he gov-
> erns all things, and knows all things that are or can be
> done. He endures forever, and is everywhere present
> . . . Blind metaphysical necessity, which is certainly the
> same always and everywhere, could produce no variety of
> things. All that diversity of natural things which we find
> suited to different times and places could arise from noth-
> ing but the ideas and will of a Being necessarily existing.[130]

Bruce Gordon, research director at the Discovery Institute's
Center for Science and Culture:

> When the logical and metaphysical necessity of an
> efficient cause, the demonstrable absence of a material
> one, and the proof that there was an absolute beginning
> to any universe or multiverse are all conjoined with the
> fact that our universe exists and its conditions are fine-
> tuned immeasurably beyond the capacity of any mindless
> process, the scientific evidence points inexorably toward

transcendent intelligent agency as the most plausible, if not the only reasonable explanation.[131]

Others were Catholic clergymen who were top scientists of their day:[132]

Robert Grosseteste (ca. 1168–1253), bishop of Lincoln in England who pioneered that branch of science called "optics."

Roger Bacon (c. 1214–1294), English Franciscan monk whose writings predicted the construction of the telescope and laid the groundwork for the scientific method.

St. Albert the Great (1200–1280), bishop who taught St. Thomas Aquinas and who did a great amount of observational work in botany and zoology.

Thomas Bradwardine (1290–1349), archbishop of Canterbury who proved Aristotle's scientific ideas on motion to be inconsistent and was the first to attempt to formulate a mathematical law of motion.

Nicholas of Oresme (1323–1382), bishop of Lisieux in France who made significant contributions to psychology, physics, mathematics, and economics.

Nicolas of Cusa (1401–1464), German cardinal who posed bold ideas such as the universe being infinitely large and that the sun and earth were in motion in infinite space.

Marin Mersenne (1588–1648), historic figure in mathematics referred to as the "father of acoustics."

Christoph Scheiner (1573–1650), Jesuit priest who was one of the first five people to discover sunspots with a telescope independently of one another. His sunspot data is still used by scientists today.

Giambattista Riccioli (1598–1671), Jesuit priest who was the first person to observe a binary star, perfected the pendulum for measuring time in a precise manner, and mapped the surface of the moon with his fellow Jesuit, Francesco Grimaldi.

Francesco Grimaldi (1613–1653), who helped Fr. Riccioli map the surface of the moon and is best known for his discovery and naming of the diffraction of light.

Lazzaro Spallanzani (1729–1799), top biologist of the eighteenth century whose investigative work and experiments served as the foundation for the work of Louis Pasteur.

Giuseppe Piazzi (1746–1826), director of the Palermo Observatory who discovered the first known asteroid.

Pietro Secchi (1818–1878), a founder of modern astrophysics who initiated the study and classification of stars using spectroscopy (color classification).

Gregor Mendel (1822–1884), Augustinian monk and priest who was the founder of genetics.

Abbe Henri Breuil (1877–1962), one of the leading paleontologists of his time and known for his expertise on cave paintings and prehistoric art.

Julius A. Nieuwland (1878–1936), professor of chemistry at Notre Dame whose work led to the development of "neoprene," the first synthetic rubber.

George Lemaitre (1894–1966), director of the Pontifical

Academy of Sciences who was one of the two origina-
tors of the Big Bang theory.

By now your friend will see that to believe in God is to be in good intellectual company.

THE WAY PREPARED: Many reasonable people believe in God, and therefore there is no need to fear that belief in God puts one in an anti-intellectual crowd.

> *If any one imagines that he knows something, he does not yet know as he ought to know.*
> —1 Corinthians 8:2

PART III

PREPARE THE WAY FOR JESUS

13

How can I believe in Jesus when I can't trust the historicity of the Gospels?

The historical reliability of the Gospels is essential to Christianity. If the historical records of Jesus' life are not trustworthy as accounts of things that actually happened, there would be little reason to believe that Christianity is true. Sure, there would be the testimony of oral tradition. But skeptics aren't privy to such testimony. So, promotion of the Christian faith in our secular world rises or falls with its historical validity.

Skeptics want to view the historical records of Jesus' life as untrustworthy. Christopher Hitchens opined, "The New Testament is itself a highly dubious source."[133] H.L. Mencken referred to the New Testament as "a helter-skelter accumulation of more or less discordant documents."[134]

This view, which continues among skeptics today, constitutes a major obstacle to encountering the truth of Jesus. Therefore, it is imperative that we remove this obstacle to prepare the way of the Lord. The strategies below can be summarized in the acronym, A.I.D.[135]

- **A**id—the Gospel writers were *ABLE* to write reliable history.

- **I**ntention—the Gospel writers *INTENDED* to write reliable history.

- **D**id—the Gospel writers *DID* write reliable history.

STRATEGY 1

Show that the Gospel writers were *able* to write reliable history.

There are three reasons to believe that the Gospel writers were able to write reliable history.

First, they were either eyewitnesses, as in the case of Matthew and John, or close associates of eyewitnesses—Mark was a disciple of Peter[136] and Luke was a companion of Paul,[137] each having close collaboration with the apostles. Eyewitness testimony is gold for historiographical research.

If your friend doubts the traditional authorship of the Gospels (that Matthew, John, etc., actually wrote the Gospels attributed to them), point out that *all* of the ancient manuscripts have the traditional names ascribed to them.[138] Furthermore, it would have made no sense to have misrepresented the authorship of at least three of those Gospels, since Matthew was a despised tax collector and Mark and Luke were not eyewitnesses.

A second reason is that the Gospels were written in close temporal proximity to the events recorded.

> *Q:* "Wouldn't you agree that the less time there is between the records of events and the events themselves, the better the writer would be able to remember what happened?"

All historians agree that the closer the written records of an event are to the event, the better. Proximity also decreases the chance of legendary influences altering the core facts.

So how close in time was Gospel authorship to the events the Gospels record? You can start with Matthew and Mark, which could not have been written any later than A.D. 68. The early Christian writer Irenaeus makes clear that Matthew wrote his Gospel while Peter and Paul were still alive,[139] and Peter and Paul died during Nero's persecution, which lasted from 64 to 68. Most scholars agree that Mark wrote his

Gospel before Matthew, placing it prior to A.D. 68 as well.

There is evidence that suggests Matthew and Mark may have written their Gospels even earlier—before A.D. 62. Luke wrote the Acts of the Apostles after he wrote his Gospel, and he wrote his Gospel after Matthew and Mark's Gospels (see Luke 1:1–4). In Acts 28:16–31, Luke describes how he was with Paul while Paul was under his two-year house arrest in Rome, which many scholars date to around A.D. 60, putting the composition of Acts at A.D. 62.[140] Some scholars even push Paul's imprisonment back two years, thus dating Acts to the year 60.[141] Upon finishing the chapter, and consequently the book, you'll notice an abrupt ending.

Luke doesn't give any information as to what happened after Paul's appeal to Caesar—nothing on Caesar's response, or Paul's death, which took place a few years later.

> *Q:* "Wouldn't Luke, who saw it fit to record the martyrdom of Stephen (Acts 7) and James the greater (Acts 12:2), have written about Paul's martyrdom, especially after devoting ten chapters to the events leading up to and including his arrest and trials?"

The likely conclusion we can draw from the omission of the remaining events of Paul's life is that Luke was writing at the time of Paul's house arrest, and didn't continue afterward. If this is true, we must date the Acts of Apostles no later than A.D. 62, which dates Luke's Gospel to earlier than 62 and the Gospels of Matthew and Mark earlier still. This means that eyewitnesses surely would have still been alive at the time those *synoptic* Gospels were composed, thus giving the Gospel writers reliable sources to consult with and restricting legendary developments.

So it's reasonable to conclude that the Gospels of Matthew, Mark, and Luke were written no more than thirty-five years after the events they record, and likely even within thirty years. Compare this with other ancient texts that are considered reliable. Ask your friend these questions:

Q: "If historians trust the biographies of Alexander the Great and Siddhartha Gautama (the Buddha), which are roughly 400 years removed from the events they record,[142] or the six sources for the life of Caesar Augustus, which range from ninety to 200 years after the events they record,[143] shouldn't we trust the synoptic Gospels, which are no more than thirty-five years removed from events, and John's Gospel, which is roughly sixty years removed?"

I think the answer is clear. A thirty-five or sixty-year time gap is far preferable to 400 years when evaluating the historical reliability of ancient documents.

Finally, lest your friend think that even thirty-five years is still too long to accurately remember Jesus' words and actions, especially since many of us can't remember what we ate for breakfast yesterday, share with him the following points:

- The apostles were students of Jesus who lived with him for three years receiving daily instruction, not one flyby lecture in an auditorium.

- The apostles would have frequently rehearsed Jesus' teaching in their own teaching and preaching before writing them down (see Matt. 10:1–23), and thus would have solidified them in their memory.

- The apostles lived in a cultural milieu where the ability to memorize and retain large amounts of information was a highly prized and developed skill (ancient Greeks memorized epics from Homer,[144] Seneca the Elder could repeat 2,000 names in exactly the sequence in which he had just heard them,[145] and the Jews memorized large portions of the Old Testament).[146]

- The Gospel writers had oral sources that predate their final written form.[147]

- It is very likely that the apostles would have made written notes while traveling with Jesus.[148]

- There was leadership present to ensure faithful transmission.[149]

At this point your friend may concede that the Gospel writers were able to record events accurately. But was it their *intention* to write history? They could have been intending to write folklore. This brings us to strategy two.

STRATEGY 2

Show that the Gospel writers *intended* to write reliable history.

There are three reasons to think the Gospel writers intended to write reliable history. The first is that the Gospel writers record details that are not commonly found in myths and legends.

> *Q:* "Why would the Gospels include actual historical events (e.g., the Passover, the festival of tabernacles), and historical individuals with high-ranking positions (e.g., Pontius Pilate, Caiaphas the high priest, Caesar Augustus, Tiberius Caesar) if they were writing mythology?"

Legends or myths usually are not concerned with real-life details. In this case, the events and names in the Gospels would have been easily subject to verification during the first century. These facts suggest that the Gospel authors meant to root their narratives in history.

A second reason is that at least two Gospel writers *explicitly express their intention* to write history. For example, John says, "He who saw it has borne witness—his testimony is true, and he knows that he tells the truth—that you also may believe" (John 19:35).

Luke also makes his historical intention clear in the prologue to his Gospel:

> Inasmuch as many have undertaken to compile a narrative of the things which have been accomplished among us, just as they were delivered to us by those who from the beginning were eyewitnesses and ministers of the word, it seemed good to me also, having followed all things closely for some time past, to write an orderly account for you, most excellent Theophilus, that you may know the truth concerning the things of which you have been informed (1:1–4).

Scholars note that Luke's prologue is similar to historical prologues written by Greco-Roman authors such as Herodotus, Thucydides, and Josephus.[150]

There are three clues that suggest Luke's historical intent. The first is Luke's usage of *degesin*, the Greek word for "narrative." Greco-Roman authors used this word to specify "the writing of history."[151]

A second clue is Luke's emphasis on "eyewitnesses." Luke knows that by basing his narrative on eyewitnesses he makes it possible for his readers to corroborate his testimony about Jesus.

Finally, Luke identifies the purpose of his Gospel as to give "the truth" about what has been taught. Luke uses the Greek word *asphaleian*, which is a word he uses elsewhere for "the facts" (Acts 21:34).

> *Q:* "Why would Luke use a word that means 'writing history,' emphasize 'eyewitnesses,' and identify his purpose in presenting 'the facts,' if he intended to write folklore?"

The reasonable conclusion is that Luke's intention was to write a factual narrative, not a mythical one.

The third reason is similar: there are clear formal similarities between the Gospels and ancient historical biographies of the era, such as the *Life of Josephus* (A.D. 100) and *Lives of the Caesars* written by Roman historian Suetonius (A.D. 120). For example, the Gospels' tripartite focus on Jesus' birth, public life, and death is also an essential part of ancient biographies.[152]

Another parallel can be seen in Matthew and Luke, who begin their biographies with Jesus' ancestry (Matt. 1:1–16; Luke 3:23–38). Just as the phrase "once upon a time" signifies a fairytale, and "Paul, to the church in Rome" signifies a letter, so "genealogy" signifies an ancient biography. For example, Josephus's autobiography and Lucian's biography of Demonax both begin by listing the subject's ancestry.[153]

Scholars point to a third parallel between the Gospels and ancient biographies: the flexibility authors take with arranging material topically or thematically. For example, Suetonius writes about Caesar August "not in chronological order, but by categories."[154] This is similar to what the early Christian writer Papias says of Mark: "[He] wrote down everything he remembered, though not in order, of the things either said or done by Christ."[155]

Finally, the Gospels parallel ancient biographies in that they do not intend to tell the reader *everything* about the person. Consider what John the apostle says:

> But there are also many other things which Jesus did; were every one of them to be written, I suppose that the world itself could not contain the books that would be written (John 21:25).

This is very similar to what the Greek historian Plutarch says in his biography of Alexander the Great:

> [M]ultitude of deeds is so great that I shall make no other preface than to entreat my readers, in case I do not tell of all the famous actions of these men, nor even speak exhaustively at all in each particular case.[156]

Lucian is another example. He writes in the *Life of Demonax,*

These are a very few things out of many which I might have mentioned, but they will suffice to give my readers a notion of the sort of man [Demonax] he was.[157]

When the Gospel writers' *intention* to write history is coupled with the fact that they were *able* to write history, one has good reason to approach the Gospels with a sense of trust.

STRATEGY 3

Show that the Gospel writers *did* write reliable history.

There are three ways you can show that the Gospel writers actually did write reliable history. First, explain how critical sayings and events in Jesus' life meet the criteria that historians use to determine the historicity of a saying or event. There are many, but the most popular are *multiple attestation* (more than one independent source), *embarrassment* (details that might seem to contradict the writer's purpose), and *coherence* (one detail fits with other known details that are historical).

Take, for example, Jesus' death. The four Gospels, Paul's epistles, the writings of the early Church Fathers, the first-century Jewish historian Josephus,[158] and the first-century Roman historian Tacitus[159] attest to it, thus satisfying the criterion of multiple attestation.

Furthermore, Jesus' crucifixion *coheres* with other details we know about Jesus' life. As we will see later, Jesus claims to be God. In the eyes of first-century Jews, such a claim is punishable by death. Therefore, Jesus' death coheres with his claims to be divine. And since Jesus' death coheres with his claims to be God, it is most likely his death is a historical fact.

The criterion of embarrassment is found on multiple occasions, but the most clear is the Gospel writers' account of women witnessing the Resurrection. As we shall see in a later chapter, the testimony of women in first-century Judaism was not taken seriously. Given such a cultural milieu, why would the Gospel writers make women the first witnesses of the Resurrection unless it was true?

These are just a few, but there are many more details that meet the historiographical criteria, and thus indicate the historical accuracy of the Gospel writers.[160]

A second way you can show that the Gospel writers *did* write history is by listing archaeological evidence that confirms Gospel details:

- The nineteenth-century discovery of the Pool of Bethesda mentioned in John 5.[161]

- The 1961 discovery in Caesarea of an inscription with Pontius Pilate's name.[162]

- The 1961 discovery in Caesarea Maritima of a third-century mosaic that had the name "Nazareth" in it—the first known ancient non-biblical reference.[163]

- Coins with references to the names of the Herodian dynasty—Herod the king, Herod the tetrarch of Galilee (killed John the Baptist), Herod Agrippa I (killed James Zebedee), and Herod Agrippa II (before whom Paul testified).[164]

- The 1990 ossuary discovered that had the Aramaic words, "Joseph son of Caiaphas" inscribed on it.[165]

- The 1968 ossuary discovered near Jerusalem that contained the bones of a first-century man who had been crucified, details of which confirm the Gospel narratives of Jesus' crucifixion.[166]

Finally, we know the Gospel writers did write history because many Gospel details are confirmed by ancient non-Christian sources. For example, the first-century Jewish historian Josephus mentions in his writings Caiaphas the high priest,[167] Annas the high priest,[168] Pontius Pilate,[169] King Herod and his descendants,[170] John the Baptist being killed by Herod,[171] James the "brother of Jesus,"[172] and even refers to Jesus as a "wise man," a "doer of startling deeds," and a figure who was condemned to death by "Pontius Pilate."[173]

In his work the *Annals*, the first-century Roman historian Cornelius Tacitus refers to a group of people called "Christians" and describes their leader as "Christus, the founder of the name, [who] was put to death by Pontius Pilate, procurator of Judea in the reign of Tiberius."[174]

In light of the historiographical criteria, the archeological evidence, and the corroboration of Gospel details in ancient non-Christian sources, it is reasonable to conclude that the Gospel writers were not only able to write reliable history and indeed meant to do so, but that they in fact *did* write a trustworthy record of the life of Jesus.

THE WAY PREPARED: The Gospels are historically trustworthy.

> *Historical rigor does not consist in fundamental skepticism toward historical testimony but in fundamental trust along with testing by critical questioning.*[175]
> —Richard Bauckham
>   (English New Testament scholar)

14

How can I believe that Jesus even existed when the only evidence for him comes from the Bible?

Many skeptics doubt the Gospels because its authors were believers. Since these Christians had an investment in Jesus' life, they argue, they probably used those writings to push an agenda rather than to relate accurate history.

Is this true? Should we discount the Gospels' accounts about Jesus' existence because their authors were Christians?

The perceived lack of non-Christian evidence for Jesus' existence makes this obstacle like a valley instead of a mountain. The three strategies below will help you fill the valley and prepare the way of the Lord.

STRATEGY 1

Show that the demand for non-biblical references to Jesus' existence is unreasonable.

You can do this in four ways. First, point out to your friend that the argument assumes what has just been disproven: that the Gospels are historically unreliable. If the Gospels are trustworthy as historical documents, it follows that we can accept their claim that Jesus was a real historical person. For the "bias" argument to even get off the ground, the skeptic would have to first prove that the Gospels are not generally trustworthy.

Second, the skeptic's demand for non-Christian sources is based on the assumption that the Gospel writers cannot be trusted since they are Christian. But this is unsound reasoning. Just because someone cares about the content he is reporting doesn't make him untrustworthy.

> Q: "Should we not trust what Plato tells us of Socrates since he was Socrates' disciple? Should we not trust what American historians say about George Washington? Should we not trust what a Jewish author writes about the Holocaust?"

If we cannot accept an historical account just because a reporter is "invested" in the event he describes, then we would have to reject a lot of historical accounts! That is not a price a reasonable person should be willing to pay.

You can also suggest that having Christian sources actually *ensures* accuracy. It is precisely because the early Christian writers were passionate and committed to their cause that they would have worked hard to tell the story straight.

Finally, the skeptic's insistence that we ignore the New Testament as evidence of Jesus' existence is simply bad historiography.[176]

> Q: "Why would we ignore the earliest, primary sources about Jesus in favor of sources that are much later, secondary, and less reliable? Does that sound like good history?"

Since the skeptic's demand to use only extra-biblical sources is both unreasonable and a bad approach to historical research, Christians do not have to shoulder the burden of providing such sources for the existence of Jesus.

STRATEGY 2

Show that ancient non-Christian sources do affirm that Jesus was a historical person.

Although you are not required to shoulder the burden of providing non-Christian sources that affirm the historical Jesus, your second strategy concedes to the skeptic's request for argument's sake.

A first source is Cornelius Tacitus, a Roman senator and the most important Roman historian of the first century. Share with your friend this quote from his *Annals* (c. A.D. 115):

> Nero fastened the guilt and inflicted the most exquisite punishments on a class hated for their disgraceful acts, called Christians by the populace. *Christ, from whom the name had its origin, suffered the extreme penalty [Crucifixion] during the reign of Tiberius at the hands of one of our procurators, Pontius Pilatus,* and a most mischievous superstition, thus checked for the moment, again broke out not only in Judea, the first source of the evil, but even in Rome, where all things hideous and shameful from every part of the world find their center and become popular.[177]

Here we have an unsympathetic witness affirming not only Jesus' existence but also his crucifixion and death under Pontius Pilate, which corroborates the Gospel accounts. The agnostic New Testament scholar Bart Ehrman concurs:

> Tacitus's report confirms what we know from other sources, that Jesus was executed by order of the Roman governor of Judea, Pontius Pilate, sometime during Tiberius's reign.[178]

The next source outside the Christian scriptures is the Jewish historian Flavius Josephus. In his *Antiquities of the Jews* (published in A.D. 93), he includes two references to the historical Jesus. The first is found in Book 18, which is often referred to as the *Testimonium Flavianum*:

> About this time there lived Jesus, a wise man. For he was one who performed surprising deeds. He won over

many. And when, upon the accusation of the principal men among us, Pilate had condemned him to a cross, those who had first come to love him did not forsake him. And the tribe of the Christians, so called after him, has still to this day not disappeared.[179]

Explain to your friend that most modern scholars regard the above quote as the authentic nucleus written by Josephus himself, with possible later Christian interpolations deleted.[180]

Josephus's second reference to Jesus in *Antiquities* is found in Book 20, where he refers to a high priest named Ananias who convened the Sanhedrin (the highest Jewish court/governing body) to oversee the stoning of lawbreakers in A.D. 62. One of the criminals Josephus describes is "the brother of Jesus, who was called Christ, whose name was James."[181] This is the same James, "the brother of the Lord," that Paul refers to in Galatians 1:19.

Point out to your friend that the great majority of scholars see this passage as authentic because it lacks Christian terms like "the Lord," because it fits into the context of this section of the *Antiquities*, and because it is found in every manuscript copy of the *Antiquities*.[182]

> Q: "Are you willing to still doubt the existence of Jesus when the most respected historians of the first and second centuries affirm that he was a real historical person and confirm key details in the Gospel narratives?"

Point out to your friend that even scholars who are unsympathetic to traditional orthodox Christianity think continuing in such doubt is unreasonable. For example, John Dominic Crossan, an ex–priest and generally skeptical Scripture scholar, admits that nothing is more historical than Jesus' crucifixion, which of course implies that he existed:

> That he was crucified is as sure as anything historical can ever be, since both Josephus and Tacitus . . . agree with the Christian accounts on at least that basic fact.[183]

Even Ehrman dismisses the view that Jesus never existed: "The view that Jesus existed is held by virtually every expert on the planet."[184]

> Q: "If the vast majority of scholars in related fields acknowledge these non-Christian sources as sufficient evidence to show that Jesus was a real person, wouldn't it be unreasonable to continue doubting it?"

With evidence from both Christian and non-Christian sources affirming the historical Jesus, there is no reason your friend should doubt that Jesus was a real historical person.

STRATEGY 3

Explain that the rise of Christianity and its rapid growth are unintelligible if Jesus never existed.

You can start your third strategy by sharing with your friend this quote from Tacitus, which comes right after the quote mentioned above in strategy two:

> Accordingly, an arrest was first made of all who pleaded guilty [Christians]; then, upon their information, *an immense multitude was convicted*, not so much of the crime of firing the city, as of hatred against mankind. Mockery of every sort was added to their deaths. Covered with the skins of beasts, they were torn by dogs and perished, or were nailed to crosses, or were doomed to the flames and burnt, to serve as a nightly illumination, when daylight had expired.[185]

Notice that Tacitus reports "an immense multitude" suffered death instead of denying their Christian beliefs.

Q: "If Jesus never existed, how do you explain the success and spread of the Christian movement? How do you explain that these Christians, some of whom claimed to have known Jesus personally, were willing to endure such torture if Jesus wasn't real?"

To say that the Christian movement could have spread so quickly based on a made-up person, and that the Christians were willing to die rather than renounce their faith in someone they knew was a fictional character, strains reason to a breaking point.

THE WAY PREPARED: Although there is evidence for Jesus outside the New Testament, it's unreasonable to deny the New Testament evidence for Jesus simply because it's Christian.

> *People who insist on evidence taken only from writings outside the New Testament . . . [are] demanding that we ignore the earliest, primary sources about Jesus in favor of sources that are later, secondary, and less reliable, which is just crazy as historical methodology.*[186]
> —William Lane Craig (American Christian apologist)

15

How can I believe in Jesus when he was just a wise teacher?

For many there is no need to believe *in* Jesus, because he was just one wise teacher among many in world history. Sure, he had some great things to say, but so did other wise men.

But when one looks carefully at the evidence, it's impossible to conclude that Jesus was *merely* a wise teacher. As we'll see in the strategies below, Jesus claimed to be God. And anyone who claims to be God when he is not is not a "wise teacher."

I think this obstacle fits the valley metaphor since it is a lack of something, namely, the evidence that Jesus is God. The strategies below will serve to prepare the way of the Lord by filling in the valley. They constitute what is commonly known as the *Trilemma* argument. The argument goes as follows:[187]

> Jesus' claim to be God is either true or false.
> If false, then he either knew it was false or he didn't know it was false.
> If he knew it was false, then he would be a liar.
> If he didn't know it was false, then he would be a lunatic.
> Yet we perceive that he is neither a liar nor a lunatic.
> Therefore, Jesus' claim to be God can't be false.
> Therefore, Jesus' claim to be God must be true.

STRATEGY 1

Show that Jesus claimed to be God—the omnipotent divine being in the Jewish conception.

As you begin your first strategy, remind your friend that we've already established the historical reliability of the Gospels. This gives us rational grounds for looking to them in order to determine what Jesus thought about himself.

So what did Jesus think about himself? Start with examples from the Gospel of John.

- *John 8:58*: Jesus said to them, "Truly, truly, I say to you, before Abraham was, I am." So they took up stones to throw at him; but Jesus hid himself, and went out of the temple.

Explain that "I Am" is the divine name that God revealed to Moses in Exodus 3:14. Here Jesus is applying it to himself. This is why the Jews picked up stones to throw at him. In their mind, Jesus was blaspheming, and thus was worthy of death (see Lev. 24:16).

- John 10:30–33: "I and the Father are one." The Jews took up stones again to stone him. Jesus answered them, "I have shown you many good works from the Father; for which of these do you stone me?" The Jews answered him, "It is not for a good work that we stone you but for blasphemy; because you, being a man, make yourself God."

As in John 8:58, the Jews understood Jesus to be blaspheming. They perceived his claim to unity with the Father to be not merely a moral union (such as union of purpose or allegiance), but a *substantial* union—a union by nature.

After being presented these passages from John, your friend may dismiss them as unhistorical, since John's Gospel was written later, around A.D. 90. Although this is not a strong rebuttal, you can also share Mark 2:1–12.

This event is considered solidly historical because both Matthew (Matt. 9:1–8) and Luke (Luke 5:17–26) attest to it. Although small details differ in each version, all of them agree on three essential points that pertain to Jesus' claim to be God:

- Jesus says he has the power to "forgive sins."

- The scribes charge him with blasphemy in the secret of their hearts, and Jesus is aware of it.

- Jesus identifies himself as the "Son of Man."

Why do the scribes charge Jesus with blasphemy? He claimed to do what only God can do: forgive sins. This is why the scribes question in their hearts, "Who can forgive sins but God alone?" (Mark 2:6). I would venture to say that Old Testament passages like Isaiah 43:25 were running through their minds: "I, I am he who blots out your transgressions for my own sake, and I will not remember your sins."

It's interesting to note that while Jesus is claiming to have the same power as God in forgiving sins, he's manifesting another divine power—the power to read hearts (see Jer. 17:10, 1 Kings 8:39).

Jesus doesn't back down from the charge of blasphemy. Instead he affirms the scribes' thoughts concerning his divine claim by saying, "that you may know that the Son of man has authority on earth to forgive sins . . . rise take up your pallet and go home" (v.11). Jesus' response is significant not only because he validates his claim with a miracle, but because he also refers to himself as the "Son of Man." This is yet another clue in the narrative that supports Jesus' claim to be God.

"Son of Man" is an allusion to the figure in Daniel 7 that is described as "one like a son of man" who comes "with the clouds of heaven" (Dan. 7:13). This figure is commonly seen as the messianic king, but, as New Testament scholar Brant Pitre argues, this king is not just a human king—he's a divine one.[188]

Pitre highlights two details that suggest the figure's divinity. First, Daniel describes him as "coming on the clouds." According to the Old Testament, this is something only God does (see Jer. 4:13). Second, Daniel doesn't say, "He *is* a son of man," but he is "*like* a son of man" (Dan. 7:13; emphasis added). Pitre writes, "He *appears* to be a merely human figure but is in fact a heavenly being."[189]

The contemporary Jewish scholar Daniel Boyarin describes this figure as a "second divine figure" (the first being the ancient of days) and "a God who looks like a human being."[190]

So, let's recap. 1) Jesus claims to forgive sins and merits the charge of blasphemy. 2) He reads the hearts of the scribes, which is a power that belongs to God. 3) He claims to be the "Son of Man," which is a reference to the divine figure of Daniel 7.

Twenty-first-century Americans may complain that Jesus could have made it clearer by saying, "Hey, I'm God." But for first-century Jews, that's exactly what they heard when Jesus claimed to be the Son of Man with power to forgive sins.

The Jewishness of Jesus' claim to divinity provides a response to another possible objection. Your friend might say that Jesus claimed divinity in an Eastern sense of being one with the divine consciousness. Perhaps Jesus was an enlightened mystic, a guru, who realized that we're *all* actually God.

This makes no sense, first of all, because Jesus was not an Eastern pantheist but a Jew. As Peter Kreeft and Robert Tacelli put it, "No guru was ever a Jew and no Jew was ever a guru."[191]

No, Jesus claimed to be the *Jewish* God, the absolutely unique God that is the Creator and sustainer of all that is *beside himself.* If Jesus claimed to be *this* God, then he couldn't possibly have claimed to be "God" in the Eastern mystical sense, for that understanding of divinity makes us all equally divine.

The differences, and outright contradictions, between the Jewishness of Jesus' claims to be divine, and the teachings of Eastern gurus, lead Kreeft and Tacelli to conclude, "it is utterly unhistorical, uprooted and deracinated to see Jesus as a Hindu and not a Jew."[192] Therefore, we can exclude the idea that Jesus was divine like a guru, and affirm his claim to be divine in the Jewish sense.

STRATEGY 2

Show that it's unreasonable to believe that Jesus was lying about his claim.

There are three reasons that you can give to suggest Jesus wasn't lying. First, Jesus performed miracles.[193]

> *Q:* "If Jesus were lying about his claim to be God, then why would God permit him to perform miracles that require divine power—such as raising the dead (Mark 5:21-43, Luke 7:11-17; John 11) and healing the blind (John 9:31-33)?"

If Jesus were lying about being God, it doesn't make sense that God would perform miracles in direct association with Jesus' false claim.

A second reason to believe Jesus wasn't lying is that even most skeptics believe that Jesus was *at least* a good, moral man. The evidence for Jesus' good moral character is abundant:

- He was humble (he washed his disciples' feet—John 13:1–17).

- He didn't exclude people based on social status (he welcomed the rich and poor alike—Luke 19:1–10; 4:18, and even tax-collectors and sinners—Mark 2:15).

- He preached on the importance of forgiving people (Matt. 6:14).

- He insisted that we love others as ourselves (John 13:34).

- His Sermon on the Mount is widely revered as an example of moral perfection (Matt. 5–7).

> *Q:* "If Jesus was a good, moral man, wouldn't it be reasonable to trust him for who he says he is, namely God?"

Good, moral men don't lie about their identity.

Finally, there is no evidence that Jesus would have had selfish motives or reasons to lie.

> *Q:* "Don't people usually lie for selfish reasons?"

Point out that Jesus had nothing to gain from lying. He wasn't seeking political power. He spoke of his kingdom not being of this world (John 18:36), and declared he came to serve and "not to be served" (Matt. 20:28). He even told the rulers of his kingdom, the apostles, not to exercise their authority like the Gentiles do, but to become servants (Luke 22:24–30).

The Gospel portrait of Jesus definitely doesn't give any evidence that he was seeking fame or fortune. He often sought time alone in prayer (Mark 1:12–13; 1:35; 6:45–46), and spoke out against the love of riches (Mark 10:23–27).

The only thing Jesus had to gain from lying about being God was death. Since he had everything to lose and nothing to gain, his testimony is credible. People don't die for what they know to be a lie.

STRATEGY 3

Show that it's unreasonable to believe that Jesus was a lunatic.

Your third strategy doesn't require much work. There are three simple reasons why it's unreasonable to think Jesus was just insane, a conclusion that even most critics of Christianity are not willing to make.

First, Jesus spoke in ways that captivated his audiences—*they* surely didn't think he was a lunatic:

- John 7:46: "No man ever spoke like this man."

- Mark 1:27: And they were all amazed, so that they questioned among themselves, saying, "What is this? A new teaching! With authority he commands even the unclean spirits, and they obey him."

It's possible that a lunatic—someone crazy enough to believe that he's almighty God— might briefly say a few good things here and there, but given the depth of Jesus' teachings over such a long time, and the impact they had on people's lives, it's unreasonable to say that Jesus was such a lunatic.

Second, Jesus was able to read the hearts and minds of those with whom he was speaking:

- *Mark 2:8*: And immediately Jesus, perceiving in his spirit that they thus questioned within themselves, said to them, "Why do you question thus in your hearts?"

  > *Q:* "How could a person with severe mental delusions be so perceptive of the thoughts of people?"

I think it's more plausible to say that Jesus was not mentally deluded.

Finally, Jesus argued with the smartest people of his day and beat them at their mind games time and time again:

- Over the woman caught in adultery (John 8:1–11)

- Over the question of paying taxes to Caesar (Mark 12:13–17)

- Over the question of marriage in the resurrection (Mark 12:18–27)

Mentally addled people are usually not skilled at debate.

> *Q:* "If the evidence that Jesus was wise and astute is so overwhelming, as even critics of Christianity accept, then how could you conclude that he was a lunatic?"

Wise men aren't crazy men. They know who they are. And if Jesus was a wise man and not a liar, and claimed to be God, then he was.

THE WAY PREPARED: Jesus is Lord because he is neither a liar nor a lunatic.

> *A man who was merely a man and said the sort of things Jesus said would not be a great moral teacher. He would either be a lunatic . . . or else he would be the Devil of Hell. You must make your choice.*[194]
> —C.S. Lewis

16

How can I believe in Jesus when he sounds like a legend?

Jesus is said to have cast out demons, raised people from the dead, and healed the blind and deaf. But to many skeptics such things sound like the stuff of legend, too fantastic to believe.

I think the valley is a fitting metaphor for this obstacle. The skeptic lacks evidence that would persuade him to think these reports are historically trustworthy. So how do we argue for the historicity of Jesus' miracles in order to fill the valley and prepare the way of the Lord?

There are two ways to do this: a general way and a specific way. The latter, which includes looking at each miracle in light of the criteria for historicity, is too detailed for the scope of this chapter.[195] So our strategies below will employ a general assessment.

STRATEGY 1

Show that the Gospel writers record things about Jesus' miracles that actually have the potential to undermine their efforts to persuade people to believe.

Your first strategy employs the *embarrassment criterion* we noted in an earlier chapter. In short, details embarrassing to the figure written about are presumed true, since the author would have no reason to make them up.

One example of this is Mark's account of the Pharisees' accusation that Jesus performed miracles by the power of the devil:

"He is possessed by Be-elzebul, and by the prince of demons he casts out the demons" (Mark 3:22).

> Q: "Why would Mark make up this story when it has the potential to undermine Jesus' reputation?"

Jews did in fact make such a charge hundreds of years later in the Talmud. For example, Kallah 1b claims that Mary confessed that on her wedding day Joseph left her and she conceived Jesus by an evil spirit. This gave rise to the Jewish tradition that Jesus had a literal demon as his father.

> Q: "If the embarrassment criterion suggests that the Pharisees' accusation is historical, wouldn't it be reasonable to conclude that Jesus' contemporaries really did see him as a man with remarkable powers who performed remarkable deeds? Why else would they make such a charge?"

It's not likely that Jesus' toughest critics would acknowledge that he had supernatural powers unless it was common knowledge that he was exercising them.

STRATEGY 2

Show that Jesus' miracles were far different from the first-century milieu of wonder-workers.

Your second strategy employs yet another criterion of historicity, the criterion of dissimilarity. Applied to our case, it states that if a saying or deed attributed to Jesus is dissimilar to the Jewish traditions, or even dissimilar to the broader historical milieu of the time, it is likely to be authentic.

The dissimilarities between Jesus' miracles and ancient stories of wonder-workers, both Jewish and pagan, suggest to historians that the wonders Jesus performed were historical, not part of a local myth tradition. In his book, *An Introduction to New Testament Christology*, Bible scholar Raymond Brown identifies five ways in which Jesus' miracles differ from those found in ancient Greek and Jewish stories. For brevity's sake, we'll look at two.

One unique characteristic is that Jesus performs miracles *by his own authority.*

- *Mark 2:9*: "Rise, take up your pallet and walk."
- *Mark 5:41*: "Little girl, *I say* to you, arise."

Point out that Jesus doesn't say, *"In the name of God,* rise and walk."

> Q: "If Jesus didn't have to invoke the name of God
> to perform the miracles, wouldn't it be reasonable to
> conclude that he performed them by his own power?"

Perhaps if there were no other wonder-workers to compare this to, it would be hard to answer this question. But there *are* others with whom we can contrast Jesus' miraculous deeds.

For example, the Old Testament prophets Elijah and Elisha call on the power of God in order to raise the dead (1 Kings 17:17–22; 2 Kings 4:32–35). The first-century B.C. Jewish wonder-worker Honi (Onias) is said to have brought down rain by praying to God while standing in the middle of a circle.[196] Among the Greeks and Romans, similar methods of miracle-working were commonly reported—whether through magical formulas, paraphernalia, or prayers to the gods.[197] But this is not how Jesus worked.

Another unique characteristic that Raymond Brown points out is that Jesus doesn't perform miracles for the sake of showing off. Whereas pagan wonder-workers, such as Apollonius of Tyana (first century A.D.), sought to astonish and gain admiration,[198] Jesus shied away from drawing attention to himself.

- Jesus refused Herod's request to show off his power (Luke 23:8–12).

- Jesus gets frustrated with the Pharisees' constant requests for a sign (Mark 8:11–12).

- Jesus refuses Satan's request for him to show off his power (Matt. 4:5–7).

- Jesus commands the healed leper to remain silent (Mark 1:44).

Many people allow a reflexive tendency to lump in Jesus' miracles with other accounts of wonder-working in the ancient world to be an obstacle to the Lord. But you can show them how the many dissimilarities between Jesus' wondrous deeds and those of other ancient accounts—both Jewish and pagan—argue in favor of their historicity. What may at first glance seem like the stuff of legend does not have to keep reasonable people from considering the gospel.

STRATEGY 3

Explain how the Gospel narratives are restrained in their description of Jesus' miracles.

Your third strategy argues from the fact that the Gospel narratives of Jesus' miracles stand in stark contrast with the frivolous and exaggerated elements found in the fraudulent Gnostic Gospels that appeared in the early centuries of the Church.

You can use Mark's account of the Resurrection as an example. Point out how it's simple and unembellished—he doesn't even include the actual event of Jesus rising.

> Q: "If Mark was making this stuff up, don't you think he would have described the actual moment when Jesus came back to life? Wouldn't that have made it more interesting?"

Mark's restraint is glaringly different from the extraordinary details found in the apocryphal Gospel of Peter—giant angels, a talking cross, a voice from heaven, and Jesus coming out of the tomb as a gigantic figure whose head reaches to the clouds!

The Gospel narratives of Jesus' miracles contrast with that of another Gnostic text, the *Infancy Gospel of Thomas*, which illustrates the child Jesus making clay sparrows fly and twice cursing other children to death—one for spilling water and one for bumping into Jesus on the street. Such frivolous details are generally absent from the Gospels, with the possible exceptions of the coin in the fish's mouth (Matt. 17:24–27) and Jesus cursing the fig tree (Mark 11:12–14, 20–21). But even these miracles prove to be non-frivolous upon further investigation.[199]

This editorial restraint is found in many other ways. Consider, for example, how the Gospel writers don't portray Jesus as performing miracles to convert the hardened of heart. He doesn't do so for those relatives that "take offense at him" in his hometown (Mark 6:4), the Pharisees who demanded he give a "sign from heaven" (Mark 8:11–13), and his enemies who tempted him to come down off the cross so that they might believe (Mark 8:31–32).

It's amazing that the Gospel writers didn't take advantage of the opportunity to showcase Jesus' power to convince his own skeptics, especially since they were trying to convince their own skeptics. This is exactly what you would expect if they were fabricating these events.

We also see this editorial restraint in the *number* of "raisings from the dead" that Jesus performed. There is the raising of Jairus's daughter from the Marcan tradition (Mark 5:21–43), the raising of the son of the widow of Nain in the special Luke tradition (Luke 7:11–17), the Johannine account of the raising of Lazarus (John 11:1–46), and a saying in the Q tradition[200] that speaks in passing of Jesus raising the dead (Matt. 11:5). Fr. Robert J. Spitzer reflects on the implications of this restraint:

Curiously, despite the spectacular character of the "raisings", none of the Gospel writers felt a need to multiply them. Mark, Matthew, and John limit themselves to one, and Luke limits himself to two. The fact that the evangelists do not multiply these stories indicates a mature editorial restraint and respect for the truth.[201]

The Gospel accounts of Jesus' miracles in his public ministry are as spare and restrained as the accounts of his birth, early life, and resurrection. Even though making the miracle stories more dramatic would have given them more appeal to potential converts, the Gospel writers did not give in to the temptation to exaggerate them. Their restraint, along with Jesus' unique style and the testimony of his enemies, are all evidence for the historical reliability of the accounts of Jesus' miracles.

THE WAY PREPARED: The accounts of Jesus' miracles are historically trustworthy and do not fit the genre of legend.

The statement that Jesus acted as and was viewed as an exorcist and healer . . . has as much historical corroboration as almost any other statement we can make about the Jesus of history.[202]
—John P. Meier (American biblical scholar)

17

How can I believe in Jesus when his prophecies didn't come true?

Certain skeptics claim to reject Jesus because he was a failed apocalyptic prophet—that is to say, his prophecy about the end of the world didn't come true.

Their argument centers around the Olivet Discourse in Matthew, where Jesus promises that the "current generation" would not pass away before his coming (Matt. 24:34). Skeptics like Bart Ehrman[203] and the late Albert Schweitzer[204] interpret Jesus' words to mean that he is predicting his return in glory prior to the death of the disciples. Since this didn't happen, they conclude, Jesus is proven to be a false prophet. Even C.S. Lewis, in his essay "The World's Last Night," says that Matthew 24:34 "is certainly the most embarrassing verse in the Bible."[205]

How can we remove the mountain that is the skeptic's false understanding of Jesus' teaching and prepare the way of the Lord?

The key is to give skeptics good reasons to think that Jesus' prediction doesn't primarily[206] refer to his second coming at the end of time, but to the Roman siege of Jerusalem that resulted in the destruction of the temple in A.D. 70. In other words, he's not predicting the end of *the* world, but *a* world—the world of temple Judaism.[207]

STRATEGY 1

Show that various details in Jesus' teaching parallel

prophecies of the Babylonian invasion of Jerusalem and the destruction of the first temple in 586 B.C.

In 586 B.C., King Nebuchadnezzar II laid siege to Jerusalem in response to a revolt begun by the tributary king of Judah, Zedekiah. Nebuchadnezzar destroyed the city and its temple, exiling the inhabitants to Babylon (see 2 Kings. 25:2; 2 Chr. 36). These events came to pass as the prophets of Israel had foretold (2 Kings. 20:16–18; Jer. 15:1–14, 21:8–14; Ezek. 4–5; Amos 2:4–5; Mic. 3:12).

The first detail in Jesus' teaching that parallels these events is the movement of the setting from the temple in Jerusalem to the Mount of Olives, which is directly east of Jerusalem (Matt. 24:3). This seems to parallel Ezekiel's description of the Shekinah ("the glory of the Lord") crossing the threshold of the temple and hovering over the cherubim at the east gate, then moving "straight forward" in the direction of the Mount of Olives (Ezek. 10:18–23).

This relates to our proposed interpretation because Ezekiel describes this event within the context of prophesying about Jerusalem's impending destruction in 586 B.C. In Matthew 24, we have Jesus, the glory of God made flesh, prophesying, leaving the temple, and heading east toward the Mount of Olives. Such a parallel is too direct to be a mere coincidence.

A second detail that parallels the prophecies of the 586 B.C. Babylonian siege on Jerusalem and the destruction of the temple is the famine warning (Matt. 24:8). Ezekiel prophesied the same thing in Ezekiel 7:14–16.

Third, Jesus' command for the Christians to "flee" into the mountains parallels the prophecies of Zechariah (Zech. 14:1–2,5) and Joel (Joel 2:32), who both incorporate this motif within the context of foretelling the destruction of Jerusalem in 586 B.C.

Q: "If fleeing the city was central to the prophecies of the destruction of Jerusalem in the sixth century B.C., and Jesus speaks of fleeing the city in his prophecy,

then wouldn't it be reasonable to wonder if Jesus
is foretelling the Roman siege of Jerusalem and the
destruction of the temple in A.D. 70?"

Not only do the above Old Testament texts make it a reasonable conclusion, but the fourth-century Church historian Eusebius of Caesarea supports it, too. He recounts in his *Ecclesiastical History* how the Christians fled to an ancient Greek city called Pella right before the destruction of Jerusalem in A.D. 70.[208]

STRATEGY 2

Show that the various signs preceding Jesus' coming match up with Josephus's records of the historical events that led up to the Roman siege of Jerusalem in A.D. 70.

For strategy two, you want to begin by reading Matthew 24:6–14 and then highlighting each detail that is corroborated by the first-century Jewish historian Josephus.

First, Jesus speaks of "wars" (v.6). Josephus recounts how civil war raged in the Roman Empire right at the time before the siege of Jerusalem (around A.D. 69).[209]

Second, Jesus speaks of "famine" and "earthquakes" (v.7). Josephus records both catastrophic events in his *Wars of the Jews*. With regard to earthquakes, he writes:

[F]or there broke out a prodigious storm in the night, with the utmost violence, and very strong winds, with the largest showers of rain, with continual lightnings, terrible thunderings, and amazing concussions and bellowings of the earth, that was in an earthquake . . . anyone would guess that these wonders foreshadowed some grand calamities that were coming.[210]

Josephus talks about famine elsewhere in Book Six:

[T]here perished, for want of food, eleven thousand . . .
they were in want even of corn for their sustenance . . .
there came a pestilential destruction upon them, and
soon afterward such a famine, as destroyed them more
suddenly . . . there were also found slain . . . but chiefly
destroyed by the famine.[211]

A third detail in Jesus' prophecy that is directly corroborated
by Josephus, and the final one for our consideration in this chapter, is the advent of "false prophets" (Matt. 24:11).

In his *Antiquities,* Josephus describes an Egyptian who declared himself a prophet and developed a group of followers that
was later brought to ruins by Marcus Felix, the Roman procurator of the Judean Province from A.D. 52–58.[212] The Egyptian
disappeared, never to be heard from again.

Josephus also records the advent, around the time of A.D. 44–
46, of a man named Theudas who persuaded many people that
he was a prophet leading them to the Jordan River—promising
to divide it like Joshua. Theudas and his followers were slaughtered by the Romans under the direction of the then reigning
procurator of Judea, Cuspius Fadus.

STRATEGY 3

Explain that various contextual details point toward the interpretation of Jesus' prophecy of Jerusalem's destruction in A.D. 70.

The first detail is the explicit prophecy of the destruction of the
temple that precedes the prophetical utterances in question:

Jesus left the temple and was going away, when his disciples
came to point out to him the buildings of the temple. But
he answered them, "You see all these, do you not? Truly,
I say to you, there will not be left here one stone upon
another, that will not be thrown down" (Matt. 24:2).

Second, all the signs, language, and details that make up Jesus' teaching are in response to the disciples' question: "Tell us, when will this be, and what will be the sign of your coming and of the close of the age?" (Matt. 24:3). This verse bridges the destruction of the temple and the signs of impending judgment.

A third detail is the cosmic cataclysmic imagery that Jesus uses:

> [T]he sun will be darkened, and the moon will not give its light, and the stars will fall from heaven, and the powers of the heavens will be shaken (Matt. 24:35).

Prophets used this kind of imagery in the Old Testament when they were prophesying the *impending destruction of God's enemies*:

- The destruction of Babylon: "sun," "moon," and "stars" no longer give their light (Isaiah 13).

- The destruction of wicked nations: stars "fall" from heaven (Isaiah 34).

- The destruction of Egypt: "sun," "moon," and "stars" are darkened (Ezekiel 32).

> *Q:* "If this cataclysmic imagery was used by Jewish prophets not to foretell a cosmic apocalypse but to warn of the impending destruction of cities, then wouldn't it be reasonable to conclude that Jesus, a Jewish prophet, would use the same imagery in the same way?"

Jerusalem, in rejecting the Messiah and persecuting the fledgling Church, had in effect become God's enemy just as Babylon and Egypt were. When Jesus' prophecy is read against this Old Testament backdrop, the destruction of Jerusalem seems to be a reasonable interpretation.

The cataclysmic imagery also suggests the fall of Jerusalem because the temple was for the Jews a symbol of the whole universe.

The outer veil before the court of Israel had "embroidered upon it all that was mystical in the heavens" (stars and constellations).[213] The seven lights of the menorah represented the sun, the moon, and the known planets at the time (Mercury, Venus, Mars, Jupiter, and Saturn).[214] The Old Testament affirms this parallel between the temple and the cosmos: "He built his sanctuary like the high heavens, like the earth, which he has founded forever" (Psalm 78:69).

Josephus even describes the temple in like manner in his *Antiquities of the Jews*:

> If anyone without prejudice, and with judgment, look upon these things [in the Tabernacle], he will find they were in every one made in way of imitation and representation of the universe. When Moses distinguished the tabernacle into three parts, and allowed two of them to the priests, as a place accessible and common, he denoted the land and the sea, these being of general access to all; but he set apart the third division for God, because heaven is inaccessible to men.[215]

Q: "If the Jerusalem temple had cosmic elements to it and was understood to be a mini-cosmos, then wouldn't it be appropriate to describe its destruction in cosmic terms?"

Another detail is found in Luke's version of the same prophecy, in which Jesus *localizes* the events in Jerusalem:

> But when you see *Jerusalem* surrounded by armies, then know that its desolation has come near. Then let those who are *in Judea* flee to *the mountains*, and let those who are *inside the city* depart, and let not those who are out in the country enter it; for these are days of vengeance, to fulfill all that is written" (Luke 21:20–22; emphasis added).

By placing the events inside the city of Jerusalem, Jesus

doesn't seem to be referring to a worldwide event like the end of the world at the second coming of Christ. Which, if you think about it, makes more sense. After all, what if someone doesn't have mountains to run to?

Finally, Jesus says that everything he describes would take place within a *generation*, which for the Jews was forty years: "Amen I say to you, this generation will not pass away until all these things have taken place" (Matt. 25:34).

> Q: "If Jesus made this prophecy around A.D. 30 to 33, and the temple was destroyed in A.D. 70 during the Roman siege, then wouldn't that put the event within a generation?"

These details give a strong indication that Jesus was not wrong in his prophecy concerning his impending return. Rather than prophesying about his glorious coming at the end of time (CCC 668–682), he intended his coming to be understood in the sense of *God's coming in the Old Testament*, namely, that judgment is imminent (Jer. 4:11–13).

Some of the early Church Fathers saw these details as pointing to Jerusalem's destruction in A.D. 70 as well. For example, when commenting on Luke's version of Jesus' prophecy about the destruction of the temple (Luke 21:5–6), the fifth-century patriarch Cyril of Alexandria writes,

> The power of the Romans would tear it down and burn Jerusalem with fire, and retribution would be required from Israel for the Lord's murder. They had to suffer these things after the Savior's crucifixion.[216]

When Cyril comments on Jesus' prophecy of the temple's destruction in Matthew 24:1, he says the same thing, but adds that it was punishment for "slaying of the Lord."[217]

Jerome was another Father who was open to this interpretation. In commenting on Matthew 24:23, where Jesus speaks of false christs and prophets arising to perform great signs and wonders to lead the elect into error, he offers three possible interpretations, one of which is the Roman siege in A.D. 70.[218]

You can assure your friend that there is no need to worry about this obstacle. Christianity has been dealing with it for centuries.

STRATEGY 4

Explain how the "failed prophet" interpretation doesn't jibe with the early Christian belief that Jesus was God.

Q: "If the early Christians believed that Jesus was wrong about his second coming, wouldn't it be strange that they continued to profess his divinity? How could they have believed that Jesus was God if he erred?"

We can hope that your friend sees the underlying assumption: divinity and error cannot co-exist. If it's not clear to him, then simply point it out.

The early Christians didn't back down from professing Jesus' divinity. For example, John the evangelist identifies Jesus as the Word, and says that "the word was God" (John 1:1). After saying that we as Christians are in Jesus in 1 John 5:20, he writes, "This is the true God and eternal life."

It doesn't make sense that the early Christians would have said such things knowing that Jesus was wrong about his second coming. That they *do* say such things, therefore, gives us reason to think the early Christians didn't believe Jesus was speaking merely of his second coming at the end of time. They must have understood him to mean something else, and as we've seen above, Jerusalem's destruction in A.D. 70 is a very good candidate.

THE WAY PREPARED: The destruction of Jerusalem and the temple in A.D. 70 happened exactly as Jesus foretold.

> *When the people saw the sign which he had performed, they said, "This is truly the Prophet who is to come into the world."*
> —John 6:14

18

How can I believe in Jesus when he threatened to send people to hell?

In John 15:6 Jesus says, "If a man does not abide in me, he is cast forth as a branch and withers; and the branches are gathered, thrown into the fire and burned." In Matthew 25:41, he says to those who failed to serve him by serving others, "Depart from me, you cursed, into the eternal fire prepared for the devil and his angels."

For some people, these threats of hell for failure to follow Jesus are a major obstacle. How could Jesus be good, loving, and merciful if he threatens to damn people for eternity? For many, hell is incompatible with Jesus' love. How can we remove this obstacle to prepare the way?

The three strategies below provide reasonable ways of reconciling God's goodness and the reality of hell. Keep in mind that these strategies presuppose Jesus' divinity, which we have already covered. Therefore, whatever is said of God can be applied to Jesus.

STRATEGY 1

Explain how it belongs to God's goodness not to coerce human beings into loving him.

Your first strategy appeals to the good of man's freedom, and how such freedom is necessary for a relationship of love. You can begin by asking your friend this question:

> *Q:* "Imagine a man makes a modest romantic
> advance to a woman and she rejects him. But then
> he grabs her and tries to kiss her anyway. Is this a
> good man?"

No, this man is a creep, which probably is what the woman would say as she slapped him across the face.

This example shows that it is not befitting of goodness to coerce someone into a loving relationship. The same principle applies to God and those who reject him.

> *Q:* "If someone rejects God, and doesn't wish to be
> with him for an eternity, wouldn't it belong to God's
> goodness to respect the person's free will and not
> coerce the person into loving him?"

I think it would. As C.S. Lewis writes in *The Great Divorce*, "There are only two kinds of people in the end: those who say to God, 'Thy will be done,' and those to whom God says, 'Thy will be done.'"[219] Hell is for the latter. All those there choose it.

If that's the case, then the possibility of hell, which the *Catechism of the Catholic Church* defines as "definitive self-exclusion from God" (1033), is not incompatible with God's goodness.[220]

STRATEGY 2

**Explain that the everlasting punishment of hell
is a matter of justice.**

Your second strategy appeals to justice. There are three lines of reasoning that you can take.

First, the gravity of the free and willful rejection of God— what the Catholic Church calls a "mortal sin" (CCC 1855) or, as the apostle John calls it, "a sin unto death" (1 John 5:16; Douay Rheims)—reasonably calls for permanent exclusion from the presence of God. As St. Thomas Aquinas teaches,[221] the gravity of an offense is determined according to the dignity of the person sinned against.

> Q: "Is it reasonable to inflict a greater punishment on an individual for striking the president of the United States than for striking a fellow citizen in a bar brawl?"

The law does this very thing. You can now apply the principle to God.

> Q: "If God is infinite in dignity and majesty, wouldn't he have an absolute and infinite right to obedience from his reasonable creatures?"

Since there is no greater dignity than *infinite* dignity, you can connect the dots:

> Q: "If God is infinite in dignity and majesty, and has an absolute and infinite right to obedience from rational creatures, wouldn't it follow that a willful violation of this right, which is what a mortal sin is, would be the most severe offense a human being can commit?"

It would seem reasonable that such a violation would be the highest and gravest offense.[222] Since the rejection of God's absolute right to our obedience, worship, and love is a moral disorder of the highest degree, it deserves a penalty of the highest degree. Everlasting punishment seems to fit the bill.

You could also argue that the alternatives to everlasting punishment don't jibe with God's goodness and justice. Let's say for argument's sake that a damned soul would instead receive an intense dose of punishment and then enter heaven. Would this be just?

Imagine I find out that my twelve-year-old son ditched school, went to a party with his older teen friends, then got drunk (this is merely hypothetical, mind you). What if I punished him by saying, "Son, you've been a bad boy, and as a result you're going to stay in your room for ten minutes. But when that time is up, pack your bags because we're going to Legoland!"

> Q: "How does this register on your justice monitor—
> especially if my son refuses to apologize for his
> misconduct?"

I'm pretty sure your friend would agree that the punishment is too small and that it makes no sense to follow with a reward.

Similarly, a temporary stint in hell—no matter how long the term—is much too small relative to the everlasting happiness of heaven that follows. It would be unjust for God to give heaven as a reward, after any amount of temporal punishment, to a person who committed the most grievous offense of all: the permanent, unrepentant rejection of God's absolute right to obedience, worship, and love.

Annihilation of the soul is also an unreasonable alternative.

> Q: "How could a person experience just punishment
> for permanently rejecting God if he ceased to exist?
> Wouldn't that reduce to zero the gravity of violating
> God's absolute right?"

You can also explain how annihilation of the soul would violate God's wisdom.

> Q: "Why would God create a soul with an immortal
> nature only to thwart it?"

It doesn't make sense. Moreover, Aquinas argues that God's power is manifest in preserving things in existence; therefore to take a soul out of being would hinder that manifestation.[223]

Finally, you can explain how it belongs to God's goodness to make a distinction between loyal and disloyal subjects, and to give them their just deserts.

> *Q:* "Let's say your parents gave their inheritance to
> one of your siblings who had rejected them all their
> life and continued to reject them right up to their
> death. Would it be just for your parents to give that
> sibling their inheritance, especially when you had
> been faithful to your parents throughout your entire
> life and remained faithful till their death?"

Hopefully your friend can see how it would be an injustice for his parents to do such a thing. The same applies to God. It wouldn't be good for God to give heaven as a reward to his children that refuse to love him even until their death.

STRATEGY 3

Explain that the torment of hell is not arbitrary vengeance but flows from the nature of sin.

Your third strategy addresses the nature of the punishment of hell. The *Catechism* teaches that the eternal punishment of hell is not "a kind of vengeance inflicted by God from without, but as following from the very nature of sin" (1472).

What the *Catechism* means is that the torment in hell is a natural consequence of being separated from the ultimate source of joy and happiness, God himself. Kreeft and Tacelli sum it up best:

> Since the God to whom we choose to open and love and
> obey is the sole source of all the joy in reality, our refusal
> of this God must necessarily be joyless and painful. Thus
> hell must have the aspect of pain as well as punishment. If
> God is joy, hell must be pain.[224]

In other words, hell is painful because it is a *privation* of God, the source of all joy. As St. Augustine taught, our hearts are made for God and they are restless until they rest in him.[225] If a person chooses to separate himself from God for eternity, the state of restlessness or misery is simply a natural consequence. The torment follows from the way God has made human nature.

Consider these two scenarios. Suppose a father tells his son, "If you want to go to the movies, then you have to clean your room," and the son chooses not to clean his room. The result of his choice is that he doesn't get to go to the movies. He throws a fit. His "pain," the deprivation of not seeing a movie, is a consequence of his choice. But notice that the connection between the consequence and the choice is not natural. The father *imposes* it.

Contrast this with the scenario of an individual who intentionally puts a plastic bag over his head and dies of asphyxiation. The painful effect of death is a *natural* consequence of stopping his supply of oxygen. It belongs to his nature that he needs oxygen to live. If he doesn't have oxygen, then he doesn't have life.

Similarly, it belongs to human nature for a person to be united to God in order to have happiness. If he's not united to God, then no happiness, and only misery.

> Q: "Why would it be contrary to God's goodness to allow human nature to function according to the design he created?"

If God decides to create something with a particular nature, then it belongs to his goodness to treat that thing according to its nature. God made humans to be in union with him for an eternity. Therefore, if anyone chooses to reject such union and end up separated from God for an eternity, which is the essence of hell, his misery would be the natural result given his nature. And there is nothing contrary to God's goodness to allow nature to take its course—whether it takes it in beatitude with God in heaven or misery without him in hell.

Now, lest your friend think this is cold and clinical, emphasize the point that God never ceases drawing us to himself with his grace in this life. Given that God made us to be united with him in heaven, it's necessary that he provide the means to achieve that union. That means is grace. As Jesus told Paul, "My grace is sufficient for you" (2 Cor. 12:9).

Moreover, because God wills that *all* be saved (1 Tim. 2:4; cf. 2 Pet. 3:9), he offers this grace of salvation to all. But God also wills that we not impede this grace from achieving its salvific end. Therefore, on condition that we do not forfeit this grace by committing a mortal sin (CCC 1855–1859), we will be saved. There is no injustice in God's providing everything necessary for us to achieve happiness through union with him in heaven and at the same time respecting our choice to choose our own misery by rejecting the means to achieve such union.

The only alternative is for God to make it so that we can't reject his grace—by revealing his essence to us as he does to the blessed in heaven. But then we would lose the dignity of being real causes of our own perfection and the dignity of meriting our final reward, which as we've already seen is not as good as having the dignity (see strategy three, chapter eight).

THE WAY PREPARED: The existence of hell stems from Jesus' will that we have the dignity to determine whether we want to enter into an everlasting loving relationship with him or not.

> *The thought of hell . . . must not create anxiety or despair, but is a necessary and healthy reminder of freedom within the proclamation that the risen Jesus has conquered Satan.*[226]
> —Pope St. John Paul II

19

How can I believe in Jesus when he's nothing but a rip-off of pagan gods?

Although the claim that the Jesus story is a rehash of old pagan myths is something that the majority of scholars don't consider a topic worthy of debate,[227] it is alive on the popular level—via the internet, television, and movies.

Take for example the movie *Zeitgeist,* which has some twenty-five million views on YouTube and has stoked the idea that Christianity is merely a mishmash of other religious ideas, and thus a total fiction. This presents a formidable obstacle. Mark Foreman, professor of philosophy and religion at Liberty University, recounts the story of a student who approached him after watching *Zeitgeist,* concerned that "all the stuff I was taught in church [is] just a big hoax."[228]

How do we lay low this mountain? The strategies below do not constitute a comprehensive response to every accusation skeptics make relating to Christianity and pagan myths. However, they do provide a general method of investigation, and the endnotes point to excellent resources on this topic.

STRATEGY 1

Explain how there are several historical problems with asserting that the Jesus story was a rip-off of pagan deities.

There are three ways you can do this. First, if your friend puts forward this objection to imply that Jesus didn't exist, then share with him the historical evidence for Jesus' existence that we covered in chapter fourteen.

If your friend acknowledges Jesus as a historical person, but argues that the *details of his life* (birth, death, resurrection, etc.) are taken from the mythological stories of pagan deities, then you want to draw your friend's attention to the marked difference between the verifiable historical details of Jesus' life and the non-verifiable details of pagan myths.

> *Q:* "Why should I believe that the Jesus story is a myth similar to pagan myths when the Gospel writers ground their narratives in historical details that can be corroborated but the pagan myths do not?"

Sure the Osirian myths mention the Nile River, a few cities in Egypt, and some people, but this doesn't come close to the verifiable time-and-place details mentioned in the Gospels. With regard to Roman mythology, one scholar writes, "The Roman mystery cult of Mithras has no substantive written record; therefore there is no way of checking for accuracy of dates, people, places, events, and such."[229]

Consider the historical setting of Luke's Gospel:

> In the fifteenth year of the reign of Tiberius Caesar, Pontius Pilate being governor of Judea, and Herod being tetrarch of Galilee, and his brother Philip tetrarch of the region of Ituraea and Trachonitis, and Lysanias tetrarch of Abilene, in the high-priesthood of Annas and Caiaphas, the word of God came to John the son of Zechariah in the wilderness; and he went into all the region about the Jordan, preaching a baptism of repentance for the forgiveness of sins (Luke 3:1–2).

Notice Luke gives us a time period ("fifteenth year of the reign of Tiberius Caesar"), names of rulers (Tiberius Caesar,

Pontius Pilate, Herod, Philip, Trachonitis, Lysani, Annas, Caiaphas), places (Judea, Ituraea, Abilene, the Jordan), and locals (Zechariah).

This stands in stark contrast with the pagan myths that are cosmic epics set in heavenly realms and that rarely, if at all, reference historical places, events, and people. Unlike the Gospels they simply are indifferent to historical settings.

Finally, and perhaps most importantly, some of the popular forms of pagan myths post-date Christianity. For example, for many years scholars believed the Roman military god Mithras (whose cult was popular from the first to the fourth century A.D.) could be traced back to the ancient Persian god Mithra (also called Mitra), whose name is found in a treaty found in Iran that dates to 1400 B.C. The catalyst for this idea was the twentieth-century Belgian archaeologist and historian Franz Cumont.[230]

If this were true, then Mithraism would actually predate Christianity, and could be considered (as many skeptics allege) source material for the Jesus story. But according to scholar John Hinnells, modern research shows that there is no connection between the Roman god and the ancient Persian god Mithra:

> We must now conclude that [Cumont's] reconstruction simply will not stand. It receives no support from the Iranian material and is in fact in conflict with the ideas of that tradition as they are represented in the extant texts. Above all, it is a theoretical reconstruction which does not accord with the actual Roman iconography.[231]

German historian Manfred Claus concurs with Hinnells conclusion: "The mysteries cannot be shown to have developed from Persian religious ideas, nor does it make sense to interpret them as a forerunner of Christianity."[232]

Q: "How can Jesus be ripped off from Mithraism when the Mithraic narrative comes after Christianity?"

Even the full account of Osiris's story, "Concerning Isis and Osiris," didn't come on the scene until the Greek writer Plutarch put it down in writing in the second century A.D. Only a basic outline exists in the Pyramid Texts (c. 2686–2160), and other information is scattered in Egyptian and Greek sources.

Skeptics who appeal to these types of stories to support the idea that Jesus is a rehash of pagan mystery religions fail to distinguish between the ancient cults, which predate Jesus, and the second- and third-century reconstructions of the cults.[233] The details that they claim are comparable to parts of the Jesus story come from the latter—*after* the appearance of Jesus and the gospels.

STRATEGY 2

Show how the alleged similarities are exaggerated, and sometimes not true.

Your second strategy challenges the alleged parallels. Some of them are simply bogus, and some are greatly exaggerated. We can't go into all of the parallels here, but the two events that are most emphasized are Jesus' birth and resurrection.

You can start with Jesus' birth, which skeptics say was influenced by the virgin birth of Mithras. Ask this question:

> *Q:* "How can Mithras be said to have had a virgin birth when according to Roman mythology it is believed that he emerged from a rock?[234] Could one even call this a birth?"

Concerning the Roman Mithras's so-called birth, Claus writes, "The literary sources here are few but unmistakable: Mithras was known as the rock-born god."[235]

If your friend has been reading mythicist books or websites, he may object that in the Persian legends Anahita, mother of Mithra (the Persian version of the name), was a virgin when Mithra was conceived. An inscription at a dedicatory temple in

Iran dating from 200 B.C. reads, "Anahita, the Immaculate Virgin Mother Goddess of the Lord Mithra."[236] But in the Persian legends Anahita (once worshiped as a fertility goddess) conceived Mithra by coming into contact with Zoroaster's 400-year-old sperm while she swam in a lake.[237] Although Anahita is a virgin, it is hardly a conception like Jesus, where no material causes are used whatsoever. His conception is a direct act of God.

Other pagan gods that skeptics claim are models for the Jesus story, such as Horus and Osiris, don't even come close to a virgin birth. Both were conceived through weird forms of sexual intercourse.[238]

With regard to the claimed resurrection parallels, the most common is that of Osiris. But legitimate scholars are quick to point out that Osiris never really rose from the dead—he reigned as king of the underworld. Egyptologist Henri Frankfort explains:

> Osiris, in fact, was not a dying god at all but a dead god. He never returned among the living; he was not liberated from the world of the dead . . . on the contrary, Osiris altogether belonged to the world of the dead; it was from there that he bestowed his blessings upon Egypt. He was always depicted as a mummy, a dead king.[239]

This is why the Book of the Dead has a prayer that the Egyptian believer prayed to Osiris, requesting a permanent place in the netherworld: "Grant thou [Osiris] to me a place in the netherworld, near the lords of right and truth, my estate may it be permanent in Sekhet-hetep."[240]

Q: "Is reigning as king of the underworld really the same as being raised from the dead?"

When you lay bare this and other bogus or wishful-thinking parallels between Jesus and ancient pagan gods, you can help your friend see that they are no obstacle at all.

STRATEGY 3

Explain that correlation doesn't mean causation.

Your third strategy grants for argument's sake that at least some genuine similarities between Jesus' life story and the pagan deities might exist. But the conclusion that Jesus' story was taken from the pagan stories doesn't follow from that premise. By themselves, the similarities do not constitute evidence that Christianity was influenced by or based on pagan mystery religions. Correlation does not entail causation.

To show how this reasoning is fallacious, share with your friend some correlations between John F. Kennedy and Abraham Lincoln:[241]

- Lincoln was elected to Congress in 1846; Kennedy was elected to Congress in 1946.

- Lincoln was elected president in 1860; Kennedy was elected President in 1960.

- The names "Lincoln" and "Kennedy" each have seven letters.

- Lincoln had a secretary named Kennedy; Kennedy had a secretary named Lincoln.

- Both married, in their thirties, a twenty-four-year-old socially prominent girl who could speak fluent French.

- Both presidents dealt with civil rights movements for African-Americans.

- Both presidents were shot in the back of the head, on a Friday before a major holiday, while sitting next to their wives.

- Both their assassins were known by three names consisting of fifteen letters (John Wilkes Booth, Lee Harvey Oswald).

- Oswald shot Kennedy from a warehouse and was captured in a theater; Booth shot Lincoln in a theater and was captured in a warehouse.

- Both assassins were shot and killed with a Colt revolver days after they assassinated the president and before they could be brought to trial.

- Both presidents were succeeded by vice presidents named Johnson, from the South, born in 1808 and 1908 respectively.

> Q: "Are we to conclude that the story of John F. Kennedy's life is ripped off from the story of Abraham Lincoln's life simply because of these uncanny similarities?"

To repeat, correlation does not mean causation. You have to give *evidence* that one was caused by the other. Just asserting the similarities doesn't prove anything.

THE WAY PREPARED: The Jesus story recounted in the Gospels is not a rip-off of pagan mythology.

> *Alleged parallels between Jesus and the pagan savior-gods in most instances reside in the modern imagination.*[242]
> —Bart Ehrman (agnostic New Testament scholar)

20

How can I believe in Jesus when there is no evidence that he rose from the dead?

The resurrection of Jesus lies at the heart of Christianity. If Jesus didn't rise from the dead, then Christianity is false. St. Paul makes this clear: "If Christ has not been raised, then our preaching is in vain and your faith is in vain" (1 Cor. 15:14).

Skeptics affirm the antecedent—Jesus didn't rise from the dead—and therefore conclude that Christianity is false. Their reason is that they don't see any evidence for it. How do we fill this valley and make a way for the Lord?

We must embark on a historical investigation to determine if Jesus' resurrection is the best explanation of the facts. If the competing hypotheses fail to account for the circumstantial details but the resurrection hypothesis succeeds, we're justified in affirming Jesus' resurrection as a historical event.[243]

STRATEGY 1

Prove the historicity of the circumstantial details surrounding Jesus' resurrection.

The first two details are Jesus' death and burial. Jesus' death is the most well-established fact about him—perhaps the most well-established fact in all of ancient history, with multiple independent sources confirming it.

Under the Christian mantle, we have all four Gospels, the Acts of the Apostles, Paul's writings, and the writings of the early Church Fathers. The non-Christian sources that confirm Jesus' death are Josephus, Tacitus, Lucian of Samosata, Mara Bar-Serapion, and the Talmud.[244]

The historicity of Jesus' burial is supported by the criterion of early testimony. Scholars date Paul's creedal statement in 1 Corinthians 15:3–5—"Christ died . . . he was buried . . . and he was raised"—to within five years of Jesus' death and resurrection. Paul informs us that this saying was a part of the apostolic preaching (1 Cor. 15:11), which leads many to conclude that he most likely received it in A.D. 39 when he visited Peter and James in Jerusalem three years after his conversion in 36 (Gal. 1:18–19).[245] If he received it in the year 39, that means the saying must have been formulated prior to that: within five to six years after Jesus' death (A.D. 33).

The report that Joseph of Arimathea, a member of the Sanhedrin (a sort of Supreme Court that dealt with matters of Jewish law), buried Jesus is another datum that supports the historicity of Jesus' burial. It's unlikely that the apostles would have made up a fictional character and placed him on the well-known Sanhedrin. Given that Joseph of Arimathea was a real person, the apostles' testimony that he buried Jesus meets the historiographical criterion of embarrassment.

> *Q:* "Why would the apostles make a member of the council that sentenced Jesus to death a sympathizer of Jesus? Wouldn't this have worked against their purposes?"

The next circumstantial detail is the empty tomb. There are several lines of evidence that you could use to show that the empty tomb is a historical fact,[246] but let's focus on just one: the empty tomb is attested to by six different sources that range in dating from six to thirty years after the reported event.

- Paul's preaching in 1 Corinthians 15:1–3 is one. He preaches that Jesus was buried and raised, which implies that the tomb was empty.

- Scholars argue that Mark's account of the empty tomb is part of the source material he used for his Gospel, which dates to within seven years after the actual event (another reason why it's considered historically reliable).[247]

- Matthew's account of the empty tomb comes from a different source as well, because he records things the others do not: the guard at the tomb and the narrative of the Jews conspiring to fabricate a story that the apostles stole the body.

- Luke's account reveals that he used an independent source. He narrates how the two disciples went to the tomb to verify the women's claim that the tomb was empty. He didn't get this from Mark because Mark doesn't record it, and as all scholars agree, the synoptic Gospels (Matthew, Mark, and Luke) are independent of John.

- Because John's account of the empty tomb is independent, he is a fifth source.

- Finally, Luke's record of Peter's first sermon on Jesus' resurrection in Acts 2 comes from an independent source. Peter's message about David prophesying the resurrection of the Christ is unique (Acts 2:25–32), thus indicating its independence from the source material for the four Gospels and Paul.

Since multiple attestation and early testimony are key indicators for historical reliability, we can confidently judge, as a matter of historical inquiry, that Jesus' tomb was empty as the New Testament records.

Along with the empty tomb, historians can also evaluate the historical reliability of the alleged glorious resurrected appearances to different people on different occasions.[248] For example, Jesus' appearance to Mary Magdalene and the women is multiply attested to by Mark (Mark. 16:9), John (John 20:11–18), and Matthew (Matt. 28:8–10).

The report of Jesus' appearance to women also satisfies the embarrassment criterion. In the world of first-century Judaism, the testimony of women was not held in high esteem.[249] This being the case, it would be an embarrassment to suggest that women were the first witnesses of the resurrected Jesus.

> Q: "Why would the apostles record such a detail unless it were true?"

Jesus' appearance to Peter by himself is historically reliable because both Luke (Luke 24:34) and Paul (1 Cor. 15:5) testify to it; thus satisfying the multiple attestation criterion. We also learn from different sources that Jesus appeared to "the twelve." Paul, Luke, and John record the immediate appearance after the Resurrection (1 Cor. 15:5; Luke 24:36–43; John 20:19–20), John records Jesus' later appearance on the seashore (John 21), and Matthew records Jesus' final appearance to the twelve before the Ascension (Matt. 28:19–20).

In 1 Corinthians 15:6, Paul tells us that Jesus appeared to more than 500 brethren at once. He also records that Jesus appeared to James, which we can evaluate historically in light of Paul's conversation with James when he traveled to Jerusalem (Gal. 1:19). Finally, Jesus' appearance to "all the apostles" is affirmed by three independent sources—Paul (1 Cor. 15:7), Luke's Gospel source (Luke 24:50–51), and Luke's source for Acts (Acts 1:2, 6–11).

The final two circumstantial details that need to be taken into account are:

- Jesus' resurrection was central to the early Christians' belief (1 Cor. 15:14) and was something worth dying for.

- The early Christians didn't find another (living) Messiah to follow, but continued professing Jesus as Savior and Lord after his death.

STRATEGY 2

Show that the conspiracy and swoon theories

do not adequately account for the historical facts surrounding Jesus' resurrection.

Your second strategy addresses two common alternative theories to the literal resurrection of Jesus: the conspiracy theory and the swoon theory. Let's take the conspiracy theory first.

The conspiracy theory suggests that the early Christians stole Jesus' body and lied about the resurrected appearances. This theory explains the empty tomb, the alleged post-mortem appearances, and even the Christian claim that Jesus was Lord; however, it doesn't adequately explain why the Gospel writers record women as the first witnesses of the empty tomb and the resurrected Jesus—a detail that harms rather than helps their credibility.

> Q: "Couldn't have the Gospel-writing conspirators just as easily chosen men to be the first witnesses— perhaps Joseph of Arimathea and Nicodemus—to make their story more persuasive?"

Furthermore, the conspiracy theory doesn't fit with the early Christian belief in a resurrected *Messiah*. First-century Jews were not expecting *anyone* to rise before the end of time.[250] This is not something that would persuade the Jews to join the new religion.

> Q: "Why would the conspirators make this up when a resurrected Messiah was not even a hope for first-century Jews?"[251]

Finally, this theory fails to explain why the early Christians believed the Resurrection was worth dying for.

> Q: "Do you know anyone who would die for what he knew to be a lie? Isn't it unreasonable to think that the early Christians would undergo harsh persecution and death for a hoax?"

The Christians had nothing to gain and everything to lose. This makes them credible witnesses. Therefore, to say that they lied strains credulity.

The swoon theory says Jesus didn't die on the cross, but merely fell unconscious, later revived in the tomb, and then walked out. This alternative theory, too, fails as a reasonable explanation of the historical facts.

First, it totally disregards the historical evidence that Jesus died. Second, it doesn't adequately explain the detail it attempts to explain: namely the empty tomb.

> Q: "Is it reasonable to believe that a half-dead Jesus, who had been tortured and nailed to a cross for hours before passing out, would have had enough strength to roll away the heavy stone covering the tomb? Is it credible to think Jesus would then have been able to get past the guards stationed there and make his way to safety unseen?"

The swoon theory also fails to explain why the early Christians believed Jesus was raised in a glorified and incorruptible state.[252] A half-dead man covered in blood is a far cry from the idea of a glorious victor over death.

STRATEGY 3

Show that the subjective experience theories don't adequately account for the historical facts surrounding Jesus' resurrection.

Your third strategy addresses the *subjective experience* theories that seek to explain the early Christian belief in Jesus' resurrection. For example, the hallucination theory suggests that the Christians only *imagined* that they saw Jesus. The vision theory puts forward the idea that Jesus appeared to certain early Christians in visions, causing them to believe mistakenly that he had risen from the dead.

Although these explanations could possibly explain the alleged appearances of a resurrected Jesus, they fall short in accounting for the other facts. For example, they don't explain the empty tomb.

Q: "If the Christians were merely hallucinating or having visions of Jesus, why didn't the skeptics simply produce the body?"

Given that Jesus of was so popular, and was placed in a tomb that belonged to Joseph of Arimathea, a prominent member of the Sanhedrin, it's reasonable to conclude that the location of Jesus' tomb would have been known and his corpse easily verified.

Moreover, the subjective explanations might be adequate to explain a single appearance of Jesus, but they fail to explain the multiple appearances to different people on different occasions.

For example, we know Jesus appeared privately to Mary Magdalene (Mark 16:9), the women at the tomb (Luke 24:10), Peter (1 Cor. 15:5), and James (1 Cor. 15:7). He appeared to the twelve (1 Cor. 15:5) and did so on many different occasions—in the upper room on the night of the Resurrection (John 20:19–23), on the seashore (John 21), for a succession of forty days (Acts 1:3), and on the Mount of Olives before his ascension (Matt. 28:18–20). Paul writes that Jesus even appeared to more than 500 brethren at the same time, many of whom were still alive when Paul penned his letter (1 Cor. 15:6).

Q: "How can so many different people hallucinate the same thing or have the same vision (drawing from it the same erroneous conclusion) at different times and in different places?"

The bodily nature of the encounters with the resurrected Jesus is another problem for the hallucination and vision theories. For example, there were two times when the resurrected Jesus ate with his disciples—with his apostles on the seashore (John 21:9–

14) and in the home of the two disciples traveling on the road to Emmaus (Luke 24:28–30). Jesus even told the apostle Thomas to touch the wounds in his hands and side from his crucifixion (John 20:27). Hallucinations and visions don't eat food and can't be touched.

These subjective theories are also bankrupt when it comes to explaining the unique characteristics of Jesus' resurrection and the early Christian belief in Jesus as Lord. The existence of Jesus' resurrected, *glorified* body is not something that would have been present in the Christians' minds to project onto reality.

> *Q:* "Why would Christians have imagined the glorified body of Jesus when the Jewish conception of resurrection was a return to the same kind of bodily life as before death[253] and the pagans at the time didn't even have a conception of bodily resurrection?"[254]

In order for the Christians to project this idea onto reality, it would have had to be in their minds. But there is no explanation for how this could have happened. For this reason, the hallucination theory fails.

Furthermore, visions of dead people were not unheard of in the first century. Such an occurrence would not give the Christians reason to think Jesus was actually risen from the dead, much less to continue professing their crucified leader as Messiah and Lord and making the Resurrection a central doctrine.

STRATEGY 4

Explain that the glorious and literal resurrection of Jesus succeeds in explaining all the facts.

Obviously if Jesus rose from the dead, the tomb would be empty. His glorious resurrection would also explain the alleged postmortem appearances, the unique qualities of Jesus' resurrected body, and why the Christians professed a resurrected Messiah. Finally, the resurrection hypothesis adequately explains how the early Christians could continue to profess Jesus as God despite the fact that he was crucified and died.

As with all historical events, it's impossible to have absolute certitude of the Resurrection based on the historical evidence. However, when you consider the historical details surrounding the accounts of Jesus' resurrection, and the fact that alternative explanations fail to explain these details, it's reasonable to conclude Jesus' resurrection was a historical event.

THE WAY PREPARED: We can know with historical certainty that Jesus rose from the dead.

> *For I delivered to you as of first importance what I also received, that Christ died for our sins in accordance with the scriptures, that he was buried, that he was raised on the third day in accordance with the scriptures.*
> —1 Corinthians 15:3-4

PART IV

PREPARE THE WAY FOR CHRISTIANITY

21

How can I be a Christian when so many religious people become violent fanatics?

If you could wave a magic wand and get rid of either rape or religion, which would you choose? Popular atheist Sam Harris chooses religion: "I would not hesitate to get rid of religion. I think more people are dying as a result of our religious myths than as a result of any other ideology."[255]

This is a common charge among many "new atheists." Their belief that religion is a cause of violence in the world is a stumbling block that keeps many from considering Christianity.

I don't blame unbelievers for being repulsed by violent religious fanatics. But the existence of violent religious fanatics is not a good reason to reject Christianity. Moreover, religion *itself* is not the real problem.

STRATEGY 1

Show how the argument commits the *non sequitur* fallacy.

Recall from chapter two that a *non sequitur* is a logical fallacy in which the conclusion does not follow from the premise.

> *Q:* "If we should reject religion in general because it is a source of violent conflict, shouldn't we also reject the idea of owning land, since land has been and still is a source of violent conflict?"

The conclusion "religion is bad" no more follows from the premise "religion is a source of violence" than the conclusion "land is bad" follows from the premise "land is a source of violence." Kings and countries have fought and still fight over disputed land. But that doesn't mean we should rid ourselves of private property.

Similarly, just because individuals fight in the name of religion it doesn't follow that we should rid our world of religion. There may be other grounds on which your friend rejects Christianity, but he cannot reasonably do so on the grounds that religion has been a source of violence.

STRATEGY 2

Turn the table and apply the same logic to atheism.

Strategy two works only if your friend is an atheist. It's possible for someone to believe in God and still reject organized religion based on the above argument. If your friend fits the latter description, then proceed to strategy three.

But let's assume for the present strategy that he is an atheist, since strategy two logically follows strategy one. Point out to your friend that the "religion is dangerous" argument proves too much for an atheist.

> Q: "If you're going to reject religion, and thus Christianity, because you think it leads to violent conflict, then wouldn't you also have to reject atheism for the same reason?"

In fact, atheist violence surpasses religious violence in staggering proportions. Christian author Dinesh D'Souza explains:

The world's population rose from around 500 million in 1450 A.D. to 2.5 billion in 1950, a fivefold increase. Taken together, the Crusades, the Inquisition, and the witch burnings killed approximately 200,000 people. Adjusting for the increase in population, that's the equivalent of one million deaths today. Even so, these deaths caused by Christian rulers over a 500-year period amount to only 1 percent of the deaths caused by Stalin, Hitler, and Mao in the space of a few decades.[256]

I think it's safe to say that if your friend is an atheist, he will not want to give up his atheism. Therefore, he must reject the "religion is dangerous" argument.

STRATEGY 3

Explain how the argument wrongly assumes that violent fanaticism belongs to the essence of Christianity.

Notice that your friend rejects Christianity because he automatically thinks all religions, including Christianity, encourage violence in the name of God. But this is not true.

Explain that although it may belong to the essence of *some* religions to do violence in the name of God, it doesn't belong to *all* religions. We have to distinguish between the commitments that different religions require. Since you are trying to remove obstacles to Christianity, you need only focus on whether *Christianity* encourages violence (such as conversion by the sword). You could start with Jesus' own words:

- *Matthew 5:43–44*: "You have heard that it was said, 'You shall love your neighbor and hate your enemy.' But I say to you, Love your enemies and pray for those who persecute you."

- *Matthew 25:42*: "Put your sword back for all who take the sword will perish by the sword."

> *Q:* "Do these words sound anything like an encouragement to spread the Christian message by violence?"

Also share with your friend these quotes from early Christian writers:

Lactantius (c. 250–c. 325): "There is no occasion for violence and injury, for religion cannot be imposed by force; the matter must be carried on by words rather than by blows, that the will may be affected."[257]

Hilary of Poitiers (c. 310–c. 367): "God does not want unwilling worship, nor does he require a forced repentance."[258]

Isidore of Pelusium (d. c. 450): "Since it seems not good forcibly to draw over to the faith those who are gifted with a free will, employ at the proper time conviction and by your life enlighten those who are in darkness."[259]

Tertullian (c. 155–c. 240): "It is not proper for religion to compel men to religion, which should be accepted of one's own accord, not by force, since sacrifices also are required of a willing mind."[260]

John Chrysostom (c. 349–407): "Such is the character of our doctrine; what about yours? No one ever persecuted it, nor is it right for Christians to eradicate error by constraint and force, but to save humanity by persuasion and reason and gentleness."[261]

Athanasius (c. 297–373): "It is that the devil, when he has no truth on his side, attacks and breaks down the doors of them that admit him with axes and hammers . . . . For the truth is not preached with swords or with darts, nor by means of soldiers; but by persuasion and counsel."[262]

Your friend can rest assured that persuasion by violence is not part of the Christian religion. Christians who have carried out violent acts in the name of God throughout history only show their failure to live up to Christian standards. Such violence is an *abuse* of the Christian name, and thus a *perversion* of Christianity. But just because someone abuses something doesn't mean that the thing is bad in itself.

Here your friend may still object: "Sure, I can see the distinction between what Christianity teaches and Christians who fail to live up to the standard. But my problem is with the claim that one is right and the other is wrong. That's the source of the violence, since it breeds competition."

Sociologically, there may be some truth to this. But for Christianity, one doesn't necessarily follow from the other. Although Christianity, and in particular Catholic Christianity, claims to have the full truth about God and his son Jesus Christ, it also promotes at the same time the respect of every person's dignity as a free human being. As the Second Vatican Council teaches, "man's response to God in faith must be free: no one therefore is to be forced to embrace the Christian faith against his own will" (*Dignitatis Humanae* 10). In imitation of Jesus who bore witness to the truth (John 8:32), Christians are called to propose the gospel of Jesus and invite others to believe in it, but not "to use force to impose it" (DH 11).

So, if a Christian becomes violent toward others he thinks are wrong, then he would be, once again, abusing the Christian name and thus promoting a perversion of Christianity. Perhaps your friend's revulsion to violence in the name of religion should be the very reason why he should become Christian. He would fit right in.

THE WAY PREPARED: Violent acts in the name of religion shouldn't be taken as evidence that violence is an essential component of all religions, especially Christianity.

> *Belief in God can be abused . . . and we need to confront and oppose this. But abuse of an ideal does not negate its validity.*[263]
> —Alister McGrath (Irish Christian apologist)

22

How can I be a Christian when so many Christians are hypocrites?

No one wants to belong to a religion where everyone is a phony. This is why many unbelievers are hesitant to embrace the Christian faith. They know Christianity teaches one thing, but they see so many Christians doing the opposite. Who wants to join a religion of hypocrites?

The *Catechism of the Catholic Church* acknowledges this obstacle with regard to atheists:

> Believers can have more than a little to do with the rise of atheism. To the extent that they are careless about their instruction in the faith, or present its teaching falsely, or *even fail in their religious, moral, or social life*, they must be said to conceal rather than to reveal the true nature of God and of religion (2125; emphasis added).

We can sympathize with those for whom Christian hypocrisy is an obstacle to faith. But we must also show why this is not a good reason to reject the Christian religion. The strategies below will help you lower this mountain to prepare a way for the Lord.

STRATEGY 1

Explain that Christians who sin are not necessarily hypocrites.

This obstacle presupposes a flawed understanding of the connection between sin and hypocrisy. Your friend thinks that just because a Christian sins he necessarily is a hypocrite. Your first strategy must show that this is not the case.

Begin by defining hypocrisy. The word comes from the Greek *hypokrites,* which literally means "actor" or "stage player." Therefore, religious hypocrisy is an act of *pretending* to be holy or observant when one is not.

> *Q:* "Is it reasonable to think that all Christians who sin are fakers, only pretending to be Christian? Isn't it more likely that most Christians sin out of weakness, just like non-Christians do?"

Most Christians do not fit the description of a religious hypocrite because most Christians aren't pretending to be adherents of the faith while willfully breaking its commandments. Rather, most Christians *want* to follow Christianity's teachings but fail to do so consistently because of the imperfections that all humans have. This is the difference between the sinner and the hypocrite. Help your friend to see it.

STRATEGY 2

Explain how we shouldn't judge the truth of Christianity based on its adherents but on its teachings.

For your second strategy, you want to help your friend understand that he shouldn't judge Christianity based on what its adherents do but on its principles. The fundamental question is, "Is it *true*?"

> *Q:* "If you found out that one of Einstein's students was a child molester, would you reject the theory of relativity?"

In religion as in science, the good or bad behavior of those who adhere to a teaching does not determine the truth of that teaching. A belief can be true even though persons who adhere to it are immoral. Thus the behavior of individual Christians does not determine whether or not Jesus is God, or if his teachings are true. Those things must be considered independently.

> *Q:* "Isn't it possible that the Christian faith could be true even though individual Christians don't live out its teachings perfectly?"

When faced with Christians who fail to live up to the Christian standard of living, we must remember to ask, "Yes, but is Christianity *true*?" If the Christian religion is true, then we ought to embrace it no matter how bad some of its members practice it.

STRATEGY 3

Show that Christianity condemns hypocrisy.

Your third strategy seeks to affirm your friend in his repulsion from hypocritical behavior. You want to explain that this is something Christianity rejects as well. Start with a list of things Jesus identified as hypocrisy:

- Giving to the poor in order to be publicly recognized (Matt. 6:2).

- Praying in public in order to be publicly recognized as a godly man (Matt. 6:5, 23:14).

- Making your appearance gloomy in order that others may know you're fasting (Matt. 6:16).

- Complaining about the sins of others when you don't even recognize your own (Matt. 7:5; Luke 6:42).

- Honoring God in words alone without corresponding belief in the heart (Matt. 15:7–9; Mark 7:6).

- Testing others for the sake of looking superior (Matt. 22:18; Mark 12:15).

- Keeping people from knowing about God through immoral behavior (Matt. 23:13).

- Taking advantage of the poor and widows (Matt. 23:14).

- Malformation of converts (Matt. 23:15).

- Tithing but neglecting the more important things, like justice and mercy (Matt. 23:23).

- Doing pious things for show while being corrupt within (Matt. 23:25, 27, 28, 29, 34).

- Taking care of animals on the Sabbath while neglecting the needs of human beings (Luke 13:15).

- Having the ability to analyze the weather, but unable to discern right from wrong (Luke 12:56–57).

Jesus may have spent more time on the topic of hypocrisy than any other! He also made clear what the reward of such hypocrisy would be:

> [T]he master of that servant will come on a day when he does not expect him and at an hour he does not know, and will punish him, and put him with the hypocrites; there men will weep and gnash their teeth (Matt. 24:51).

You can also share with your friend some biblical passages where the early Christians condemn hypocrisy:

- Hypocrisy is contrary to love and is evil (Rom. 12:9).

- Hypocrisy is identified as lying and comes from deceitful spirits (1 Tim. 4:1–2).

- Hypocrisy is listed among malice, deceit, slander, and envy, which all must be rejected (1 Pet. 2:1).

- Hypocrisy is listed among things said to be demonic (James 3:14–17).

You can leave your friend with this challenge:

> *Q:* "If you're repulsed by hypocrisy, and the Christian faith is repulsed by hypocrisy, then wouldn't the Christian religion be a good fit for you?"

In the end your friend's dislike of hypocrisy shouldn't be a reason to reject the Christian religion, but a reason to embrace it.

STRATEGY 4

Explain that there is an abundance of evidence of Christians who have lived extraordinary lives of holiness.

> *Q:* "Would you judge a doctor's ability to practice medicine based on his patients who refused to take their medicine?"

Your friend shouldn't have trouble seeing the absurdity of this line of reasoning.

Point out to him that his obstacle arises only because he's assuming that no patients have actually taken Jesus' medicine. If he is to be fair in his judgment about Christianity, your friend needs to look into the lives of those Christians who *did* take Jesus' medicine—that is to say those who made the effort to live their lives according to what Jesus prescribed for the spiritual illness of sin. Such Christians provide a sort of experiential proof that when the teachings of Christianity are put into practice they are transformative. This gives your friend good reason to believe that Jesus is a doctor worth going to.

There are instances of extraordinary holiness and upright living both within and outside the visible boundaries of the Catholic Church. But as one author puts it, "The comparison between the exceptionally good lives of non-Catholics and Catholics is like the relationship between isolated trickling streams and the main flow of the river: a river as long as the Christian era and nearly as broad as the world."[264]

The array of Catholic saints throughout its history is so vast and varied that it would take a lifetime to study it. No justice can be done here. To get your friend started, pick a couple of your favorite saints, those you are passionate talking about, and testify to their life and witness. Encourage him, in the name of fair enquiry, to do his own study. In doing so, he will satisfy the desire that undergirds his objection—namely, the desire to know that Christianity is not just informative (a body of truths with no practical life application) but also *transformative* (truth that changes lives for the better).[265]

Also, point out that it's not just the saints of history that manifest this transformative nature of Christian teaching. There are countless testimonies of everyday Christians, among us right now, who once were in the darkness of sin, depression, addiction, and many other forms of misery, and have come out through the healing power of Jesus Christ. Your friend need only go to a local Christian community, whether Catholic or non-Catholic, and talk to the folks there for his evidence.

Point out that there will always be the bad mixed with the good. Jesus taught this on several different occasions:

- The parable of the kingdom of God which is like a field where the weeds are allowed to grow alongside the wheat (Matt. 13:24–37).

- The parable of the kingdom of God being like a net that brings in both the good and bad fish (Matt. 13:47).

But assure your friend that in both of the above parables Jesus promises that the bad will only remain for a while, for there will be a time of reckoning when he will separate the good from the bad. That time will be at his second and glorious coming.

THE WAY PREPARED: The truth of Christianity is not dependent on whether all its members live up to its teachings.

> *"Those who are well have no need of a physician, but those who are sick; I came not to call the righteous, but sinners."*
> —Mark 2:17

23

How can I be a Christian when Christianity discriminates against women?

It's puzzling how in a culture saturated with pornography, a multi-billion-dollar enterprise that portrays women as objects to be used for men's sexual gratification, there could be an objection that *Christianity* is anti-women.

Nonetheless, it's there in many people's minds, so it's necessary to consider the obstacle—since we ought to reject any religion that views women as less valuable than men. So where do critics get off saying that Christianity is unjust toward women? They usually turn to the following Pauline passages:

- "I want you to understand that the head of every man is Christ, the head of a woman is her husband" (1 Cor. 11:3).

- "As in all the churches of the saints, the women should keep silence in the churches. For they are not permitted to speak, but should be subordinate, as even the law says. If there is anything they desire to know, let them ask their husbands at home. For it is shameful for a woman to speak in church" (1 Cor. 14:34–35).

- "Let a woman learn in silence with all submissiveness. I permit no woman to teach or to have authority over men; she is to keep silent" (1 Tim. 2:11).

Following our metaphor, these passages definitely constitute the *presence* of something that blocks the Lord. So let's see how we can lower this mountain to prepare the way.

STRATEGY 1

Explain that Christianity views women as equal to men in dignity.

Your first strategy sets the context in which one is to deal with the above problematic passages. It shows that in the Christian milieu women are *not* viewed as inferior to men. They are considered equal in dignity before God.

Start with the teaching and practice of Jesus. He interacted with women in a way that suggests he had a view of women that broke the boundaries of his time and culture. For example, he performed his first public miracle in Cana at the request of a woman, namely, his mother (see John 2:1–11). He healed women of their spiritual and physical ailments (Luke 8:1–3; Mark 5:24–34), saved the life of a woman caught in adultery (John 8:7), and held casual conversation with a Samaritan woman (John 4:10), all of which broke the sexual and racial customs of his day.

Also, Jesus allowed women to accompany him and the twelve in their ministry. Luke tells us that several of them "provided for them [Jesus and the twelve] out of their means" (Luke 8:2–3). Matthew records that many of the women who followed Jesus "ministered to him" (Matt. 27:55). You can also remind your friend that Jesus chose women to be the first witnesses of his resurrection, which given the cultural background of first-century Judaism was totally unique (see chapter 20).

Jesus' teaching on divorce and remarriage is yet another example of his view on the dignity of women. It holds men and women to the same standard of behavior:

> Whoever divorces his wife and marries another, commits adultery against her; and if she divorces her husband and marries another, she commits adultery (Mark 10:11–12).

Given that in first-century Judaism the Mosaic Law didn't permit wives to put away their husbands, Jesus' teaching here is radical. Philosopher Christopher Kaczor comments:

By establishing one moral code obligatory on men and
women alike, Christianity fostered a lasting commitment
of unconditional covenantal love, protecting the family
structure and putting the sexes on an equal footing.[266]

Moreover, Jesus' strict teaching protects women from the dire
economic and social difficulties that divorce brought on women
in the ancient world. And it is the first of its kind in the history
of world religions.[267]

With Jesus' teaching now in place, you can turn to Paul's
teaching. Start with 1 Corinthians 11:11–12:

Nevertheless, in the Lord woman is not independent of
man nor man of woman; for as woman was made from
man, so man is now born of woman. And all things are
from God.

Notice that Paul recognizes there is a mutual dependence between man and woman. Ask your friend this question:

Q: "How could Paul see men as superior to women if
he acknowledges that they mutually depend on one
another?"

Surely this is a far cry from misogyny.

The mutuality motif is also found in Paul's famous teaching
about wives submitting to their husbands. Right before Paul
says, "Wives, be subject to your husbands" (Eph. 5:22), he says,
"Be subject to one another out of reverence for Christ" (Eph.
5:21). For Paul, subjection is a two-way street. Wives are called
to submit to the role of the husbands, and husbands are called
to submit to the role of their wives. Paul seems to imply that
although husbands and wives have different roles they are equal
in dignity.

Paul gives further hints to the dignity of women in the same
passage. For example, when he says, "Husbands love your wives

as Christ loved the Church" (Eph. 5:25), he is saying that the wife's value in relation to the husband is analogous to the value of the Church in relation to Jesus. That's a pretty high value.

How valuable was the Church to Jesus? He died for her. How valuable should the wife be to his husband? He should die for her. Paul goes on to say in v. 29 that the husband should "nourish" and "cherish" his wife as Christ does the Church. To compare wives to the Church is to bestow a great dignity upon women. Women are not things to be dispensed with and treated as garbage.

Paul also hints to the dignity of women when he teaches that husbands should "love their wives as their own bodies," since "he who loves his wife loves himself" (Eph. 5:28). Notice that for Paul, to mistreat one's wife is to violate one's own dignity. This belief contradicts the idea that men are superior to women in dignity.

> *Q:* "How could a husband violate himself when he mistreats his wife unless he and his wife were equal in dignity?"

You can also share with your friend examples of how Paul did not conform to cultural norms when it came to the roles of women:[268]

- He recognizes several women as fellow workers in Christ Jesus (Rom. 16:1–16).

- He insists that a husband should give his wife her conjugal rights (1 Cor. 7:3–4).

- He teaches that in the Church there is neither male nor female (Gal. 3:28).

Paul's teaching that women are equal in dignity with men precludes any sort of misogynistic interpretation of the Scripture passages mentioned above. So what do those passages mean? Strategies two and three will answer this question.

But before we get there, point out that this Christian perspective of women gives a plausible explanation for why so many women converted in the early centuries after Christ. What woman wouldn't want to belong to such a religion? Historian Henry Chadwick makes this observation:

> Christianity seems to have been especially successful among women. It was often through the wives that it penetrated the upper classes of society in the first instance. Christians believed in the equality of men and women before God and found in the New Testament commands that husbands should treat their wives with such consideration and love as Christ manifested for his Church. Christian teaching about the sanctity of marriage offered a powerful safeguard to married women.[269]

Of course, individual members of the Church, including members of the hierarchy, have mistreated women.[270] Even some of the early Church Fathers misinterpreted the revelation that Christ gave and promoted false views of women.[271] But similar to what we said in the previous chapter, anyone who acts against the dignity of women is failing to live up to the standard set by Christ and his apostles—not to mention the various magisterial documents written in support of the dignity of women.[272]

"Okay, this is all fine and dandy," your friend might say, "but those Pauline passages still seem to be misogynistic. What do you have to say about that?" Let's turn to those and see what we can make of them.

STRATEGY 2

Explain what Paul means in 1 Corinthians 11:3 by the husband being the "head" of his wife.

You can start with 1 Corinthians 11:3, where Paul says that the husband is the "head" of his wife. The key to understanding this passage is Paul's teaching on the Mystical Body of Christ in 1 Corinthians 12:14–31.

For Paul, all members of Christ's body are equal in value, but yet he recognizes they are not the same. They all have different roles to play as does each part of a human body. Every member functions in a unique way for the good of the whole. This is why he teaches that one member of the body cannot say to another member, "I have no need of you" (1 Cor. 12:21).

The same is true with regard to husbands and wives. Although the husband and wife have distinct roles to play in the family, they work together for the good of the *whole*. The husband's role as leader in relation to his wife doesn't mean his wife is of less importance. Just as the eye can't say to the hand, "I have no need of you," so to the husband can't say to the wife, "I have no need of you." This is why Paul teaches in 1 Corinthians 11:11, which was quoted above, "[I]n the Lord woman is not independent of man nor man of woman."

STRATEGY 3

Explain what Paul means by women keeping silent in the Christian assembly.

The next problematic passage that needs explanation is 1 Corinthians 14:34–35. Keep in mind that the reasoning below can also be applied to 1 Timothy 2:11.

> *Q:* "Wouldn't it be odd for Paul to have meant that women can't speak in church in an absolute sense since he already said in 1 Corinthians 11:5 that women could 'pray' and 'prophesy' in church?[273] Do you think Paul is dumb enough to contradict himself in such an obvious manner?"

It's hard to imagine. So if women could speak in church just like men were able, then what did Paul mean?

There are two possible interpretations. The first is that women were not allowed to give *official instruction* in the Christian assembly. This would be akin to the Church's prohibition of someone who doesn't have clerical authority giving the homily at Mass.[274] The Congregation for the Doctrine of the Faith approved this interpretation in its 1976 document *Inter Insigniores*:

> [T]he apostle's forbidding of women to speak in the assemblies (1 Cor. 14:34–35; 1 Tim. 2:12) is of a different nature, and exegetes define its meaning in this way: Paul in no way opposes the right, which he elsewhere recognizes as possessed by women, to prophesy in the assembly (1 Cor. 11:15); *the prohibition solely concerns the official function of teaching in the Christian assembly.* For St. Paul this prescription is bound up with the divine plan of creation (1 Cor. 11:7; Gen. 2:18–24): it would be difficult to see in it the expression of a cultural fact (4; emphasis added).

Such a prohibition would no more be unjust discrimination than the Church saying a layman can't give a sermon at Mass. Most people can see that this is reasonable. Not just anybody can get up and give an official teaching.[275]

Another possible interpretation is that Paul is attending to a specific pastoral problem in the church of Corinth involving women.[276] Notice how Paul gives the instruction, "If there is anything they [women] desire to know, let them ask their husbands at home."

> *Q:* "Why would Paul have to give such an instruction unless the women were asking questions in the Christian assembly?"

Imagine that a teacher in a classroom said, "Kids, hold your questions until after the lecture." What would you surmise? I think it would be reasonable to conclude that the kids kept interrupting the teacher with questions.

Similarly, it's possible that when Christians gathered together for worship in Corinth, women were interrupting the service with questions about the Faith. This is not that farfetched, given that the first Christian services were held in believers' homes, thus occasioning the temptation to treat them too informally.

Your friend may object, "But doesn't it seem that Paul is picking on women here? Why single them out?" Explain that Paul's instruction to be silent is not directed *only* at women. He gave the same sort of instruction to others more generally:

- To those inspired to speak in different tongues, he says, "But if there is no one to interpret, let each of them keep silence in church and speak to himself and to God" (1 Cor. 14:28).

- He instructs *everyone* to be silent if someone receives a revelation in order that all may hear: "If a revelation is made to another sitting by, let the first be silent. For you can all prophesy one by one, so that all may learn and all be encouraged" (v. 30–31).

In light of the context, it seems that Paul's instruction for women to keep silent may be merely a specific application of a general principle that applies to everyone.

Apparently Paul has to address the issue involving women because it was a big-enough problem that required his attention. As the New Testament scholar Ben Witherington explains,

> One must assume that he singles these women out for comment because he has heard that some of them were notable violators of these principles. Throughout the chapter Paul is correcting abuses, and his words must be read in that context.[277]

What the above two interpretations show is that Paul's teaching is more about the division between clergy and laity than about men and women. Therefore, Paul is not advocating misogyny.

THE WAY PREPARED: Christianity is the foremost promoter of the dignity of women.

> *The feminine sex is ennobled by virtue of the Savior's being born of a human mother; a woman was the gateway through which God found entrance to humankind.*[278]
> —Edith Stein (St. Teresa Benedicta of the Cross)

24

How can I be a Christian when Christianity encourages blind faith?

There are many charges unbelievers level at Christians, but one of the most common is that their faith is *blind*—that is to say, belief without evidence.

Leading atheist Richard Dawkins writes, "Faith, being belief that isn't based on evidence, is the principal vice of any religion."[279] Julian Baginni, British atheistic philosopher, concurs: "Belief in the supernatural is belief in what there is a lack of strong evidence to believe in."[280]

Such digs may seem justified with regard to Christianity, since Jesus said, "Blessed is he who believes and does not see" (John 20:28). It is this verse that led Baginni to think that Christianity endorses blind faith.[281] It is also a common source of confusion for callers to *Catholic Answers Live.*

So how can we remove this obstacle that stands in the way of the Lord? The three strategies below will help you lower the mountain and prepare the way.

STRATEGY 1

Explain the true meaning of Jesus' words in John 20:28.

Jesus is emphasizing belief without *physical sight and touch*, not belief without evidence. Recall how Thomas said, "Unless I *see* in his hands the print of the nails, and *place my finger* in the mark

of the nails, and *place my hand* in his side, I will not believe"
(John 20:25; emphasis added).

> Q: "Wouldn't you agree that there is a difference
> between belief without physical sight or touch and
> belief without evidence?"

Your friend has to agree; otherwise, his belief that George
Washington was the first president of the United States would
be "belief without evidence," since he never physically saw or
touched George Washington. But that's absurd.

Even though your friend hasn't seen or touched George Washington, his belief that George Washington was the first president
of the United States is not without evidence. As Christian apologist John Lennox argues, to verify something by touch and sight
is just *one kind* of evidence.[282] Therefore, it doesn't follow that
Jesus is endorsing "blind faith" the way that skeptics mean.

A logical question arises at this point: "So what other kind of
evidence is there?" The narrative itself tells us. Notice Thomas's
doubt is in response to the testimony of the apostles, "We have
seen the Lord" (John 20:25).

> Q: "Although Thomas's belief would have been
> without sight if he had believed the apostles, wouldn't
> their testimony serve as a kind of evidence?"

This provides a possible rationale behind Jesus' rebuke of
Thomas—namely, the apostles' testimony should have been sufficient for rational belief.

STRATEGY 2

**Show how it belongs to the Christian faith to base
belief on the evidence of testimony.**

John the Evangelist viewed his own Gospel and epistles as

reasonable evidence for belief. With regard to his Gospel, he writes, "[Jesus' signs] are written that you may believe that Jesus is the Christ, the Son of God, and that believing you may have life in his name" (John 20:31). John sees his testimony of Jesus' miracles ("signs") as sufficient evidence to merit belief by those who couldn't see him perform the signs.

He writes in a similar way in his first epistle:

> That which was from the beginning, which we have heard, which we have seen with our eyes, which we have looked upon and touched with our hands, concerning the word of life . . . that which we have seen and heard we proclaim also to you, so that you may have fellowship with us (1 John 1:1, 3).

Challenge your friend with this question:

> Q: "How could John be intending for Christians to practice blind faith if he is offering his testimony, along with the testimony of the other apostles, as evidence for rational belief?"

To the non-believer who asks, "Why should I believe in Jesus?" John says, "Because we saw him perform miracles, and we saw him risen from the dead." This is a far cry from blind faith.

Your friend may object that we need to assess whether John's testimony is credible. And your response is, "Sure we would." Is John lying? Is he reliable in telling us what Jesus said and did? Fortunately, John and the other Gospel writers root their narratives in history, thus making it possible to historically investigate the reliability of the Gospels. And as we've shown in chapter thirteen, there is enough good evidence to merit a general approach of trust in what they report.

It would be different if John were saying, "I proclaim to you, Jesus, whom I, and everyone else, have never seen or touched. You just have to believe!" In this case there would be nothing subject to historical investigation, and thus one would have to make a blind act of faith. But this is not what John is requiring of non-believers.

Therefore, it belongs to the Christian faith to believe based on evidence rather than make a "blind impulse of the mind" (CCC 156).

STRATEGY 3

Show how the objection undermines science as a rational form of knowledge.

Your third strategy shows how saying that belief without sight is without evidence puts your friend in a pickle with regard to science.

> *Q:* "Would you say that your belief in gravity and subatomic particles is not evidence-based since you have never physically seen these things?"

If he were to be consistent with the logic of his critique of faith, he would have to make such an absurd conclusion. Indeed, if he applies the logic of his argument to science in general, he would have to reject the majority of the scientific enterprise.

> *Q:* "If belief without sight or touch is belief without evidence, shouldn't you limit your scientific beliefs only to those theories that you empirically verify for yourself?"

I don't think any reasonable person would say yes—including Baginni and Dawkins. But that's exactly what the logic of the argument demands.

The logic further undermines science because science presupposes a non-empirical *belief* that the universe is rationally intelligible. As Paul Davies writes, "Even the most atheistic scientist accepts as an act of faith the existence of a law-like order in nature that is at least in part comprehensible to us."[283] Without the belief that order and intelligibility exist in the universe, science would never get off the ground.

You can assure your friend that the faith Christians are called to have in Jesus is not belief without evidence, but a *response* to the evidence. It is not "a blind impulse of the mind" because there are "motives of credibility"—such as miracles, prophecies fulfilled, the Church's growth, the Church's holiness, and the Church's stability (CCC 156) that support it. Neither, as we have seen, is belief in God a blind impulse of the mind, for there are many good arguments that make God's existence more reasonable than not.

Unfortunately, many critics fail to distinguish warranted belief and unwarranted belief, thinking all belief is unwarranted. As a result, some think they have to leave reason at the door of faith, but nothing could be further from the truth.

THE WAY PREPARED: Christianity does not require that you leave reason at the doorstep of faith.

> *The Catholic tradition, from the outset, rejected the so-called "fideism," which is the desire to believe against reason.*[284]
> —Pope Benedict XVI

25

How can I be a Christian when the Bible contradicts science?

The six "days" of creation in the first chapter of Genesis are a major obstacle for many who consider the Christian religion. The reasoning usually goes as follows: "Why would anybody in his right mind belong to a religion whose sacred writings say the universe and everything in it was created in six twenty-four hour periods? Don't they know that science tells us the universe was evolving for a little over 9 billion years before the earth was formed, and that *homo sapiens* didn't come on the scene until billions of years later?"[285]

Our three strategies below will show that such an obstacle is merely illusory. It exists only in the minds of unbelievers, because of a false understanding of the creation story's intended meaning.

STRATEGY 1

Explain how the author of the creation story in Genesis is not doing science.

The author of the creation story is not intending to give a scientific account of the beginning of the universe. Conveying the mathematical truths about the laws of nature was not his purpose.

And even if God wanted to reveal such truths to the biblical author, the author wouldn't have been able to understand it any more than my six-year-old son would be able to understand calculus if I taught it to him.

Instead, the author intended to convey explanations about God and human beings that countered rival myths among the pagans (e.g., the Epic of Gilgamesh). He had to explain five things in particular:

- The God who created the universe is *one*—and *only* one—in contrast to the pagan belief in many gods

- God created everything outside of himself, in contrast to the belief that created things were gods.

- Human beings were made in the image and likeness of God, not to be playthings for the gods.

- Creation is good and is meant to be pleasing and helpful to humankind, in contrast to the pagan belief that creation was evil.

- Creation was the result of God's divine plan and not a product of chaotic warring among the gods.

The *Catechism of the Catholic Church* describes the purpose of the creation story this way:

> Among all the scriptural texts about creation, the first three chapters of Genesis occupy a unique place. From a literary standpoint these texts may have had diverse sources. The inspired authors have placed them at the beginning of Scripture to express in their solemn language the truths of creation—its origin and its end in God, its order and goodness, the vocation of man, and, finally, the drama of sin and the hope of salvation (289).

The late philosopher and historian of science Stanley Jaki puts it succinctly:

> This purpose was not to instruct man about cosmogenesis, but to enlighten him about the manner of reverencing the One on whom all depends.[286]

If we don't take the creation story primarily as "a lesson in world-making,"[287] then the problem of trying to reconcile the creation narrative in Genesis with the modern scientific narrative goes away. Your friend must realize that the biblical revelation was given "not [as] an instruction about how the heavens go, but how to go to heaven."[288] Science is only competent on the former point, not the latter. You need theology for that.

And lest your friend think that this view of the creation story is a weak concession to modern scientific discovery, point out that even back in the fifth century St. Augustine didn't believe that the creation story was intended to scientifically describe the universe's beginning. In his work *The Literal Meaning of Genesis,* he taught that the author symbolically portrays God creating the sun and moon on the fourth day to signify that God made them to rule the realms he created on the first three days (day-night, sky-water, land).

His symbolic view of the text is further supported where he teaches that what God created instantly the author separated in time: "[T]he sacred writer was able to separate in the time of his narrative what God did not separate in time in his creative act."[289] Augustine even concedes that ultimately we don't know exactly what the days mean in the creation story: "What kind of days these were is extremely difficult or perhaps impossible for us to conceive, and how much more to say!"[290]

Wrap up this strategy with the following questions:

> *Q:* "How could the creation story be criticized for containing scientific errors when it wasn't even attempting to do science? Would you accuse the weatherman with scientific error for saying the sun is going to 'rise' at 6 a.m.?"

Just as the weatherman's language is not subject to scientific criticism since he's not intending to make a scientific statement, so too the author of the creation story is not subject to scientific criticism since he wasn't intending to make a scientific statement about the origin of the universe.

STRATEGY 2

Explain that the author uses a different methodology from science to affirm primeval truths, and that he doesn't intend all details to be taken as historical facts.

Your second strategy addresses the method that the ancient author uses to communicate inspired truths about God and mankind. In his 1950 encyclical *Humani Generis*, Pope Pius XII affirmed that the author intended to convey certain historical truths, but that he did so in a manner that is unique to the ancient writing style of his time:

> [T]he first eleven chapters of Genesis, although properly speaking not conforming to the historical method used by the best Greek and Latin writers or by competent authors of our time, do nevertheless pertain to history in a true sense, which however must be further studied and determined by exegetes; the same chapters . . . in simple and metaphorical language adapted to the mentality of a people but little cultured, both state the principal truths which are fundamental for our salvation, and also give a popular description of the origin of the human race and the chosen people (38).

Notice that Pius XII acknowledges the presence of "metaphorical language" and "popular descriptions" in the creation story. This means that the reader doesn't have to take every detail as a historical fact.

For example, the *Catechism* teaches that the six-day succession in the creation story is a symbolic presentation of the Creator's divine work (397). This means that the six days of creation are not literal time periods.

The third-century Christian writer Origen believed this was obvious, since the author begins counting days before the sun, moon, and stars even existed. In a bit of a snarky way, he writes,

Now who is there, pray, possessed of understanding, that will regard the statement as appropriate, that the first day, and the second, and the third, in which also both evening and morning are mentioned, existed without sun, and moon, and stars—the first day even without a sky?...I do not suppose that anyone doubts that these things figuratively indicate certain mysteries, the history having taken place in appearance, and not literally.[291]

So, even some 1,800 years ago, a Christian writer was interpreting the six-day succession as a literary device rather than a literal chronology.

The *Catechism* also acknowledges that the account of the fall in Genesis 3 "uses figurative language" while affirming the truth of a primeval event involving our first parents' sin against God (390). It even recognizes the tree of the knowledge of good and evil as symbolic, in that it "evokes the insurmountable limits that man, being a creature, must freely recognize and respect with trust" (396).

This reiterates past teaching. For example, in reference to the authors of the Old Testament, Pope Leo XIII writes,

[T]hey did not seek to penetrate the secrets of nature, but rather described and dealt with things in more or less figurative language, or in terms which were commonly used at the time, and which in many instances are in daily use at this day, even by the most eminent men of science (*Providentissimus Deus* 18).

Pope Leo explains that the authors used figurative language to put down in writing what God wanted "in a way men could understand and were accustomed to" (PD 18).

Knowing that a Christian is not required to take every detail of the creation story as literal and historical, your friend need no longer see its supposed contradiction of science as an obstacle.

STRATEGY 3

Explain how the framework interpretation is a plausible way to understand the text.

Your third strategy offers a plausible interpretation of the six-day motif. It is called the framework interpretation. This view holds that rather than conveying facts about the time or sequence in which God created, the six days of creation represent a *literary framework* into which the events of creation can be fitted.

Explain to your friend that there seems to be embedded in the six days of creation a kind of poetic structure in which the first three days correspond with the last three. On the first three days God creates realms or regions by way of separation: day from night, sky from sea, and sea from land.

On the following three days, God fills these realms. For example, he places the sun, moon, and stars to rule the day and night. He populates the sky with birds and the sea with fish. He then fills the dry land with animals and man.

Scholars call the first three days the days of *distinction* because God separates the realms from one another. The next three are called the days of *adornment* since God adds new things to the regions he separated.

It's possible that this literary framework signifies what was mentioned in strategy one, namely, that God ordered things in a rational way, contrary to pagan belief at the time.

Moreover, there seems to be a progression in the days from the least significant things of the physical world to the most significant—human beings. Perhaps this is yet another way the author is responding to the pagan view of man. He is trying to show that man is essentially good, and that the physical world and everything in it is ordered toward him. It's possible this is what is meant by Adam and Eve receiving "dominion over the fish of the sea, and over the birds of the air, and over the cattle, and over all the earth, and over every creeping thing that creeps upon the earth" (Gen. 1:26).

Over the centuries, theologians have given many other inter-pretations of the six days of creation. But none of them require abandoning scientific truth in order to believe.

THE WAY PREPARED: The creation story is not intended to be taken as a scientific account of the origins of the universe, and therefore doesn't contradict science.

> *The language in question is a mythical one . . . the term "myth" does not designate a fabulous content, but merely an archaic way of expressing a deeper content. Without any difficulty we discover that content, under the layer of the ancient narrative.*[292]
> —Pope St. John Paul II

26

How can I be a Christian when the Bible is full of contradictions?

It's common among skeptics to mock Christians for believing in a Bible that is full of contradictions, especially when it comes to the Gospels. For example, the late atheist Christopher Hitchens called the New Testament "a work of crude carpentry, hammered together long after its purported events, and full of improvised attempts to make things come out right."[293]

The popular agnostic and New Testament scholar Bart Ehrman similarly complains about the sources for Jesus' resurrection: "[They] are hopelessly contradictory, as we can see by doing a detail comparison of the accounts in the Gospels."[294]

If the sources for the life and teachings of Jesus are filled with contradictions, then why should anyone trust them? Wouldn't that be a reason not to be a Christian? Our strategies will show you how to lower this mountain and prepare a way for the Lord.

STRATEGY 1

Explain that even if there were real contradictions in the Gospels, these would not automatically negate their general reliability.

Let's say for argument's sake the Gospels do contain contradictions. This doesn't mean we must reject wholesale the historicity of the events they record. There are four ways that you can explain this to your friend.

First, we've already established the general reliability of the Gospels in chapter thirteen. This means that even if a Gospel writer contradicts another and gets a detail wrong, it only proves that he was wrong about *that* particular detail. It doesn't follow that he is wrong about every detail in his Gospel, nor does it undermine the general trust that we can have in his reports.

Second, it's possible that other details could be proven as historically probable in light of the historiographical criteria—criteria that historians use to determine the historicity of a saying or event. We looked at a few of them in chapter thirteen.

For example, Jesus' death meets the criterion of *multiple attestation*. The four Gospels, Paul's epistles, the writings of the early Church Fathers, the first-century Jewish historian Josephus,[295] and the first-century Roman historian Tacitus[296] all attest to it. His crucifixion satisfies the criterion of *coherence* because it coheres with his claims to be God, which for the Jews was punishable by death. That women were the first witnesses of the resurrection is a detail that is most likely historical because it satisfies the criterion of *embarrassment*.

There are many more examples, but suffice to say that even if the Gospels contradicted one another on some details, we would be justified in taking as historical those sayings and events of Jesus' life that meet the historiographical criteria.

Third, we may look at small contradictions as evidence *for* rather than against historical reliability. Why would the Gospel writers include contradictions if they were making things up? If they were conspiring to make up a story, you would think that they would make everything perfectly coherent. And such perfect coherence would have been possible, given, as we know, that some authors (Matthew and Luke) used the material of another (Mark) to draw from. This would have prevented their conspiracy from breaking down like it does when police question people's fake alibis, or like it did in the story of the two elders whose conspiracy broke down when Daniel questioned them separate from each other (Dan. 13:47–64).

Finally, common experience tells us that we don't have to discount an event in its entirety just because there are contradictory accounts of some of its details.

> Q: "Should we conclude the *Titanic* didn't sink because some survivors of the *Titanic* said that the ship broke in two pieces prior to sinking but others said it went down intact?"

You can also use the example of the fire in Rome during Nero's reign. The second-century Roman historian Cornelius Tacitus says that Nero was not responsible for the fire, since he was away in the city of Antium while the fire raged.[297] Suetonius, another second-century Roman historian, says that Nero sent men to burn the city and watched from the tower of Maecenas.[298] And the third-century Roman statesman and historian Dio Cassius reports that Nero started the fire himself and watched from the rooftop of the imperial palace.[299]

> Q: "Must we conclude from these discrepancies that the fire in Rome didn't happen?"

Just because there are contradictions with regard to the details of how the fire started and who was responsible for it, we shouldn't conclude that these historical accounts aren't talking about a real fire. Similarly, even if the alleged contradictory details surrounding the resurrection of Jesus (for example) were real, that alone would not be enough to conclude it didn't happen.

Remember that the above strategy presumes for the sake of argument that there *are* real contradictions. Therefore it only seeks to show that your friend, despite the contradictions, would be justified in accepting the historical fact that Jesus rose from the dead and responding to that evidence by making an act of faith to believe in him. Although he could then become a Christian inasmuch as he believes in Jesus, he still might be hesitant to profess being a member of the Christian religion because Christianity professes the New Testament to be inspired and inerrant.

But that's where the work of showing that the contradictions are only *apparent* comes into play. Our next two strategies will give you some tools to at least begin this work.

STRATEGY 2

Explain the key principles to keep in mind when dealing with apparent contradictions in the Gospels.

The first principle is that *incompleteness* doesn't mean *inaccuracy*. As apologist Trent Horn writes, "Just because the sacred author did not record something another author recorded does not mean his text is in error."[300]

For example, John seems to indicate that Mary Magdalene was the only woman that went to the tomb (John 20:1), yet we know from Matthew, Mark, and Luke that she was among other women. This is not a contradiction, because John didn't say that Mary Magdalene was the *only* woman. He simply focused on Mary Magdalene and her later response to Peter and John. In fact, that response indicates she *was* with other women: "she ran . . . and said to them . . . *we* do not know where they have laid him" (John 20:2; emphasis added).

The second key principle is that ancient authors did not always order events chronologically. They could order events topically instead,[301] or they could *telescope events*—a literary device that makes events in a narrative appear closer together in time than they actually were.

A topical ordering approach provides a possible resolution of the apparent contradiction between Mark and John with regard to what Jesus did after his baptism. Mark says Jesus "immediately" went out into the desert after his baptism (Mark 1:12) whereas John says Jesus spent time with two of John the Baptist's former disciples—one of them being Andrew—who then began to follow him (John 20:35–42).

Mark's use of the word "immediately" (Greek: *euthys*) could suggest that he was trying to emphasize the motif that Jesus is a man of action. Mark is fond of this term, using it forty-seven times in his Gospel compared to the *combined ten* times in Matthew, Luke, John, and Acts.

It may be that Mark's concern was not chronology but the excitement and urgency of Jesus' ministry—that is to say, he did this, this, and this. The early Christian writer Papias argues along these same lines:

> Mark having become the interpreter of Peter, wrote down accurately whatsoever he remembered. It was not, however, in exact order that he related the sayings or deeds of Christ.[302]

Luke seems to employ the telescoping technique in Luke 24:36–53, when he describes the events following the Resurrection. He makes it seem that everything happened in one day when we know from the other Gospels that these events occurred over the course of several days.[303]

> *Q:* "Why should we accuse the Gospel writers of chronological contradictions when the literary techniques of the era did not require perfect chronological details?"

It's simply a mistake to apply modern standards of chronology to ancient writers.

A third principle is that ancient-world biographies were not expected to have verbatim transcribing (*ipsissima verba*—actual words). It was sufficient that they paraphrase their reports so long as what they wrote remained faithful to the meaning of the original utterance (*ipsissima vox*—actual voice).[304]

For example, with regard to his records of speeches given during the Peloponnesian War, the Greek historian Thucydides admits "it was in all cases difficult to carry them word for

word in one's memory" but he adhered "closely as possible to
the general sense of what they really said."[305] Jonas Grethlein,
a German historiography scholar, confirms this principle: "It is
widely agreed that most speeches in ancient historiography do
not reproduce *verba ipsissima*."[306]

This principle helps resolve the apparent contradictions that
exist between the synoptic Gospels' narratives of the words of
institution at the Last Supper. Compare Matthew 26:26–28,
Mark 14:22–25, and Luke 22:19–20 and you'll see that they differ. Here is a good question for your friend:

> *Q:* "Why should we assume that the ancient authors
> of the Bible had to record speeches and events in the
> exact same manner as modern historians do (verbatim
> transcription) when it was perfectly within their rights
> as authors to paraphrase Jesus' teachings while at the
> same time being faithful to his original meaning?"

The apparent contradictions only arise if we demand from
ancient historians what we demand from modern ones, namely,
verbatim transcription. But that contradicts what scholars know
about how ancient historians worked.

Finally, it's important that your friend realize that some of
the alleged contradictions are due to copyist mistakes that found
their way into the copied manuscripts. This is to be expected,
given the long and arduous process of copying texts.

For example, 1 Kings 4:26 says Solomon had 40,000 stalls of
horses but 2 Chronicles 9:25 says he had 4,000. The latter number is probably correct, since there were no stables big enough
at the time of Solomon to hold 40,000 stalls. Trent Horn gives
a plausible explanation for how the large number made its way
into the manuscript:

> [I]n Hebrew the word for "four" is spelled with the He-
> brew letters "aleph-resh-bet-ayin-heh," and the word
> for "forty" is spelled "aleph-resh-bet-ayin-yodh-mem."

A copyist simply added the wrong ending to the word and transformed "four" into "forty."[307]

The presence of copyist errors, however, doesn't mean that we can't generally trust that copied manuscripts faithfully reproduce the original autographs. Given the number of manuscripts we have, and the close temporal proximity they have with the autographs compared to other ancient texts, the evidence for the reliability of the New Testament manuscripts is solid.[308]

STRATEGY 3

Explain how common apparent contradictions can be resolved.

There are many alleged contradictions, but one of the most popular involves the genealogies of Jesus presented in Matthew 1 and Luke 3. Skeptics attack many aspects of the genealogies, but a favorite is the discrepancy involving Joseph's father. Matthew tells us that Joseph's father was Jacob, and Luke tells us his father was Heli. How do we reconcile this?

A possible way to harmonize these passages is with evidence that Joseph was the biological son of Jacob and the legal son of Heli. The early Church historian Eusebius records that Jacob and Heli were half-brothers, and that when Heli died childless, Jacob married Heli's widowed wife and fathered Joseph in accord with the Jewish Levirate law (Deut. 25:5–6).[309] This provides a possible rationale behind Matthew's usage of *begot* in his genealogy and Luke's description of people being *of* a father in his. Matthew's language bespeaks physical lineage, whereas Luke's language allows for both physical and adoptive lineage.

Another popular example is Matthew and Luke's account of the centurion and his servants requesting Jesus' help. Matthew reports that a centurion made an appeal to Jesus to heal his servant (Matt. 8:5). But according to Luke 7:3 it was the centurion's servants who made the appeal. Although it could have been both, in which case Matthew is simply emphasizing one and Luke is emphasizing the other, there is another plausible explanation.

In the first century it was common to speak of someone performing an action when the act was done by someone else at his bidding, on his behalf, or by his authority. It's similar to the old legal maxim: *Qui facit per alium, facit per se*—he who acts through another does the act himself.

For example, Matthew tells us that Joseph of Arimathea cut the rock out for his tomb in which he laid Jesus (Matt. 27:59–60). But Joseph likely didn't do the actual cutting—he probably commissioned a mason to do it for him. In the centurion story above, Jewish leaders say the centurion built their synagogue (Luke 7:5). Obviously the centurion didn't build the synagogue himself; he commissioned and paid for it.

Similarly, Matthew credits the centurion with the appeal because he sent the messengers to make the request on his behalf, which is the detail that Luke gives us. The objection only arises because of a failure to understand the cultural and linguistic context.

Another apparent contradiction that is commonly used is Judas's death, as recorded by Matthew (Matt. 27:3–10) and Luke (Acts 1:18). Matthew reports that the chief priests bought the field and Judas hung himself. Yet Luke records that Judas acquired the field and fell headlong, causing his bowels to burst out.

How did Judas die? Who purchased the field?

Let's consider the first question. When someone falls he normally doesn't burst open.

> *Q:* "Did you ever fall down when you were a kid? Did your guts burst out of your stomach?"

But that might be what we would expect if a) Judas was already dead and it was his dead body that fell, and b) the body fell from a considerable height. What's interesting is that outside Jerusalem trees grow right on the edge of steep cliffs with their branches extending over the valley. It's possible that Judas hung himself from a tree extending over the cliff to ensure his death.

And when the rope broke, his dead body fell to the ground and burst open upon impact. This is not proof that it happened this way, but it does provide a plausible explanation given the circumstantial details.

Concerning the question of who purchased the field, we must remember the maxim above: he who acts through another does the act himself. The chief priests physically purchased the field, but they did so with Judas's money. This is why Peter attributes the act to Judas in Acts 1:18.

Obviously, we can't go into all the alleged contradictions in the Bible. But the plausible reconciliations for the three examples above at least show that alleged contradictions, after closer examination, can be overcome. This can give your friend confidence that other apparent contradictions can be similarly resolved. And when you add to this the general reliability of the Gospels, one has good reason to believe that what the Gospels record about the life and teachings of Jesus is accurate.

THE WAY PREPARED: When closely examined, the apparent contradictions in the Bible turn out to be just that: apparent.

> *Despite two centuries of skeptical onslaught, it is fair to say that all the alleged inconsistencies among the Gospels have received at least plausible resolutions.*[310]
> —Craig Blomberg
> (American New Testament scholar)

27

How can I be a Christian when the Bible depicts God as a wrathful monster?

Christianity teaches that God is all-good, and at the same time believes the Bible is the inspired word of God. But in the Bible God commands followers to exterminate whole peoples (Deut. 7:1–2; 20:16–17; 1 Sam. 15:1–3). This naturally leads skeptics to object: "How can God be all-good if he commands genocide? Why would I belong to a religion that believes this sort of thing?"

Apart from the problem of evil, this is perhaps the biggest obstacle a skeptic faces when considering the Christian faith. But there are several ways we can respond.

One way is to say these commands are purely symbolic, merely warfare rhetoric—similar to how athletes might say "we slaughtered them" in order to describe their victory over another team.[311]

Another way is to say that the author attributed the Israelites' actions to God's commands because of the common cultural belief at the time that God is the *direct* cause of everything.[312] The author may have taken the Israelites' success in the various wars as divine sanction.[313] Trent Horn calls the ancient writer's expression of this divine sanction "divine command language," and compares it to the common use of anthropomorphic language, which describes God in human terms, and phenomenological language, which describes the natural world according to sense perception.[314]

A third way sees the commands as literal. This is the approach we will defend, since it's the hardest for skeptics to swallow, and since skeptics often perceive the other approaches as cop-outs, though often they do so unfairly.

If we can reconcile the literal approach with God's all-good nature, then all three interpretations taken together would give a skeptic good reason to not let this issue be an obstacle to embracing the Christian faith.

STRATEGY 1

Explain that God is the author of life, and therefore it is within his divine prerogative to bring a human life to an end, even innocent human life. And he may do so by divine command.

You can begin by asking your friend this question:

> *Q:* "Wouldn't it be true to say that there are some circumstances in which it is just to kill someone, such as in just war and self-defense?"

If your friend pushes back on just war, then focus on self-defense. Few will dispute that the moral prohibition of taking human life applies only to *innocent* human beings. When an aggressor threatens our life or the life of another innocent person, it is morally permissible to use lethal means to stop the aggressor (see CCC 2264).

> *Q:* "If it's not always evil for us to end someone's life, wouldn't the same be true for God?"

The question then becomes: under what conditions is it just for God to will the end of someone's life? The answer lies is God's dignity as the author of all life. The authority that he has over us as the Creator gives him the divine prerogative to determine when a particular person's life ends, and the means by which that comes about. God does not *owe* us, as a matter of justice, the preservation of our lives. Therefore God does not commit evil in willing its end.

It is even within God's divine prerogative to deputize someone to carry out his will of bringing human life to an end. If he can do it through natural disasters or plagues,[315] then he can do it through human mediators. St. Thomas Aquinas explains:

> All men alike, both guilty and innocent, die the death of nature: which death of nature is inflicted by the power of God on account of original sin, according to 1 Samuel 2:6: "The Lord killeth and maketh alive. Consequently, by the command of God, death can be inflicted on any man, guilty or innocent, without any injustice whatever.[316]

This is the rationale that justifies God's command for the Israelites to wipe out the inhabitants of the lands mentioned in the Bible passages cited above. Your friend may wonder why God may take innocent human life but we may not. The answer is that we are not the authors of life, and thus we don't have the authority to do what God alone can do. Explain to your friend that this line of reasoning is not foreign to our common experience.

> *Q:* "Is it unreasonable for an ambulance driver to run a red light when we may not? Is it unreasonable for a principal to cancel classes for a day although a student or teacher can't?"

Your friend should be able to see that it is not contrary to reason for a person with authority to do things that someone under his authority is not permitted to do.

Similarly, we are not permitted to take the life of innocent humans because we don't have ultimate authority over human life. But God does.

STRATEGY 2

Explain how God's command is within the context of divine justice.

Your second strategy shows that God's genocidal commands in the Bible go beyond his merely exercising his authority as Creator.

> *Q:* "If Hitler had been captured and put on trial, wouldn't it have been just to give him the death sentence, or at least the maximum term of imprisonment?"

Hitler is an example that should be used sparingly! But the purpose of this question is to establish with your friend that great crimes deserve great punishment.

Similarly, God's command to destroy the inhabitants of different lands is always within the context of divine justice—rendering to each his due.[317] It is a response to the perverse wickedness of the inhabitants. Share the following examples:

• The Amalekites were the first to attack Israel after her liberation from Egypt (Exod. 17:8; Deut. 25:17–19), and they did so again later at Hormah (Num. 14:45). They also allied themselves with other nations to commit genocide against Israel (Judges 6:3–5).

• The Canaanites committed various sorts of heinous sins. Leviticus 18:1–20 gives a list of the various sorts of incestuous relations they engaged in. The most grievous of their sins was child sacrifice. This is implied in the Levitical prohibition of sacrificing children to the Canaanite deity Molech (Lev. 18:21; Lev. 20:2), and the psalmist's lamentations over the Israelites worshipping the idols of Canaan (Psalm 106:36–38). There is also archeological evidence that confirms child sacrifice among the Canaanites.[318]

God's command for the Israelites to wipe out the inhabitants of these lands is nothing more than a deputation to enact appropriate punishment. The gravity of their sins merited punishment by death (see strategy three for an explanation of why God chose this method). God also saw this as the only way to protect Israel from being ensnared by the evil ways of these nations (Deut. 20:18), which unfortunately happened no few times (Psalm 106:36–38).

It's also important to note that God's judgment on these peoples did not come immediately, but only after he gave them ample time to turn to him and spare themselves judgment. For example, the order to carry out God's command to destroy the Amalekites (1 Sam. 15:3) didn't come until some 400 years after the Amalekites became Israel's enemy (Amalekites are descendants of Amalek, the grandson of Esau, the brother of Jacob—Genesis 36:12). That is plenty of time to recognize and come to accept the unique relationship that Israel had with God.

Furthermore, God warned the Kenites, a people living among the Amalekites, about the impending judgment on the Amalekites, and gave them a chance to escape (1 Sam. 15:6). It's hard to imagine that the Amalekites would not have heard about the warning, and thus it's reasonable to assume they could have fled with the Kenites and escape judgment, but they chose not to.

The time for repentance is even more evident when it comes to the Canaanites. For example, Genesis 15:16 says, "The iniquity of the Amorites [a nation that inhabited Canaan] is not yet complete," implying there was still time for them to repent before their judgment. The book of Wisdom explains how God judged them [the Canaanites] "little by little" and "gave them a chance to repent" even though God was aware "that their way of thinking would never change" (Wis. 12:10).

There is also evidence that suggests the Canaanites would have known about the mighty works God wrought for the Israelites, thus giving them a chance to repent or at least give over their land peacefully. The harlot Rahab tells Joshua's spies that the Canaanites had heard how God led the Israelites through the water of the Red Sea, and as a result feared the Israelites (Joshua 2:9–10). But they still chose to remain and fight against Israel rather than escape their destruction.

These passages show how God tempered his justice with mercy. The opportunities he gave Israel's enemies to escape impending judgment make their destruction a consequence of their own making.

But what about God's command to kill even the innocent persons (for example, children) of these nations?

First, I think it has to do with God's condescension to the cultural limitations of the people of those times. As we will see in strategy three below, God relates to the Israelites in cultural and intellectual categories that were common at that time. In the ancient world, the rules of warfare did not involve distinguishing between combatants and noncombatants (see 2 Kings 8:12; Isa. 13:16–18; Nahum 3:10). God's command for this sort of military engagement seems to have been an example of God's divine accommodation—dealing with Israel within their limited moral and cultural framework. As apologist Jimmy Akin writes, "God was dealing with blunt instruments."[319]

Second, one could use the same answer given in the previous strategy: God is the author of all life, and therefore can justly determine when and how someone's life—even the life of an innocent person—comes to an end.

Finally, we must remember that from a Christian perspective death is not the end of the story. We continue to exist after death, and since God is all-powerful he can more than compensate the innocent who have suffered and died.[320] In other words, God can make it up to them by granting the bliss of eternal life. This is what Paul means when he writes to the Corinthians,

> So we do not lose heart . . . For this slight momentary affliction is preparing for us an eternal weight of glory beyond all comparison, because we look not to the things that are seen but to the things that are unseen; for

the things that are seen are transient, but the things that
are unseen are eternal" (2 Cor. 4:16–18).

As tragic as it may be, in human terms, for the innocent to
die, the New Testament revelation of the afterlife tells us that it's
not *ultimately* tragic.

STRATEGY 3

**Explain how the harsh consequence of capital
punishment is a divine accommodation to the moral
and cultural limitations of the Israelites at the time.**

Your third strategy addresses the common concern about the
harshness of God's punishment of these wicked nations. Your
friend may ask, "Why death? It seems so harsh."

> *Q:* "Do you agree that parents should discipline their
> children differently according to their age? Wouldn't
> it be a bit weird if a parent continued to spank his
> sixteen-year-old son as he did when his son was
> three?"

Point out that the *developmental stage* of the child is the reason
for these different disciplinary tactics. There is not much reasoning that you can do to persuade a three-year-old child why a
certain behavior is bad and that he ought not to do it. But when
the child matures and his reasoning skills advance, a parent can
use different methods to communicate moral guidance.

> *Q:* "If you were just learning to add and subtract, and
> I put a series of algebraic functions on the board,
> would you be able to understand them?"[321]

Obviously the answer is no. Your friend wouldn't have the
categorical apparatus to understand the complexities of algebraic

equations. He would be looking at the numbers and trying to figure out why a math problem has letters like "x."

These examples confirm a principle made famous by Aquinas: *quidquid recipitur ad modum recipientis recipitur*—"whatever is received into something is received according to the condition of the receiver."[322] We can apply the same principle to God's relation to Israel and its enemies.

At that time, God was dealing with barbaric and primitive peoples whose moral and cultural capacities were very limited—analogous to the intellectual limitations of the child and the student above. Recall Akin's statement above: "God was dealing with blunt instruments."[323] God's moral guidance for Israel, therefore, is going to look different from his guidance for Christians in the New Covenant. His dealings with his enemies are also going to look different.

Take his moral guidance, for example. God could have revealed to the Israelites that once they entered into the Promised Land of Canaan they should love their enemies and avoid their enemies' wicked behavior for the sake of doing what's good. But that would have been like the parent teaching a three-year-old son to reform his behavior by saying, "It is contrary to fraternal charity for you to hit your sister," or for a teacher to say to the second-grader, "Solve the equation $x^3 + 1$ and $(y^4x^2 + 2xy - y)/(x - 1) = 12$," and expect the correct answer.

Without the later revelation of God's unconditional love in the suffering and death of Jesus, the revelation of heavenly bliss, and the intellectual and cultural development present at the time of Jesus, such instructions might have been unintelligible for the Israelites. And consequently they would have been no more equipped to avoid the wickedness of their enemies after this instruction than they would have been before it.

This seems plausible given that the reason God commands the Israelites to "utterly destroy" their enemies (Deut. 20:17) is that "[their enemies] may not teach [the Israelites] to do according to all their abominable practices which they have done in the service of their gods, and so to sin against the LORD your God"

(Deut. 20:18; cf. Deut. 7:4). God knew that if the Canaanites and their surrounding inhabitants were left behind, the Israelites would take on their wicked ways, and thus impede Israel from carrying out God's plan to be a light to the nations and prepare the way for the coming Messiah (see Isa. 49:6). And given the conditions of the time, the only effective way to prevent this danger was to exterminate them.

The Israelites failure to fully carry out God's command proves this rationale true—for they later fell prey to the wickedness of their enemies:

> *They did not destroy the peoples, as the LORD commanded them,* but they mingled with the nations and learned to do as they did. They served their idols, which became a snare to them. They sacrificed their sons and their daughters to the demons; they poured out innocent blood, the blood of their sons and daughters, whom they sacrificed to the idols of Canaan; and the land was polluted with blood (Psalm 106:34–38; emphasis added).

Furthermore, along with not having the revelation of God's unconditional love and the torments of being separated from him in hell, the Israelites and their enemies didn't have the concepts of eternal damnation and the spiritual harm that sin causes. Consequently, God could not have used such things to teach the Israelites the gravity of the sins committed by their enemies and motivate them to avoid such wickedness. Also, such concepts would have been futile in trying to motivate Israel's enemies to cease their wicked behavior. Therefore, it's fitting that God would use death to communicate the gravity of rejecting him as the sovereign Lord, since death in the ancient world would be the ultimate punishment for an offense. For Israel, it was a warning. For Israel's enemies, it was judgment.

Of course, God *could* have given special graces to enlighten the Israelites and their enemies to where they would avoid war. But he didn't. And this gets us right back into the problem of evil that we dealt with in chapters seven and eight. God has the power to stop all evil. But he permits it only inasmuch as he will bring about a greater good. And just because we might not see the greater good, it doesn't follow there isn't one.

THE WAY PREPARED: God is sovereign Lord over life and has divine prerogative to take it. Moreover, his commands for the Israelites to destroy the Canaanites and surrounding inhabitants were issued for the sake of divine punishment and the preservation of the Israelites from adopting their enemies' wicked ways.

> *The infinite God, in his effort to teach finite beings, simplifies his message to be able to reach us within the limitations of our cultural circumstances. In the ancient world . . . . Laws were simple because life was brutal.*[324]
> —Mark Giszak (American biblical scholar)

PART V

PREPARE THE WAY FOR THE CHURCH

28

How can I join a church that is so superstitious?

To outsiders, Catholic piety can seem weird. We light candles and make requests that God will answer our prayers. We display pieces of bone and clothing from people who have died long ago. We even kiss these items and pray with them.

We also kiss statues and bow before them. Some Catholics bury statues in their yard thinking it will help sell their house. We wear scapulars, holy medals, and crucifixes. We have crucifixes on our walls at home, we dip our hands in holy water, we have rosaries, and all sorts of other religious items. And we actually believe that they somehow help us to be holy.

All of this can sound superstitious to those who don't understand the rationale behind these acts of piety. It can be an obstacle for many considering the Catholic Church: both for Protestants, who may think such practices are a kind of idolatry, and secular skeptics, who think they're just strange. We don't have space to cover every pious Catholic practice, but our strategies below will focus on three of them. The general principles used in explaining them can be applied to many other practices, too.

STRATEGY 1

Explain how the Church's use of relics is not superstitious.

You can start by acknowledging the fact that some Christians probably *do* use relics in a superstitious way: meaning that they think such objects have power *in themselves* to bring about miraculous effects—like an amulet or lucky charm. But the Church views this as an abuse.

Relics, whether it is a bone or other remains from a saint's body (*first class*), a piece of a saint's clothing (*second class*), or something that a piece of the saint's body or clothing has touched (*third class*), have value for Catholics because they belonged to people who served God in an exemplary way. Explain that this kind of devotion is not foreign to common human experience.

> *Q:* "Isn't it true that all of us treasure things that have belonged to someone we love, whether it be a piece of clothing, a book, a lock of hair, or some other item?"

There shouldn't be any contention here. These "relics" simply remind us of the love we shared with that person while they were alive and even after death. And it doesn't have to be someone we knew personally. If we don't blink an eye at Ford's Theater Museum keeping the bloodstained pillow on which President Lincoln died, then we shouldn't be concerned with preserving the relics of God's holy instruments. And as St. Thomas Aquinas teaches, since their bodies are "much more intimately and closely united to us than any garment," and their bodies "were temples, organs of the Holy Ghost dwelling and operating in them," we should indeed *reverence* the relics of their bodies.[325]

Relics also have value because at times God chooses to use these relics as an occasion to perform miracles. They have no power in themselves: contrary to magic, relics are not used to manipulate supernatural power for our own ends. It is God who establishes the efficacy of relics, and he uses them to produce effects that can only derive from his divine power.

Any Christian who uses relics in a way similar to an amulet or lucky charm is acting contrary to Church teaching. Therefore, your friend's repulsion to such superstition is something you can affirm.

Also share the biblical evidence for miracles accompanying relics:

- God uses Moses' staff to part the Red Sea (Exod. 14:16–22).

- A dead man was raised when his body came into contact with the bones of the prophet Elisha (2 Kings 13:21).

- The sick were healed by touching the tassels on Jesus' cloak (Matt. 14:35–36; Mark 6:56; Luke 8:43–44).

- God used Peter's shadow to cause miraculous healings of the sick (Acts 5:14–16).

- Paul's handkerchiefs and aprons were used to affect healing of diseases and to drive out demons (Acts 19:11–12).

The use of relics continued even beyond the apostolic age. For example, the Smyrnaeans in A.D. 156 wrote a letter describing the martyrdom of their bishop, Polycarp:

> We took up his bones, which are more valuable than precious stones and finer than refined gold, and laid them in a suitable place, where the Lord will permit us to gather ourselves together, as we are able, in gladness and joy and to celebrate the birthday of his martyrdom.

The fourth-century Bible scholar St. Jerome witnesses to the Catholic veneration of relics in response to those who were accusing Catholics of worshipping relics:

> We do not worship, we do not adore, for fear that we should bow down to the creature rather than to the creator, but we venerate the relics of the martyrs in order the better to adore him whose martyrs they are.[326]

The ancient Christian practice of venerating relics is ultimately meant to give glory to God. If God exists, and reverencing the relics of God's saints is not superstitious, then there is no reason why the veneration of relics should be an obstacle to joining the Catholic Church.

STRATEGY 2

Distinguish between proper and improper use of sacramentals and Catholic prayers.

Sacramentals are holy objects or practices that God uses, like relics, to accompany grace. Similar to its belief about relics, the Church does not believe sacramentals have power in themselves to produce spiritual effects. Nor does the Church believe that prayers are spiritual vending machines where you put in your request and automatically get what you want. To believe such things would be superstitious. As the *Catechism of the Catholic Church* states,

> To attribute the efficacy of prayers or of sacramental signs to their mere external performance, apart from the interior dispositions that they demand, is to fall into superstition (2111).

Sacramentals are physical things that the Church uses to represent spiritual realities. This is why they are called "sacred signs" (1667). Examples include crucifixes, incense, relics, rosaries, holy water, prayer postures, and religious medals. They are not as powerful as the seven *sacraments* (such as baptism and the Eucharist) because they do not give grace themselves but merely signify it. But they are still instruments that God, through his Church, uses to bless us and direct us to deeper holiness.

Sacramentals make our ordinary daily lives more focused on God. A crucifix hanging in our office, a sacred medal around our neck, or regularly blessing ourselves with holy water keep God front and center in our minds. By sanctifying our days with the use of sacramentals we show that our religion is not restricted to church on Sunday. Sacramentals can also serve as badges of our faith, telling the world that we belong to Jesus Christ and his Church and inviting opportunities to evangelize others. This is a far cry from superstitious belief. And any Catholic who thinks otherwise is deeply confused.

The closest example of a sacramental in the Bible is found in the Old Testament. In Numbers 21:8–9 Moses erects a bronze serpent on a pole and tells those who were bitten by serpents to look upon it for healing. The Israelites heed Moses command and are healed.

Although the New Testament does not contain any explicit examples of sacramentals as Catholics use them today, the principle that undergirds their use is present—namely, God uses matter to communicate blessings. He does this because he wills to relate to us in ways that are fitting to our nature as bodily beings.

For example, in John 9:1–7 Jesus uses mud, spit, and the waters from the pool of Siloam to heal a blind man. Matter is not evil. It is good because God created it. He loves it so much he became a human being to live among us. And it is through matter that he chooses to communicate his blessings to us.

With regard to Catholic prayers, the above teaching from the *Catechism* must always be kept in mind. Acts of prayer can never bring blessings into our lives by themselves. They must always be accompanied by a proper disposition (Matt. 6:7) and be in accord with God's will (Luke 22:42). Our knowledge that God will hear our prayers is not absolute certitude but confidence. As John the apostle writes, "And this is the confidence which we have in him, that if we ask anything according to his will he hears us" (1 John 5:14).

It is possible to pray wrongly: "You ask and do not receive, because you ask wrongly" (Luke 4:3). An example of this type of prayer would be the kind that you get in your e-mail that says, "If you say this prayer eleven times and send it to eleven people, God is guaranteed to grant your petitions!"

STRATEGY 3

Explain the proper role of statues in Catholic practice.

The Catholic Church does not teach we may worship statues. Nor, as with relics and sacramentals, does it teach that statues have some sort of mystical power.

The use of statues in Catholic life and worship is meant to remind us of those persons who have obtained the victory of eternal life, and that we must imitate them. Statues remind us that they are present with us praying for us as we run the race of salvation (Heb. 12:1). Finally, they remind us of the destiny we're all called to: union with God in heaven.

The reverence that Catholics show to the statue of a saint, such as bowing and kissing, are not necessarily acts of worship—meaning the devotion due to God alone. Consider the following examples in the Bible where someone bows without worshipping:

- Lot bows before two angels (Gen. 19:1).

- Isaac tells Jacob that nations would bow before him (Gen. 27:29).

- Jacob bows before Esau seven times (Gen. 33:3).

- Joshua bows before an angel (Joshua 5:14).

- Ruth bows before Boaz (Ruth 2:8–10).

- David bows before Saul (1 Sam. 24:8).

- Bathsheba and Nathan bow before David (1 Kings 1:16, 25).

- Solomon bows before his mother Bathsheba (1 Kings 2:19).

- A Shunamite woman bows before Elisha after raising her child (2 Kings 4:37).

- Members of the Synagogue of Satan will bow before Christians (Rev. 3:9).

Just as these acts of bowing are not acts of (idolatrous) worship but of a lesser sort of honor, so too the Catholic practice of bowing before a statue is not an act of worship.

Even kissing a statue doesn't constitute worship. Recall how Paul encourages Christians to greet one another with a kiss of peace (Rom. 16:16; 1 Cor. 16:20; 2 Cor. 13:12; 1 Thess. 5:26; 1 Pet. 5:14).

Your friend may respond, "But statues aren't people; they're just pieces of wood. Why reverence a material object?" Explain that the reverence we show is not ordered to the statue but to the *person* the statue represents. This is no different, for example, from a soldier who kisses a picture of his wife before bed.

Finally, the honor that we show the saints is in imitation of the honor that the Father shows them (John 12:26). If God can honor the saints, then so can we. Since they're not present to us in person, we just do it with physical representations of them.

THE WAY PREPARED: Catholic piety is not superstitious but a means by which we can enter deeper into a loving relationship with God.

> *We honor the martyrs' relics, so that thereby we give honor to him whose martyrs they are: we honor the servants, that the honor shown to them may reflect on their master.*[327]
> —St. Jerome

29

How can I join a church that has boring rituals?

Some skeptics often perceive Catholic worship, especially the Mass, not so much as superstitious but *boring*—just a bunch of dull rituals. It fails to engage their emotions.

I can understand where they are coming from. On the surface, Catholic worship can *seem* boring, especially when it's compared with some modern Christian worship services that seem more like a rock concert than church.

But as the strategies below will show, this lack of emotional interest does not have to be an obstacle. So, let's fill the valley and prepare a way for the Lord.

STRATEGY 1

Explain why we shouldn't use emotions as a guide for choosing which church to belong to.

You can begin by illustrating how our emotions *change*.

> *Q:* "Have you ever watched a movie that you really liked, and then later watched it again but weren't moved by it? Or perhaps you watched a movie that was boring on the first viewing but then later enjoyed it the second time around? Is there a song you liked growing up, but now you think it's cheesy?"

It's a common human experience that our emotions are inconstant. One minute we can be on cloud nine experiencing an emotional high, but then when something bad happens we can get depressed. Things we once enjoyed get old, or our interests change.

This variability in the way we experience emotion and excitement should help us see that emotions aren't the best guide to deciding which church we should belong to. Otherwise, we're going to be perpetually hopping from one church to another, always seeking a better emotional high. Pastor Bob might excite us on one Sunday but not on the next, and then we're off to another church. That's not a recipe for happiness. It's a perpetual emotional rollercoaster.

Moreover, hopping from one church to another in order to get a better emotional experience seems to miss the point about what it means to worship. Worship isn't primarily about how it makes me feel. There are a variety of other activities that I can do that will make me feel good.

Rather, worship and worship rituals are about giving the honor that is due *to God* as the sovereign Lord. It's meant to draw us out of ourselves and into a relationship with God and others, not to turn us in on ourselves in isolation. Worship is not about me; it's about God. If someone attends a worship service with only self-fulfillment as the goal, then he puts the self at the center rather than God, which undermines the whole point.

Now, since worship is about giving honor to God, we have to ask whether there is one form of worship that honors God better than another. If there were, it wouldn't matter what kind of emotional experience I get from it. It would be a matter of justice to worship him in the way that honors him best.

This is not to say that there wouldn't be any emotional satisfaction. It's reasonable to think that if we honor God in the way that is most befitting his majesty and glory, he'll reward us with emotional satisfaction. It also seems reasonable to say that an interior peace and satisfaction would arise from within since by nature we're ordered ("naturally hardwired") to worship God.

And if we worship God in the *best* way, then the satisfaction of our natural inclinations to worship him would be better satisfied. So, it would seem that an emotional experience would come both from within and without.

As to whether there *is* such a form of worship, the Catholic Church says yes—in its highest and most proper form it's the offering of the one sacrifice of Christ in the Mass.

To substantiate this claim goes beyond the scope of this book. The bottom line you want to draw for your friend is that emotional experiences alone are not a reasonable guide for choosing which church you should belong to and the form of worship that you should engage in. It doesn't bring happiness, and it misses the true meaning of worship. We have to use more fundamental criteria: Which church is the *true* church established by Jesus? Which form of worship is the *true* form of worship that befits God's majesty and glory?

STRATEGY 2

Explain how lack of understanding and conviction can be a cause of boredom.

Your second strategy seeks to articulate the reality of *acquired taste*.

> Q: "Have you ever had the experience of being bored with something the first time you were introduced to it, but later came to love it? If you haven't had this experience, would you agree that some people have?"

I used to think golf was boring to watch. I couldn't understand how my father could sit and watch golf all day on the weekends. However, after playing a few rounds myself, and learning from my father about all the intricate mechanics of the golf swing, I came to appreciate just how hard it is to hit that little white ball. I now enjoy watching golf on television because I can appreciate the talent that pro golfers have.

Another example you can share is how many adults who enjoy their work probably didn't take much interest in the profession when they were little children. If they were asked at four years of age, "What would you prefer, a big bowl of ice cream or a paid college education to become a successful accountant?" they would have opted for the ice cream. The reason is that the child doesn't understand *what* education is and the intricate connection it has with getting a job, financially supporting himself and his family, fulfilling the fundamental human desire for knowledge, and properly functioning as a human being within society.

What these examples show is that our ability to appreciate something and be engaged with it is conditioned by our understanding of that thing. And this is true no matter what the thing is: a sport, an opera performance, a movie, etc.

The same is true for Catholic worship rituals. Your friend may experience boredom at Mass, but it's possible that to some degree it's due to a lack of understanding of worship as a whole and of the rituals of the Mass in particular. He doesn't understand what's going on, so he finds it hard to get engaged.

But there's more to it than a lack of understanding of the mechanics of Catholic ritual. There is something more *glorious* going on in the Mass than what happens in a golf game or in a classroom. The Mass makes present for us the reality of Jesus' death, resurrection, and ascension, along with the graces of salvation that these events won for us. It is a participation in a heavenly worship with all the angels and saints.

The Mass also involves the reception of Jesus—body, blood, soul, and divinity—in Holy Communion. The apostles who walked with Jesus 2,000 years ago were no more in Jesus' presence than we are at the Catholic Mass, the only difference being that they could experience Jesus with their senses.

So, your friend's boredom at Mass may not be due merely to a lack of understanding of the mechanics, as with golf, but a lack of understanding or conviction regarding the glorious magnitude of the metaphysical realities that the Catholic rituals celebrate and signify.

Obviously, at this point you're not going to convince your friend that these realities are present! Nor can you at this point persuade him to *appreciate* these realities. However, you can share with him that boredom experienced at Mass ceases for those faithful Catholics who do understand and appreciate the magnitude of what's going on in the Mass. And assure him that if he comes to believe in those mysteries, boredom will cease for him, too.

STRATEGY 3

Explain how ritual or ceremony belongs to human nature.

The fact that every culture in human history has had rituals indicates that ritual corresponds to something in human nature. There are no non-ritual cultures.

Even in our American culture, which generally seems to try and rid itself of anything that smacks of formality and tradition, we have rituals. And I bet your friend doesn't mind them.

> Q: "Do you think having rituals at graduation ceremonies is a bad thing? What about the rituals that military procedures involve? Should we start doing away with rituals at weddings? Maybe the bride and groom can just say, 'Okay, we're married. Let's get on with it.'"

I think it's safe to say that your friend will not deny that these secular rituals are good.

Your task now is to draw out the reason *why* your friend intuitively believes this. You can take your cue from St. Thomas Aquinas, who teaches that it's befitting to man that he should "employ sensible signs in order to signify anything."[328]

The reason for this is that man is a *body-soul composite*. The body is essential to our personhood and thus is essential to our communicative powers. It makes sense, therefore, that we would do things in the body to signify or communicate certain things—to use "ritual," if you will. This is why in the above examples we use words and gestures to communicate the value of the things we're celebrating, and how much we appreciate those things.

If it's fitting to our human nature to use sensible signs when we're communicating our appreciation and respect for worldly things, then it's even more fitting to use sensible signs when communicating our appreciation and respect for God, since he is far superior in dignity to any worldly thing, and we have a natural obligation to order *all* things—including our bod-ies—to him.

It was this sort of reasoning that led Aquinas to conclude,

> Hence it is a dictate of natural reason that man should use certain sensibles, by offering them to God in sign of the subject and honor due to him, like those who make certain offerings to their lord in recognition of his authority.[329]

There's more to the story, however. Notice that in the above examples we recognize that *not just any* rituals will do. The mag-nitude of the events demands words and gestures outside those of everyday life.

To just have graduating students just come and grab their di-plomas all at the same time off a table set up in a parking lot would not be fitting for the event. Merely having soldiers gather together in a field and saying with a bullhorn, "Hey guys, pretty good job," and then sending them on their merry way doesn't do justice to the value of their sacrifice. And couples who get married by an Elvis impersonator in Las Vegas dressed up in their camouflage outfits does not befit the dignity of marriage. (Although even in this scenario there is *some* formality!)

So, not only do we need to use sensible things to communi-cate how much we appreciate something, we sense that we need to use *special words and gestures that befit* the dignity of the thing being celebrated. And if this is true of secular things, how much more true is it with regard to divine things?

As in strategy two, your intention here is not to persuade your friend of all that the Mass signifies. That's for another time. Your intention is simply to show that given his acceptance of other kinds of ritual, and given what Catholics *believe* the Mass signifies, he ought to at least see the reasonableness of the rituals of Catholic worship.

THE WAY PREPARED: Ritual is a human good that, when done with proper understanding, can enrich one's experience of the worship of God.

> *A feeling touching the nature of things does not only make men feel that there are certain proper things to say; it makes them feel that there are certain proper things to do.*[330]
> —G.K. Chesterton

30

How can I join a church that has so many rules?

It's not uncommon for unbelievers to look at the Church from the outside and see nothing but an overbearing rule-making machine. To take one example: Catholics are forbidden to eat meat on Fridays during Lent. "How can what foods you eat," they wonder, "have anything to do with your relationship with God?"

This precept is emblematic, say those skeptics, of many silly, pointless, and oppressive rules that the Catholic Church makes up out of thin air—and enforced by grumpy old nuns with rulers. For many, it's just too much, and they see it as sufficient grounds for not taking the Catholic seriously.

I think this obstacle has two aspects. Although the objection is framed in a way that puts the emphasis on the *kind* and *amount* of rules, it also involves an underlying aversion to rules in general. Therefore, the strategies below will deal with both aspects.

STRATEGY 1

Explain that rules are not necessarily bad and can serve the good.

You can start by asking this question:

> *Q:* "Do you think there should be rules in a household for how children should behave?"

You shouldn't get any pushback on this one. Everyone knows that you can't just do whatever you want in a family if you want peaceful coexistence. You can also use the example of sports, which wouldn't be any fun to watch if there were no rules and referees to give them structure. Even small children recognize that when there are no rules to govern a game, it's no fun. So, it's clear that rules can serve a good purpose.

Your friend may respond, "Sure, but there shouldn't be any rules when it comes to how we relate to God. He loves us just as we are." This is where the family example can be brought back into play. Explain to your friend that if rules are good for family life in a home where parents love their kids and one another, then they're good for the Church—since the Church is the family of God. Share 1 Timothy 3:15:

> [I]f I am delayed, you may know how one ought to behave in the *household of God*, which is the church of the living God, the pillar and bulwark of the truth (emphasis added).

If God's Church is his household, then it's reasonable for him to have rules to govern its members for the sake of maintaining a peaceful family life.

Furthermore, such rules can keep the members of God's family spiritually safe. Apologist Michelle Arnold states it nicely:

> Just as knowing the owner's manual can help a driver keep his car in top condition and thereby free him from worry about breakdowns, knowing "the rules of the road" in Catholicism can free a Catholic from worry about spiritual "breakdowns" so that he can more fully participate in his personal relationship with God.[331]

The household rules of the Catholic Church are ordered toward fostering our relationship with Jesus Christ. Just as knowledge of the law of gravity is necessary for man to learn to fly, these laws are the foundation from which we can spiritually soar.

The Church's rule to abstain from meat on Fridays during Lent is a great example of this. When the precept is kept in a sacrificial spirit, the hunger for meat is a helpful reminder that we hunger for God. Such hunger in turn reminds us that only in God can the deepest longings of our hearts be fulfilled. It also proves that we are not slaves to our bodily passions, and are able to govern them with reason.

If rules are not bad, and they can have a proper place in God's family, then it would be unreasonable to reject the Catholic Church on the grounds that it has rules.

STRATEGY 2

Show that the objection can't determine how many or what kind of rules are reasonable.

> *Q:* "What's the magic number of rules that a church should have? By what standard do you judge this or that kind of rule to be 'too much'?"

If your friend says, "Well, I just feel it's too much," then challenge him further.

> *Q:* "Are someone's feelings a reliable guide for determining whether a church has too many rules?"

Hopefully your friend can see they're not, since members of different churches have different feelings. Your friend may opt for a church that makes him feel better, but he would never know if it is true or not.

STRATEGY 3

Explain how the idea that the Catholic Church has an overwhelming amount of rules is a caricature.[332]

Your friend's feeling about Church rules may well also be based upon a stereotyped understanding of the Faith. The first thing you want to point out is that when compared to other groups of comparable size, the rules are relatively few in number.

For example, the United States has around 300 million citizens. The 2012 edition of its federal legislation—the United States Code—totals 45,000 pages in thirty-four volumes. By comparison, a standard English edition of the *Code of Canon Law*, which is the main legal text for the large majority of the Church's one billion members, totals a little more than *500* pages in a single volume.

> *Q:* "Why is it not okay for a billion-member Church to have 500 pages of laws, but okay for a country with 300 million people to have 45,000 pages?"

You can also explain to your friend that the minimum requirements for a Catholic are relatively few. For example, Catholics are expected to know the Ten Commandments, which is not all that difficult, follow the five precepts of the Church (CCC 2041–2043), and be familiar with the proper preparation required for receiving the sacraments they regularly partake of, particularly penance and the Eucharist.

Of course, being a Catholic is not about just meeting the minimum requirements of the law. There is much more that a Catholic should know in order to have a committed relationship with Jesus and his Church. Love demands more than the minimum. But at least your friend can see that the general "rules" for an individual Catholic in his ordinary experience are relatively few, and they pertain to things reasonable for a religion, such as worship and morality.

Finally, you might also point out that not only is the Church's code of laws relatively short, but many of its rules apply to situations that an ordinary Catholic rarely—or never—encounters. So only a fraction of them impact his daily life. As for the rest, Catholics can be instructed on the "dos and don'ts" as the situation arises.

THE WAY PREPARED: Since the Church is the household of God it's fitting that there be rules to help its members live a peaceful and holy life within it.

> *Most modern freedom is at root fear. It is not so much that we are too bold to endure rules; it is rather that we are too timid to endure responsibilities.*[333]
> —G.K. Chesterton

31

How can I join a church that hates gay people?

In today's culture, the Catholic Church takes a lot of heat for its opposition to homosexual activity and to redefining marriage to include same-sex unions. The culture perceives the Church's voicing of this belief as nothing less than hate speech.

"I can't belong to a Church that hates gay people," some say. "Aren't Christians supposed to be kind and loving to everyone?" According to a 2011 study, such opposition to homosexual behavior ranked fourth in the list of reasons why fifty-nine percent of the young-adult Christians interviewed disconnected themselves from church life after age fifteen.[334]

How does a Catholic show that the Church does not hate gay people while at the same time staying committed to the Church's disapproval of sexual acts among members of the same sex? In other words, how does a Catholic remove this obstacle and prepare a way for the Lord?

STRATEGY 1

Explain how the objection fails to distinguish between the Catholic Church's disapproval of the practice and the person.

The objection assumes that because the Catholic Church has a negative view of homosexual behavior it necessarily hates those engaged in such behavior. But this conclusion doesn't follow.

> *Q:* "Do you think adultery is wrong? Does that mean you hate all adulterers?"

(This assumes that your friend does think adultery is wrong and that he doesn't hate adulterers, but both of these still hold true for most people.)

Explain that the Church's negative attitude toward sexual activity among members of the same sex is no different. Sure, it's possible for someone to hate the person as well as the practice, but this is true of any behavior. The point is that *just because* the Church disapproves of homosexual behavior it doesn't follow that the Church hates homosexuals.

Conclude this strategy by explaining how the Catholic Church rejects all forms of unjust discrimination and hatred of people with same-sex attraction. According to the *Catechism of the Catholic Church*, "they must be accepted with respect, compassion, and sensitivity" and "every sign of unjust discrimination in their regard should be avoided" (2358).

STRATEGY 2

Show how the objection is self-refuting and inconsistent in the application of its moral principle.

Having clarified that hating the person is not really the issue, you can show your friend that the *real* moral principle underlying his objection is that we shouldn't disapprove of someone's belief or practice—such as homosexuality. To do so is "hate speech."

It's a variant of relativism, which we treated earlier. But notice that in applying the principle to the Catholic Church, the objector expresses disapproval of the Catholic belief that homosexual behavior is wrong (and marriage is between a man and a woman).

> *Q:* "Isn't your criticism of Catholic belief a kind of hate speech?"

Your friend applies his principle to the Church, but not himself. Likewise those who defend homosexuality in the name of "diversity" and "freedom of speech," but deny the Church's stance the same consideration. Once again, the critique reveals a double standard.

STRATEGY 3

Explain why the Catholic Church teaches what it does about homosexuality.

You want to start by getting your friend to put himself in the Catholic Church's shoes.

> *Q:* "If your best friend was living a lifestyle that you considered to be bad for him, and was only going to bring him misery and unhappiness, wouldn't you encourage him to stop living that lifestyle? And would your encouragement be a sign of hate or love?"

Your friend probably won't deny that he would seek to encourage his friend to stop going down the wrong path in life, and that such an attempt would be a sign of love, not hate.

Explain that this is the position that we're in as Catholics. The Church says no to same-sex sexual activity because it says yes to human happiness. It sees that behavior as violating our dignity as human beings because it contradicts our moral perfection and thus our human flourishing (happiness).

The basis of all morality is the fundamental precept to *do good and avoid evil*.[335] Our moral perfection in sexual matters, therefore, will consist in doing what is good and avoiding what is bad when it comes to our sexual powers. But this presupposes a more basic understanding of what the good is for us as human beings. You can explain this in a fairly simple way.

What is good for a living creature is determined by the purposes for which its natural faculties and capacities exist. For example, the roots of an oak tree exist for the sake of providing the tree with nutrients and stability. Anything that frustrates the achievement of these ends, such as chopping off the roots or feeding them poison, would be bad for the tree—that is to say, it would impede the tree from being what it's supposed to be, given its nature.

By contrast, anything that helps the roots of the tree to achieve these ends, such as water, fertilizer, and light, is good for the tree. It helps the tree flourish.

And these facts about what is good and bad for a tree are true no matter how we feel about them or what we choose to accept or reject.

Human beings are no different. Our faculties and capacities—whether those that we share with the animal kingdom (sight, hearing, digestion, etc.) or those that are unique to us as rational animals (intellect and free will) are ordered to what makes human nature flourish.

The same line of reasoning applies to our sexual faculties. If these exist for the sake of some end, which means something good for our human nature, then it can't be good for us to use them in a way that subverts that end. It would be viewing the order of good as an obstacle to be avoided, as if it were an evil.

Since, as we can discern through observation, the ends toward which nature orders our sexual faculties are procreation[336] and unitive love,[337] what is good for us sexually are acts that serve these ends. Acts contrary to them (such as masturbation, contraception, fornication, adultery, and same-sex sexual activity), on the other hand, feed poison to the roots. Or, to be more precise, it would be as if the tree consciously poisoned its own roots all the while sinking its roots deep into the ground.

If we ought always do what is good, and the good is determined by the ends toward which our faculties are ordered, then we *ought* to always use them in a way that is consistent with their ends and avoid using them in a way that frustrates those ends.

To use our sexual faculties in ways opposed to their ends is to act irrationally, since reason tells us what is good for our nature.

This is contrary to our human dignity, since the ability to act in accord with reason is *the* identifying mark of a human being. It is also to act immorally, since we are not doing what we *ought*. Finally, it is to harm our chances for flourishing, for succeeding in the art of being human.

To be in accord with nature's design for human sexuality, then, is to give ourselves the best chance to flourish as a human being— to be happy. And that's what the Church wants for everyone.

THE WAY PREPARED: The Church's condemnation of same-sex sexual activity is an act of love because it recognizes that such behavior is contrary to the good of human beings and impedes the achievement of human happiness.

> *What I have now said in regard to abstaining from wanton looks should be carefully observed, with due love for the persons and hatred of the sin, in observing, forbidding, reporting, reproving, and punishing of all other faults.*[338]
> —St. Augustine

32

How can I join a church that abuses children and covers it up?

There is an internet meme picturing Australian cardinal George Pell that reads, "I don't always molest children. But when I do, I make sure to belong to a powerful organization that can prevent my prosecution." This is one attack among many at the Catholic Church for sexual abuse cases involving clergy that came to light in the last couple of decades, and many bishops' inadequate response to them.

The scandal was not due only to the fact that children were abused, but that several large Catholic dioceses failed to report the cases to the police. Instead, the accused priests were transferred to other parishes (or churches).

Combining other obstacles people have about the hypocrisy of believers, Christian teachings on sexual morality, and a suspicion of hierarchical religion, this one is indeed a mountain. And it is impossible to get around or over it. The only way is to drill a hole right through.

STRATEGY 1

Empathize with your friend's frustration and show that the Church takes the matter very seriously.

We agree wholeheartedly that these abuses are gravely wrong, and that the perpetrators should be brought to justice. The Catholic Church's claim to offer moral leadership and to be a source of truth and grace makes the offenses even more deplorable. As Pope

Benedict said, "The church needs to profoundly relearn penitence, accept purification, learn forgiveness but also justice."[339] He also acknowledged that such sins brought "shame and humiliation" on the Church and expressed hope that such chastisement would "contribute to the healing of the victims."[340]

Benedict even wrote a pastoral letter to Catholics in Ireland expressing his frustration with the local church's failure to adequately deal with the abuses:

> I can only share in the dismay and the sense of betrayal that so many of you have experienced on learning of these sinful and criminal acts and the way Church authorities in Ireland dealt with them.[341]

Benedict went on to assure the people of Ireland that he was confident the meetings he had with the bishops of Ireland and senior officials of the Roman Curia put the bishops in a "stronger position to carry forward the work of repairing past injustices and confronting the broader issues associated with the abuse of minors in a way consonant with the demands of justice and the teachings of the gospel."[342]

You can also share the statement from the preamble to the *Charter for the Protection of Children and Young People,* approved by the U.S. bishops in 2002:

> The sexual abuse of children and young people by some priests and bishops, and the ways in which we bishops addressed these crimes and sins, have caused enormous pain, anger, and confusion. Innocent victims and their families have suffered terribly. In the past, secrecy has created an atmosphere that has inhibited the healing process and, in some cases, enabled sexually abusive behavior to be repeated.[343]

The bottom line is that not only do we agree with our friend that these are deplorable evils, but that the Church recognizes it, asks for forgiveness, and is taking concrete steps to ensure that it doesn't happen again. The Church has established offices of safe environment and child protection to train adults who work with children to detect signs of abuse. Dioceses throughout the world have implemented policies that mandate Catholic workers to immediately report alleged abuse to law enforcement. Pope Francis set up a special tribunal for disciplining bishops who neglect to respond to allegations of abuse.[344]

The secular press, which led the charge in criticizing the Church during the height of the scandals, has recognized the value of recent efforts such as these. In his 2012 *Washington Post* article "10 Years After Catholic Sex Abuse Reforms, What's Changed,"[345] journalist David Gibson identifies the Church as possibly "the safest place for children." He commends the Church in the U.S. for making "unparalleled strides in educating their flock about child sexual abuse and ensuring that children are safe in Catholic environments."

Neither the Church's public apologies nor its subsequent measures excuse the abuse that has been committed, but they do show that the Church is willing to make up for its mistakes. This can be a great help in starting the conversation with your friend. You can conclude this strategy by simply asking, "On behalf of the Catholic Church, please forgive us."

STRATEGY 2

Explain the truth about the numbers of the abuse.

Your second strategy seeks to put the scope of the issue into perspective. The media coverage led many to think the numbers were far greater than they were.

In 2004, the U.S. Conference of Catholic Bishops commissioned John Jay College of Criminal Justice of the City University of New York to conduct a study analyzing allegations of sexual abuse in Catholic dioceses in United States.[346] The study covered the time period from 1950 to 2002.

The final report identified 6,700 unique accusations against 4,392 clergy, or four percent of the 109,694 clergy active during the period. Of those accused, only 252 were convicted, which is less than six percent of those accused and less than one-tenth of a percent of the total clergy.

To be sure, even these numbers are too many. But they do show that the scope of the scandal, despite the coverage it received, was very small—surely too small to be a basis for rejecting the Church completely.

It's also important to point out that this kind of problem is not confined to the Catholic Church. It is found among Protestant clergy as well. In his book *Pedophiles and Priests*, Philip Jenkins, a Protestant who is an expert in the study of pedophilia, writes,

> The most-quoted survey of sexual problems among Protestant clergy states that some ten percent are involved in sexual misconduct of some kind, and that 'about two or three percent' are pedophiles, a rate equal or higher than that suggested for Catholic priests. These figures should be viewed skeptically; the methodology on which they are based is not clear, and they seem to rely disproportionately on individuals already in therapy. However, it is striking to find such a relatively high number suggested for both celibate and non-celibate clergy.[347]

Sexual abuse is not only found within Christianity. It is a problem in virtually all settings where adults have care of minors: schools, clubs, daycares, sports teams. Consider, for example, the 2014 scandal involving USA swimming coaches, ninety of whom were banned for sexual misconduct.[348] The 2011 Penn State scandal involving assistant football coach Jerry Sandusky, who was indicted on fifty-two counts of child molestation over a period of fifteen years (1994–2009),[349] is another example, as is the recent scandal involving Larry Nassar, former USA women's gymnastics team doctor and sports medicine physician at Michigan State University, who was sentenced to 175 years in prison for sexually abusing more than 150 women over the past two decades of his practice.[350] In all these cases as in many others, the allegations included evidence of cover-up and deflection from the authorities involved.

Of course, no matter where it occurs, the sexual abuse of children is a horrible crime and it needs to stop. And the standards should be higher for the Church than anywhere else. There is no other person that a child should feel safer with than a person who represents Jesus Christ. But to think this is solely or conspicuously a Catholic problem, which is the narrative the media created, is simply not true.

STRATEGY 3

Explain why we shouldn't reject the Catholic Church just because of its sinful members.

For the same reason we shouldn't reject Christianity because some Christians are sinners or hypocrites (see chapter 22), the presence of sinners in Catholicism doesn't by itself mean that the religion is false.

> *Q:* "Let's say you found out that certain doctors at five different hospitals were guilty of malpractice. Would you refuse ever to go to the doctor again?"

Your friend should see that the malpractice of a few doctors doesn't undermine the basic value of medicine—because we know that doctors and hospitals heal people and save lives. Likewise, just because a few priests were guilty of spiritual malpractice doesn't take away from the spiritual goods that the Catholic Church has to offer: the healing and salvation of souls.

Point out to your friend that all the members of the Church, including its ministers, are sinners "still on the way to holiness" (CCC 827), and "always in need of purification" (CCC 827). Consequently, there will always be a mixture of sin and holiness in the Church.

Even Jesus teaches this on several occasions. For example, in his parable about the good and evil sower (Matt. 13:24–30), he says that the weeds will grow alongside the wheat until the master comes at harvest time. But he assures us that the wheat will then be separated from the weeds.

And to those who cause scandal in the Church, Jesus gives a severe warning: "[W]hoever causes one of these little ones who believe in me to sin, it would be better for him to have a great millstone fastened round his neck and to be drowned in the depth of the sea" (Matt. 18:6).

So it's important for your friend to recognize that the Church is made up of human beings like any other institution, and human beings are sinners. At the same time, you can tell him that the Church is not *merely* a human institution. It has Jesus as its founder. He has promised that "the powers of death shall not prevail against it" (Matt. 16:18) and that the Holy Spirit will animate and guide it into truth (John 16:13).

These promises and others reveal that Christ has been and always will be with his Church, preserving it in the truth and life that is necessary for us to be saved. We don't have to reject the Church of the apostles just because one of them was Judas.

THE WAY PREPARED: Sexual predation is an unfortunate reality in many settings, not just the Catholic Church, and the crimes of certain members do not affect whether Catholicism's teachings are true. Church leaders have admitted the faults of the Church in dealing with the scandals and have taken serious steps to prevent them in the future.

We too insistently beg forgiveness from God and from the persons involved, while promising to do everything possible to ensure that such abuse will never occur again.[351]
—Pope Benedict XVI

33

How can I join a church that hoards its wealth?

"Why does the Catholic Church spend billions on golden chalices and ornate cathedrals," says the skeptic, "when it could be helping the poor?"

This is one of those objections that commonly make their way into internet memes and pop culture. For example, in a YouTube video comedian Sarah Silverman snarks, "What is the Vatican worth, like 500 billion dollars? This is great. Sell the Vatican, take a big chunk of that money . . . and . . . feed the whole $#%$ world."[352]

But this objection is not found only among those who want to mock the Church. It weighs heavy on thoughtful human beings who legitimately see the Church's perceived wealth as a strike against its credibility. It's not quite a mountain, but it's still a hill that needs to be laid low.

STRATEGY 1

Put the numbers in context.

Begin by establishing some perspective on the Church's alleged wealth.

You can start with the city-state of the Vatican itself. Its 2013 annual budget was roughly $315 million in revenue and $334 million in expenditures.[353] That's far less than Starbuck's 2017 5.34 billion in gross income and 2.46 billion in expenses.[354]

In 2010 the total annual spending for the Catholic Church in the United States was a little over 170 billion.[355] Your friend may think this number is insanely huge, but it's comparable to General Electric's $150 billion in revenue for that same year.[356] Wal-Mart made $482 billion in revenue, and only has half the employment than the million people employed by Catholic institutions in the U.S.[357]

As large as these numbers are—and the worth of the global Church is much larger, though it's hard to give an exact number—they pale in comparison to the annual amounts of money that governments spend on welfare. This is an important point if your friend stresses a belief that the Church's wealth should be given up to benefit the poor.

Consider that in the United States alone the combined amount spent on federal, state, and local poverty programs is some $1 trillion per year.[358] The Church in America *and* the Vatican would have to combine their annual revenues for five years just to meet this number. And that's just to cover one year's worth of welfare spending in one country—one of the world's richest!

It seems reasonable to say that even if the Catholic Church were to globally liquidate *everything* it has, including its art, buildings, and real estate, it would not be enough to make more than a small and temporary dent in global poverty.

And of course, liquidating the Church's alleged wealth is much easier to talk about than to do.

> *Q:* "Is someone really going to come and write a check to buy St. Peter's Basilica? How would we determine the market value of the Sistine Chapel? What about all the golden reliquaries and sacred vessels? Who's going to determine how much these things are worth? And who is going to oversee the distribution of these assets?"

The Church's art, buildings, and sacred vessels are not things that you can put a price tag on. Such items are the Church's family heirlooms. They are also memorials to the hard work of Christians past who placed their labor and treasure in service of God through the Church. The embodied heritage and the order that they have to the glory of God gives them a value that goes beyond what people might bid on eBay.

So, the talk about the Vatican's wealth is exaggerated, and the fantasies about selling it and giving it all away are unrealistic.

STRATEGY 2

Explain that the Church is a steward of its resources, directing them to the temporal and spiritual good of the world.

However you calculate the Church's material wealth, it's important to understand that the Church is not the owner of that wealth but its *steward*. That is, it uses its resources to further its mission to the world—not, like a crooked televangelist, to accumulate riches.

For example, the Church invests large amounts of money into its seminaries so that priests can get the best training possible. Preparation for the task of saving souls requires skilled professors, materials for learning, and functional facilities.

> *Q:* "If the Catholic Church should sell its seminaries and give the proceeds to the poor, shouldn't universities do the same and abort their mission of training doctors and engineers?"

The same can be said for all the other works of the Church: its parishes and schools, its missionaries, its evangelization through media and technology—in all these cases the Church directs its resources toward the world's good.

Of course, the Catholic Church doesn't think it must be a good steward with its material resources for itself alone. It uses its resources for the poor (see strategy three). It likewise is a steward of the beautiful heritage embodied in its art, buildings, and sacred vessels. The Church does not hoard these items for mere pageantry or store them as investments; it lovingly protects them because their beauty enriches the whole world.

> Q: "Do you think we should sell off secular historical treasures, buildings, art, etc., in order to feed the world? What about the Parthenon? The great pyramid of Giza? How about the statue of Zeus at Olympia, or the temple of Artemis at Ephesus? Perhaps we should sell the Mona Lisa. Wouldn't that fetch a lot of money to feed the hungry?"

Point out that just as the good lost in selling these secular treasures and giving the proceeds to the poor would outweigh the good obtained, so too the good lost in the Church selling its treasures and giving the proceeds to the poor would outweigh the good obtained. Consider, for example, the things that we've talked about so far.

There would be no more seminaries to provide priests the intellectual and spiritual training they need to minister. Humanity would be deprived of experiencing beauty and world culture. The legacy of those who labored for such beauty would be lost in the past.

We can add to this list:

- The Church would no longer be able to generate revenue from tourism in order to help the poor.

- The Church would no longer be able to offer health care in its hospitals, thus leaving thousands to fend for themselves in their physical needs.

- The Church would eventually run out of money in feeding the poor, and the poor of the future would suffer as a result.

- The person who gets the valuable items would still be subject to the demand to sell the items and give the proceeds to the poor, which would create an endless cycle of buying and selling.

STRATEGY 3

Point out that the Catholic Church actually does a great deal for the poor.

Three Catholic institutions in the United States consistently make the Forbes top 100 largest charities list: St. Jude Children's Research Hospital, Catholic Charities USA, and Catholic Relief Services. In the 2017 listing,[359] St. Jude Children's Research Hospital ranked fifth, Catholic Charities USA ranked eleventh, and Catholic Relief Services ranked thirty-eighth. Their combined contributions totaled to a little over 2.6 billion dollars. In the prior year,[360] St. Jude ranked sixth, Catholic Charities USA ranked ninth, and Catholic Relief Services ranked thirty-third, totaling almost 2.5 billion dollars in combined contributions.

In 2011, fourteen Catholic or Catholic related institutions in the United States, including Fr. Flanagan Boys' Home and Covenant House, made the philanthropy 400 published by *The Chronicle of Philanthropy*. Their combined contributions for 2010 were a little over 2.98 billion dollars.[361] And this list didn't include Catholic hospitals and groups that focus on overseas work.

According to professor David Paton at Nottingham University Business School, Caritas Internationalis estimates that its affiliates total between £2 billion and £4 billion in spending, "making it one of the biggest aid agencies in the world."[362] And keep in mind that these numbers don't include the 200,000 Catholic parishes around the world that operate their own small-scale charitable operations, along with religious orders and other Catholic charities.

If we take into consideration the many Catholic charities throughout the world, we can safely say that the Catholic Church as a whole is most likely the largest charitable organization on the planet.

THE WAY PREPARED: The Church's wealth is greatly overestimated. It is also one of the largest charitable organizations in the world and wisely uses its resources to contribute to the temporal and eternal well-being of humanity.

The rich man is not one who is in possession of much, but one who gives much.[363]
—St. John Chrysostom

34

How can I join a church that doesn't respect a woman's right to choose?

Some people look at the Catholic Church's opposition to abortion and see an attempt to oppress women by keeping them from exercising freedom of choice over their bodies. University professor Steven Morris sums it up in his claim that "the persecution of abortionists and the women who need them" are driven by "misogyny."[364]

Our strategies will focus on showing how such an obstacle is only *apparent*; the Church's opposition to abortion does not indicate misogyny and thus should not stand in the way of considering the Church's claims to truth.

STRATEGY 1

Show that the Church's position on abortion is motivated by a concern for innocent human life.

Your friend has bought into the culture's narrative as to why the Church opposes abortion; but it's likely that he hasn't considered what the Catholic Church actually says its reasons are.

You can start with the Congregation for the Doctrine of the Faith's *Declaration on Procured Abortion* (DPA), ratified by Pope Paul VI in 1974. It does not fail to recognize the hardships that mothers with crisis pregnancies may face:

> It may be a serious question of health, sometimes of life or death, for the mother; it may be the burden

represented by an additional child, especially if there are good reasons to fear that the child will be abnormal or retarded; it may be the importance attributed in different classes of society to considerations of honor or dishonor, of loss of social standing, and so forth (14).

But despite such difficulties, the Church can't approve of abortion because abortion *directly takes innocent human life*: "None of these reasons can ever objectively confer the right to dispose of another's life, even when that life is only beginning," the document continues, because, "life is too fundamental a value to be weighed against even very serious disadvantages." The Church's own writings on the matter ground its opposition to abortion on the intrinsic value of human life.

This is made even clearer in the 1987 instruction *Donum Vitae*:

> Human life is sacred because from its beginning it involves the creative action of God and it remains forever in a special relationship with the Creator, who is its sole end. God alone is the Lord of life from its beginning until its end: no one can under any circumstance claim for himself the right directly to destroy an innocent human being (5).

Human life is not only valuable but *sacred,* related to God as the Creator.

Explain to your friend that there's no need to conjecture secret or cynical reasons why the Church opposes abortion. The Church tells us why: all human beings have equal dignity and value, no matter their location (in the womb or outside the womb) or state of development. Share this quote from Pope St. John Paul II's encyclical *Evangelium Vitae*:

> As far as the right to life is concerned, every innocent human being is absolutely equal to all others. This equality is the basis of all authentic social relationships

which, to be truly such, can only be founded on truth and justice, recognizing and protecting every man and woman as a person and not as an object to be used. Before the moral norm which prohibits the direct taking of the life of an innocent human being "there are no privileges or exceptions for anyone. It makes no difference whether one is the master of the world or the 'poorest of the poor' on the face of the earth. Before the demands of morality we are all absolutely equal (57).

You can also point out that the Church's teaching on the absolute equality of human beings is not just for the protection of the unborn but of *every* innocent human being. By standing up for the rights of the weakest among us, the unborn, the Church stands up for all others whose lives may be undervalued: the poor, the elderly and sick, women, racial minorities, etc.

John Paul II spoke to this point, identifying the arbitrariness of the abortion logic:

How is it still possible to speak of the dignity of every human person when the killing of the weakest and most innocent is permitted? In the name of what justice is the most unjust of discriminations practiced: some individuals are held to be deserving of defense and others are denied that dignity?[365]

When this happens, he continued, we witness "the death of true freedom."

Remember that your strategy here is not to debate every aspect of the abortion issue but simply to dispel the myth that the Church opposes abortion because it's anti-woman. You must get him to take the Church's stated reasons at face value and to see their basic reasonableness, even if he doesn't fully agree with them.

Even if you succeed in helping him do this, your friend here might ask, "But what about the women? Doesn't the Church have to respect them, too?" This brings us to the next strategy.

STRATEGY 2

Show that the Church's position on abortion is also motivated by a concern for the health and well-being of women.

It would be odd for the Church to play the song of equality for all human beings and at the same time exclude women. Demonstrate to your friend that by trying to protect the unborn child's right to life, it also aims to protect women's lives, health, and dignity.

> Q: "Does it really benefit women when they are expected to kill the unwanted products of sexual encounters?"

For men who want to use women sexually without consequences, abortion is their best friend. It relieves them of the responsibility of following through, of showing material and emotional care for the woman and baby. They can focus solely on sexual gratification instead and, without the bond that children provide between couples, easily move on from the woman when he no longer feels as gratified. How can it be in the best interest of a woman for a man to treat her as what she's not: a sexual toy for pleasure?

So, in opposing abortion the Church also champions women's dignity. It also promotes their mental and physical health. There are many negative consequences that come with an abortion that the Church doesn't want women to experience.

One study published in the *British Journal of Psychiatry* found that ten percent of mental health problems for women are directly attributable to abortion, and that women with an abortion history have an eighty-one percent increased risk of mental health problems, along with a 155 percent increased risk of suicide.[366] Post-Abortion Syndrome (PAS), a condition related to Post Traumatic Stress Disorder (PTSD), is recognized as a source of pain and grief for many women after abortion.[367]

Studies also show that abortion increases risk of medical complications, including problems with future pregnancies,[368] infertility,[369] genital tract infections,[370] cervical cancer,[371] placenta previa,[372] and ectopic pregnancies.[373]

> Q: "How can the Catholic Church be against women when by opposing abortion it is promoting their mental and physical health?"

The Catholic Church doesn't want women to wallow in the negativity that is associated with having an abortion. By saying no to abortion, and suggesting alternatives like adoption, the Church offers women a way to avoid such misery. How can that be anti-woman?

Your friend might say that condemning women for having an abortion doesn't sound very compassionate. But although it's true that the Church condemns the *act* of abortion, it does not condemn the women who choose it. The Church understands that there are factors surrounding a woman's decision that could minimize her culpability. And the Church as well as its pro-life ministries have nothing but compassion toward post-abortive women—preaching a message of hope by extending the invitation for them to accept God's mercy.

John Paul II does this toward the end of his encyclical *Evangelium Vitae* when he addresses women who have had an abortion:

> The Church is aware of the many factors which may have influenced your decision, and she does not doubt that in many cases it was a painful and even shattering decision. The wound in your heart may not yet have healed. Certainly what happened was and remains terribly wrong. But do not give in to discouragement and do not lose hope. Try rather to understand what happened and face it honestly. If you have not already done so, give yourselves over with humility and trust to repentance. The Father of mercies is ready to give you

his forgiveness and his peace in the Sacrament of Rec-
onciliation. To the same Father and his mercy you can
with sure hope entrust your child (99).

Your friend at least can see now that the Church is not *intending* to be anti-woman. It sees abortion as an evil for both the
unborn child and women, and thus worth fighting against.

The question now that's probably lingering in the back of
your friend's mind is, "What about the woman's right to choose?
Isn't the Church fighting against that in opposing abortion?"
And this brings us to strategy three.

STRATEGY 3

Show how the real issue is not a woman's "right to choose," but the nature of abortion.

The argument that the Church is opposed to a woman's right to
choose sidesteps the fundamental question, "*What* is she choosing?" We can't begin to evaluate whether a woman has a right
to choose abortion until we first determine what she is choosing
to abort.

Here's one way you can get your friend to see that there are
some limits to what a woman can choose.

> Q: "Would you say it's a woman's right to kill her two-
> year-old child? What about her one-year-old?"

When your friend says no, point out that the reason is because
the child is an innocent human being. Notice that any talk of
women's rights is subordinate to that fact. You can now apply
the same line of reasoning to abortion.

> Q: "If a mother doesn't have a right to kill her two-
> year-old child because the child is an innocent human
> being, then wouldn't it also be true that she doesn't

have the right to kill the child in her womb if it is an
innocent human being?"

If an unborn child were an innocent human being from the
moment of his conception, which the Catholic Church—in accord with biology—believes he is, then killing him at any stage
of his development would be wrong. In that case, the issue of
women's rights with regard to abortion becomes moot. And the
Church would be no more a hater of women's rights in opposing abortion than your friend would be in saying that a woman
doesn't have a right to kill her two-year old child.

Here your friend will probably recognize that the key question to ask now is, "Is the Catholic Church *right* in saying that
the unborn child is a human being deserving protection of the
right to life from the moment of conception?"

Now you are standing on the precipice of an abortion *debate*. This is an important debate to have because either innocent human life or a woman's fundamental rights are at stake.
But it goes beyond the scope of removing the current obstacle.
The purpose here was to get your friend to see that the Church
doesn't oppose abortion in order to oppress women. In fact by
opposing abortion it protects women.

The abortion debate, however, is something that you should
be prepared for. An excellent resource for this is Trent Horn's
Persuasive Pro-Life: How to Talk About Our Culture's Toughest Issue.

THE WAY PREPARED: The Church's opposition to abortion is
motivated by a concern for both the innocent lives of unborn
babies and women's health and well-being.

> *[I]f we accept that a mother can kill even her own child, how
> can we tell other people not to kill one another?*[374]
> —St. Teresa of Calcutta

Conclusion

Tilling soil and nurturing seeds

Throughout this book we have been following the motif of *preparing the way of the Lord* in light of John the Baptist's ministry. But there is another metaphor that is appropriate for the work of preparing others for the gospel.

In Matthew 13:1–9, Jesus tells the parable of the Sower of the Seed. Some seeds fell on the path and the birds ate them. Other seeds fell on rocky ground and sprouted, but were scorched by the sun because they didn't root deep in the soil. Others fell among thorns, and the thickness of the thorns stopped the sprouts from growing. Finally, some seeds fell on good soil, and brought forth grain. As many commentators point out, the seed represents the word of God. But the Word of God is not merely some*thing*—the inspired text of the Bible. It is some*one*: Jesus.

Tilling the soil with apologetics

The ultimate goal of evangelization is to lead people into communion with Jesus. However, for many the soil (their soul) is not ready to receive the seed (Jesus). The obstacles they face are like the path, the rocky ground, and the thorns.

Now, every gardener knows that you have to first till the soil to make it hospitable for seeds to actualize their full potential once they are planted. Therefore, our job as evangelizers is to till the soil of the soul in unbelievers by removing the obstacles they face in order that the grace of Jesus can be fully actualized in them. The apologetic endeavor articulated in this book is a way to accomplish such preparatory work.

Tilling the soil by witnessing to Christ's love

But apologetics cannot be merely an intellectual enterprise. It must be animated by charity, which can only come through staying in close relationship with Jesus. We also accomplish this work, then, through witnessing to the love of Jesus.

When St. Peter gives the instruction to defend our Christian hope (1 Pet. 3:15), he says to do it "with gentleness and reverence." In other words, when we are evangelizing through apologetics we must do it with charity. As apologists, we must always fight the temptation to be triumphalistic and obnoxious. You can be right all you want, but if you are a jerk in the process then you can forget about the person believing what you have to say.

We not only prepare a way for *the Lord*, but we also prepare the unbeliever for *the Way* (Acts 24:14). If you are uncharitable to the unbeliever in the process of evangelizing him, then he is going to associate such lack of charity with all members of the Christian religion, and consequently have no desire to become a member.

Tilling the soil with prayer

Along with apologetics and being an example of Christ's love, we prepare the soil of the unbeliever's soul through prayer. Prayer is the driving force for all work in apologetics. We must pray for those we are going to encounter, and those we do encounter. We must pray even while dialoguing with the person whom we are evangelizing. It can be as simple as saying, "Come, Holy Spirit and help me!"

Invoking God's help is necessary in apologetics because he is the only one who can give growth to the seeds that we plant. St. Paul teaches as much: "I planted, Apollos watered, but God gave the growth. So neither he who plants nor he who waters is anything, but only God who gives the growth" (1 Cor. 3:6–7).

Caring for the seed through relationships

This leads to another important truth about evangelization. We are not just called to *prepare* for the planting of the seed, but also to plant and to care for the seed in order to foster its growth.

By engaging in apologetics, we prepare and plant. But we must also nurture the seed and foster its growth. One way to do this is by establishing relationships with those whom we are evangelizing, and sticking with them. Your "friend," whom we have been addressing in this book, will need more than your arguments and initial information. He will need material to read, he will have more questions that need answering, he will need direction on how to pray, and he will need help in discerning appropriate and inappropriate Catholic behavior.

Moreover, there will always be obstacles that arise and will need to be removed. Just as the gardener must always keep the garden free from the weeds lest they overtake his garden and choke out the plants, so too we must work to remove any and all obstacles that arise as a threat to faith.

Now, not all cases of evangelization afford for a long-term relationship, or sometimes even a short one! In such cases we can at least nurture seeds by prayer. I might never see the man I spoke with at the coffee shop ever again, but I can pray that God shower his graces upon him, and give growth to the seeds that I planted.

Tempering expectations for growth

One last thing: preparing the way doesn't always go according to plan. As with anything else in life, you will have to adjust to the curves. When you tend a garden, sometimes following the exact directions is not enough. You may have to till the hardened soil a little longer than what the experts say. Some seeds may sprout better than others. And for those that don't sprout as vigorously, a little extra love and care is needed as you adjust the amount of fertilizer and water.

Similarly, sometimes in conversations with unbelievers you might have to adjust your strategic plan. This book has given you the directions, but not every unbeliever is the same.

For example, the directions say employ strategy one, then two, and then three. But you may have to stay in strategy one for quite some time before you can move on to the other strategies. Or, you may have to skip around with the strategies weaving in and out of them in order to address the needs of your friend. You want to assimilate the strategies in this book in your heart and mind so that you can utilize them *as needed*. I've tried my best to order them in a way that a natural conversation would progress, but *things change*. And with change, we have to adapt.

Another way in which things don't go according to plan is that your strategies don't always provide immediate results. The seed doesn't always immediately sprout. Expect this! Remember that Jesus didn't get immediate results either. In fact, many times he got negative results. Some walked away from him (see John 6:66), and some killed him.

I doubt you'll have the same fate as Jesus. But know that your friend will not always concede your views about the topics discussed in this book. And that's okay. We strive to remove the obstacles for our friends, but sometimes the only obstacle that we can immediately remove is the idea that this whole Christian thing is unreasonable. If we can at least remove *that* obstacle, and keep our friend in prayer, then I think we can call our evangelistic endeavor a success.

Recognize your dignity, dear reader, as you are called to be "God's fellow workers" (1 Cor. 3:8). Pick up the mantle of John the Baptist to prepare a way for the Lord, removing any and all obstacles that stand between unbelievers and Jesus. Learn to prepare the soil. Learn how to plant. Learn how to water. This is what God expects of us. He expects us to prepare a way for him as he is always approaching bearing the gift of salvation.

Appendix A

Refuting universal skepticism

A year or so ago, after I gave a talk on God and science, a gentleman engaged me in a conversation in which he expressed his doubt concerning the principle of non-contradiction. This self-evident first principle of reason, upon which all knowledge is built, states that something cannot be and *not* be in the same respect at the same time. Aristotle identified it as "the most certain of all principles."[375]

The gentleman's doubt exemplifies a radical form of skepticism that tends to doubt *everything*, even the first principles of knowledge—it's called *universal* skepticism. Is there a way to refute it?

Doubting the doubt

First, the claim, "I doubt everything," is self-referentially incoherent—it refutes itself. If a skeptic doubts *everything*, then he must doubt the claim, "I doubt everything," which of course is the same as saying, "I doubt that I doubt everything." This is absurd. If a skeptic doubts his own assertion, "I doubt everything," then why is he even putting it forward?

If a skeptic responds that he is *certain* he doubts everything, then there would be one thing he doesn't doubt, namely the claim, "I doubt everything." Consequently, it wouldn't be true that he doubts everything.

Perhaps a skeptic resorts back to his original position and refuses to definitively declare his universal skepticism. Besides having to deal with the conundrum of being skeptical about his skepticism, he cannot avoid being certain about something— namely *I ought not to affirm my universal skepticism.*

Certain building blocks

If a skeptic attempted to justify his claim via argumentation, all the facts and principles he appealed to as proof would thereby be declared invalid since they imply human certitudes. As the nineteenth-century philosopher John Rickaby writes,

> [F]or this conclusion, when drawn, at once turns round on the premises and says, "Out upon you, you vile incapables, you are yourselves suspects, and can lead only to suspicious conclusions." The premises retort, "That reproach does not come well from you."[376]

No matter how a skeptic approaches his claim, whether he doubts it or affirms it, he ends in a self-contradiction.

Infinite argumentation

A third way to refute radical skepticism is to show the absurdity in the denial of first principles of knowledge. If a skeptic doubts *everything,* then he necessarily doubts self-evident first principles of knowledge such as the principle of non-contradiction. In doing so, a skeptic denies knowledge as having any foundation. But this doesn't work.

Consider trying to obtain knowledge without a principle that doesn't require further demonstration—that is, a *self-evident* principle. Any conclusion put forth would require an infinite series of reasons why that conclusion is true. For example, the skeptic's claim, "There are no self-evident first principles of knowledge," would be true only if A is true. But A would be true only if B is true and B only if C is true, *ad infinitum.* Notice the search for a true premise upon which the conclusion can rest would never come to an end—it would go on forever. No matter where one stops in the series of reasons, one would always have a reason that can't be proven true because it relies on an infinite number of other reasons we can't know to be true.

But if no reason the conclusion depends upon can ever be known to be true, then the conclusion can't be known to be true either. This is not something the skeptic wants to conclude, since it would undermine his skepticism about first principles. Therefore, a skeptic can't deny the necessity of knowledge having a foundation in first principles without undermining his own skepticism.

The absurdity

Fourth, we can show the absurdity of denying the principle of non-contradiction itself. A skeptic cannot deny the principle of non-contradiction without his speech already betraying him. He can only speak against the principle if the words he uses have that intended meaning and not the opposite. For example, if a skeptic says, "The principle of non-contradiction is false," then he must intend the statement to *mean* what it expresses and *not* the opposite, namely "the principle of non-contradiction is true."

If a skeptic affirmed the opposite, "The principle of non-contradiction is true," then he would be affirming what he initially set out to deny. But if a skeptic intends to mean what his initial statement expresses, then he presupposes the principle and thus, once again, undermines his initial attempt to deny the principle.

So, a skeptic's denial of the principle of non-contradiction ultimately ends in self-defeat.

Perhaps a skeptic could remain silent. Would that save a skeptic from the above dilemma? The answer is no, for even *understanding* what is meant by the principle presupposes its truth. The cognitional content must have the intended meaning and not the opposite.

A final way we can refute radical skepticism comes from a Jesuit priest, T.V. Fleming, in his book *Foundations of Philosophy*. He argues there are certain presupposed certitudes embedded in the statement, "I doubt everything." Consider that in order to make the statement a skeptic must know what *doubt* is. Furthermore, his statement implies that he knows that doubt *differs* from knowledge, which in turn necessarily implies he knows what *knowledge* is. Related to what was mentioned above concerning the principle of non-contradiction, a skeptic also must know the *meaning* of the proposition he wishes to doubt and the *reason* for his doubt.

Moreover, if a skeptic suspends judgment concerning a proposition, he must recognize the reasons given for it as insufficient to justify his assent. This in turn means he knows the reasons given.

The presupposed certitudes do not stop there. When a skeptic continues to hold to skepticism, he does so in order not to fall into error. But that presupposes knowledge of what *error* is. It also presupposes a desire for truth, which in turn suggests at least a tacit certitude that truth exists.

The bottom line is that a skeptic cannot doubt anything without first presupposing certitude of at least *some* things.

Yes, a skeptic may concede your airtight logic but say that it doesn't really matter because there is more to life than logic. And that's true—but what does he mean by it?

If he is trying to get out of playing the logic game, then once again he fails because the claim "there is more to life than logic" is itself a product of logic. He is making a conclusion based on certain premises that he believes to be true. It's metaphysically impossible to not play the logic game. You can only play it well or poorly.

If the skeptic intends to say that we need to make sure and not forget about other things in life *besides* logic, then we have no quarrel with that. The responses articulated above are only for those who try and *deny* the principles of reason.

So, a skeptic simply cannot doubt everything. It's impossible. The statement itself implies presupposed certitude and the denial of self-evident first principles, such as the principle of non-contradiction, is not possible for in denying it the principle is affirmed. Universal skepticism, therefore, is bankrupt. We have rational justification in being skeptical about skepticism.

Appendix B

Whatever begins to exist must have a cause

In recent times, there has been increasing skepticism, especially among New Atheism proponents, concerning the causal principle: *whatever is caused is caused by another*. Many of the arguments for God's existence rely on this principle, such as the five ways of St. Thomas Aquinas and the Kalam cosmological argument, which argues for the existence of a creator in light of the beginning of time and physical reality. It is therefore unsurprising that atheists are trying to find a way around the causal principle. Of the various forms that the causal principle takes, the one that modern atheists most frequently question is: "Whatever begins to exist must have a cause of its existence."

For example, Quentin Smith, a professor of philosophy at Western Michigan University in Kalamazoo, Michigan, writes, "the most reasonable belief is that we came from nothing, by nothing, and for nothing."[377] In a debate with Cardinal George Pell in 2012, Richard Dawkins, perhaps the most famous proponent of the New Atheism, asserted:

> Of course it's counterintuitive that you can get something from nothing! Of course common sense doesn't allow you get something from nothing! That's why it's interesting. It's got to be interesting in order to give rise to the universe at all![378]

Smith and Dawkins are in good company with the late Australian philosopher J.L. Mackie, who said, "There is *a priori* no good reason why a sheer origination of things, not determined by anything, should be unacceptable."[379]

If it is common sense that something cannot come from sheer nothingness, as Dawkins states, then why are these men of such intelligence denying common sense? Let's take a look at some possible reasons.

Modern philosophers often attempt to justify their assertion that something could begin to exist without a cause by appealing to David Hume's *imagination argument*. Hume called into question the *certainty* of the causal principle by suggesting the possibility that something could come into being without a cause. He attempted to justify his position by asserting that one can *imagine* something coming into existence without a cause.

For example, you might imagine the surface of a table with nothing on it, then you imagine a billiard ball suddenly appearing on it. Hume says that since you can *imagine* something beginning to exist without imagining a cause, and such imaginings are without contradiction, then it must be at least *possible* that no cause is needed to bring something into existence; thus the causal principle, according to Hume, is not certain. How can we respond?

First, his objection rests entirely on the false notion that our imagination serves as an accurate yardstick for determining what is possible in the real world. Consider again Hume's basic argument: if we can imagine the billiard ball popping into existence on the table *without imagining* its cause, then it's possible for the billiard ball to appear on the table without a cause. In other words, for Hume, whatever is separable in the imagination can be separated in reality.

This is simply not true. Consider the following examples. I can imagine water without at the same time imagining the molecules that make up the water.[380] But does that mean it's possible for water to exist without water molecules? According to Hume's principle, we would have to answer yes. But we know in reality that can't *be*.

I can imagine a jar of jellybeans *without imagining* the specific number of jellybeans.[381] I can also imagine the jar of jellybeans *without imagining* whether the number is even or odd. Does that mean the jar of jellybeans can *be* without a specific number or *be* without a number that is neither even nor odd? Of course not!

Since Hume bases his doubt of the causal principle on his imagination argument, and the imagination argument is demonstrably false, then it follows that Hume's imaginative argument does nothing to undermine the certainty of the causal principle in the form *whatever begins to exist must have a cause*.

A second objection against Hume is that there is nothing in his imaginative situation that necessitates the billiard ball having *no* cause as opposed to a cause that *cannot be imagined*. Recall that Hume's argument entails merely imagining the effect without imagining the cause. But, as Michael Augros argues in *Who Designed the Designer?*, perhaps there are causes that by nature cannot be imagined. Such causes could be elementary particles, forces of nature like gravity, or entities that go beyond the material realm, such as God or angels.

Now, if there are causes that are by nature not subject to the imagination, then the mere fact that we fail to imagine them when we imagine an effect (e.g., the billiard ball appearing on the table) does not prove that the effect can happen without the unimaginable cause. It simply points to the fact that the cause of the billiard ball appearing on the table might be something we *cannot imagine*.

But if this is true, then Hume's argument does not achieve what it sets out to achieve—namely, that something can begin to exist with *no* cause. Therefore, there is no need for us to doubt the causal principle based on Hume's argument.

Virtual particles example

Another rational justification for the atheist's claim that something can begin to exist without a cause comes from quantum physics. Within the study of quantum physics, scientists have observed so-called "virtual particles": particles that pop into existence *apparently* without a cause and then immediately cancel each other out, resulting in residual radiation within a vacuum. Many atheists see this phenomenon as rational justification for denying the causal principle. Lawrence Krauss, an American theoretical physicists and cosmologist, wrote a book on this subject titled *A Universe from Nothing: Why There is Something Rather than Nothing.* How is a supporter of the causal principle to respond?

First of all, the quantum vacuum in which these particles are "popping into existence" is not *nothing* (the absence of being) but *something*. This vacuum state is a low-level quantum energy field that is subject to the physical laws of nature. The virtual particles that "pop into existence" are a result of the fluctuations of energy within this quantum vacuum. In a *New York Times* review of Krauss's book, Columbia University philosopher and theoretical physicist David Albert writes,

> [V]acuum states—no less than giraffes or refrigerators or solar systems—are particular arrangements of elementary physical stuff. . . . [T]he fact that particles can pop in and out of existence, over time, as those [quantum] fields rearrange themselves, is not a whit more mysterious than the fact that fists can pop in and out of existence, over time, as my fingers rearrange themselves. And none of these poppings—if you look at them aright—amount to anything even remotely in the neighborhood of a creation from nothing.[382]

We might argue that those who appeal to the activities within a subatomic vacuum state are equivocating on the term *nothing*—sneaking something into nothing rather than just letting nothing be nothing, thus nullifying their argument against the causal principle of *whatever begins to exist must have a cause.*

Since the rational justifications for denying the causal principle do not stand to the scrutiny of reason, the question arises, "Is it possible to offer positive arguments in *defense* of the causal principle?" There are two arguments that I think succeed.

Existence and non-existence

Whatever begins to exist is also something whose non-existence is a real possibility. This is obvious, given the fact that whatever begins to exist at one time *did not* exist. Let's call this a *possible being.*[383]

Now, in the Thomistic tradition, such beings do not possess their act of existence by nature. This means that existence—*that it is*—does not belong to its essence—*what* it is.

Consider the example of a house. Prior to a house being built, the carpenter can ponder the essence of the house (*what* it is) without it yet having real existence. Notice that the mere thought of the house does not *necessitate* its existence in the real world. This means that existence does not belong to the essence of the house.

By way of contrast, think of a triangle. It is impossible to think of a triangle without thinking of a figure with three straight sides. This is so because the idea of three straight sides belongs to the *essence* of a triangle. The house, on the other hand, can be thought of *without* it existing. Therefore, the house's existence does not belong to the essence of the house—they are distinct. As some philosophers put it, knowing *what* it is does not determine *that* it is. This is why the house is merely *possible*.

Furthermore, when the carpenter builds the house and gives it real existence, the essence of the house does not change. The house's act of existence—*that* it is—makes no difference to its essence—*what* it is. Contrast this with the aforementioned triangle. The idea of three straight sides *does* make a difference to the essence of a triangle. Why? Because the idea of three straight sides belongs to the essence of a triangle—they are one and the same. But in the case of the house, its existence (*that* it is)—whether merely in the mind of the carpenter or in the real world—makes no difference to its essence (*what* it is). As such, its existence does not belong to its essence—that is to say, its act of existence is *non-essential*, making the house a *possible* being.

So, in light of the house example, we can conclude that whatever being is a possible being—a being that begins to exist—does not possess its act of existence by nature. From this it follows that we cannot conceive of such a being having its act of existence in virtue of what it is in itself. In other words, we cannot appeal to a possible being's essence to distinguish it from nothing.

Consider the house again. Can the essence of the house account for its existence in the real world as opposed to being nothing? It cannot, since the essence of the house does not contain its act of existence. The house, therefore, and every other possible being, cannot be the reason for its distinction from nothing. With this in mind, the absurdity of claiming that something can begin to exist without a cause becomes apparent.

Something or nothing at all

If a possible being's essence cannot distinguish it from nothing, then the only two options that remain are 1) something outside itself, a cause, or 2) nothing at all. The skeptic who denies the causal principle obviously rejects the former. Consequently, denying the causal principle is tantamount to saying that *nothing* distinguishes a possible being from nothing—that is, its distinction from nothing comes from neither itself nor anything else.

But how can a possible being exist and simultaneously not be distinguished from nothing? It can't! Something cannot be distinguished from nothing and not be distinguished from nothing in the same respect at the same place and time. The denial of the causal principle, therefore, at least in the form we're considering here, leads to a contradiction and thus is unreasonable—proving its affirmation to be reasonable.

The second argument in defense of the causal principle is similar to the first in that it is based on the distinction between essence (*what* something is) and existence (*that* something is). The fact that existence does not belong to the essence or nature of possible beings (things that begin to exist), one must conclude that it is non-essential and thus an accident for possible beings.

"Accident" here does not refer to a car crash but to an attribute that may or may not belong to something without affecting its essence. As the late Fr. Joseph Owens points out, "whatever there is in a thing outside its nature belongs to it accidentally."[384] For example, three straight sides belong to the essence of a triangle but the color red does not. The color red is non-essential and thus is an accident for the triangle. Similarly, because existence is non-essential in possible beings—it may or may not belong to a possible being's essence—it is considered an accident for possible beings.

Now, not only is existence accidental to the essence or nature of possible beings, it is also *ontologically prior*. This means that an essence that actually exists in the real world (say, a house or a dog) *presupposes* existence itself. Without it, an essence would not be real.

For example, my act of existence makes the essence of man *actual* in me rather than it being a mere abstraction in a mind. The same goes for Fido's act of existence, which makes the essence of dog *actual* in Fido. There can be neither an act of being a man nor an act of being a dog without existence. The bottom line is that without existence the essence of possible beings (such as Fido and me) would not exist. Existence, therefore, is an *ontologically prior accident* for the essence of things that begin to exist.

"But," one might ask, "What's the big deal?" The big deal is that it serves as the basis for defending the form of the causal principle under consideration. Consider that whatever is accidental does not exist in its own right, but is dependent upon a substance. For example, color does not exist in its own right. Red is not floating somewhere in the cosmos. It can only exist *in* something, such as a triangle or a crayon.

Now, if existence is an accident in possible beings, then it must be dependent upon a substance. But it (existence) cannot be dependent upon the substance that it makes actual. For example, Fido's existence cannot depend upon Fido's essence because, as already demonstrated, existence is *prior* to essence. Without the act of existence, the essence of dog would not be made real in Fido.

Therefore, the act of existence for a possible being must be dependent upon—received from—something *other than* the thing that it makes actual or real. Now to give existence to something (to make it real) is simply to be a cause. Therefore, everything that begins to exist must have a cause for its existence.

In conclusion, the rational justifications for denying the causal principle in the form of "whatever begins to exist must have a cause" are not grounds for undermining the force of theistic arguments of the likes of Aquinas and the Kalam cosmological argument. Furthermore, there are good positive reasons to hold to the causal principle as true. Thus, the causal principle stands on solid ground and the light of philosophical theology continues to lead the way for sojourners on the journey to theism.

Appendix C

Freedom and the vision of God

When faced with the problem of moral evil, Christian apologists often express God's dilemma in creating free human beings. The argument goes like this: since God willed to create creatures with free will, the possibility of evil necessarily exists.

The blessed in heaven

But apologists who put forward this argument don't take into account the blessed in heaven, whom the Church views as exercising free will while also being impeccable (unable to sin). If freedom necessarily involves the capacity to choose evil, then the blessed in heaven would seem to have no freedom.

It has been commonly believed,[385] however, that the blessed in heaven do have freedom. Therefore, on supposition that this common belief is true, the idea that free will necessarily involves the capacity to choose evil would be false.

St. Thomas Aquinas concurs. He writes in his work *On Evil*,

> We note a second difference regarding which there can be free choice as the difference between good and evil. But this difference does not intrinsically belong to the power of free choice but is incidentally related to the power inasmuch as natures capable of defect have such free choice. . . . And so nothing prevents there being a power of free choice that so strives for good that it is in no way capable of striving for evil, whether by nature, as in the case of God, or by the perfection of grace, as in the case of the saints and the holy angels.[386]

I believe there are two key phrases that help illuminate St. Thomas's position on this issue. The first is "natures capable of defect" and the second is "the perfection of grace." These two phrases become intelligible once we understand his understanding of man's faculty of *will* and its relation to the intellect.

Understanding human *will*

For Aquinas, the human faculty we call *will* is an intellectual appetite, a tendency to be drawn to the good apprehended by the intellect. Where the sensitive appetites respond to sensual goods presented through sense knowledge, the intellectual appetite—will—responds to the good as understood or perceived through intellectual knowledge.

The intellect presents an object (or objects) as a good, and the will responds. You might say the intellect relates to the will like a man relates to a woman he is courting. As the man, as a part of his wooing the woman, bestows her with gifts, the intellect "woos" the will by presenting to it objects under the aspect of good—providing it with a *desirable* object.

The good without qualification—not *this* good or *that* good but goodness in general—is the formal object of the will. Just as truth is the ultimate end of the intellect, goodness is the ultimate end of the will. In this we have no choice. The human will is necessarily ordered to universal goodness as "necessity of end"[387]—not "necessity of coercion," which is repugnant to freedom.

The freedom to choose

Our freedom of choice and self-determination arises when faced with *finite* or *particular* goods. Because finite goods do not express goodness in its universality (totality) but express it in this or that *particular* mode, and thus exclusive of other goods, the will is not necessitated to them. The will is free to choose among particular goods as means to its end, goodness itself. This is called "freedom of specification."

But whenever the will does choose, it only does so *sub specie boni*—under the aspect of good.[388] The human will cannot choose evil *as* evil.

"But wait a minute," you may object, "humans choose evil all the time. What gives?"

It is true humans choose evil acts. But in each case they perceive some good in them.

Misapprehension of goods

Consider, for example, a young couple who are trying to decide whether they should have sex before marriage. Suppose they perceive sexual expression of love as a good, but due to the conventions of secular culture and their lack of moral guidance from parents and teachers in their upbringing, they are totally unaware that sexual expression of love is not morally good for them in *this* circumstance.

Perhaps their only criterion for evaluating appropriate sexual behavior is whether they're in a committed relationship or not. They at least believe that you can't just shack up. And since they are in a committed relationship, they judge that it's morally good for them to have sex outside of marriage. This misapprehended moral good draws the will; the will thereby consents, chooses, and commands the action.

Lower goods for higher goods

Even when we correctly apprehend an act as evil, we still choose under the aspect of some good. In these cases, we simply choose a lower good for a higher good.

Consider, for example, how an angry man might haul off and hit someone who cut him in line at the movie theater. He acts because he perceives that relieving his tension and frustration is a good. But he chooses to pursue this lower good at the cost of higher goods: namely, the virtues of prudence and justice. Inasmuch as he didn't employ nonviolent means to deal with the situation he violated prudence. He violated justice in that his action was not due for the gravity of the offense.

The drug addict pursues the good of sensory pleasure at the cost of impeding the proper function of his intellect and will.

He chooses the lower good of his nature, his animality, over and above the higher good, his rationality.

In both cases, the will chooses under the *aspect* of good, but does evil in violating the hierarchical order of goods.

The influential will

But how can a person choose a lower good *when he knows* that by choosing it he will exclude a higher one? Here is where Aquinas's teaching on the will's influence over the intellect comes into play.[389] When it comes to immoral actions, the will can influence the intellect to reconsider an evil action as good under a *different* description.

For example, let's suppose that while the angry man deliberates whether to hit the gentleman that cut him in line, his intellect judges this action to be an inappropriate means to deal with the situation. He knows there are other, non-violent means, and he also knows that hitting him is disproportionate to the gravity of the offense.

But his intellect recognizes that this action could be considered as a good under a different aspect—e.g., this act will relieve the buildup of anger within me—and presents *that* to the will. The will influences the intellect to keep its attention on the good under the new description, which in turn keeps the intellect's attention away from the evils of imprudence and injustice. Since the good of relieving the buildup of anger wins the day, the will consents, chooses, and commands the action to be performed, resulting in the gentleman getting a bloody nose.

In the case of the drug addict, his intellect may perceive that taking the drugs is undesirable inasmuch as it's not a moral good. But his intellect also knows that the drugs will give him great pleasure. His will then influences the intellect to keep its attention on *that* good and thereby keeps it away from attending to the moral evil of the action. And since the good of bodily pleasure wins the day, the will consents, chooses, and commands the action to be performed.

The intellect's capacity to be *mistaken* in its judgment about what is good, the failure to attend to the *ordering* of goods, and the will's ability to influence the intellect to consider an act initially judged as evil as good under a different description. All this seems to be what Aquinas is getting at when he refers to the power of free choice for evil arising from "natures capable of defect."

The state of perfection precludes ability to sin

This lends itself to the question, "What if our nature, our intellect and will, was *not* capable of defect?" In other words, what if the intellect was able to *perfectly* recognize what is *truly* good and beneficial for attaining our ultimate end, and our will could never desire a lower good to a higher good, and never influence the intellect to present an evil act as good under different descriptions?

The answer is, we wouldn't be able to choose evil. Since the will is naturally ordered to the good, and the good relative to our ultimate end would *always* be perfectly known, the will would always choose appropriately. In short, we would be impeccable—unable to sin. St. Thomas explains it this way:

> Where there is no failure in apprehending and comparing, there can be no willing of evil even when there is question of means, as is clear among the blessed. For this reason it is said that to will evil is not freedom or any part of it, though it is a sign of freedom.[390]

We get a *hint* of what this might be like even in this life. Consider the act of torturing babies for fun. We can't fathom committing such a heinous crime because our wills are totally repulsed by it. Our intellect *perfectly* judges such an action for what it is—namely evil—and sees that there is no good in it (e.g., pleasure in conquest, or relief of tension) that could possibly outweigh the evil of violating the dignity of such an innocent human being. As such, our will cannot influence the intellect to consider the act as good under a different description—that is to say, we are *in no way* drawn to it. This makes us impeccable when it comes to this specific action.

In the beatific vision, which is a direct intuitive knowledge of God, who is Goodness itself, we will not be impeccable with regard to *this* sin or *that* sin, but *all* sin. Why? As Aquinas points out in the above passage from *De Malo,* our natures—intellect and will—will be perfected by grace.

The intellect will have a clear apprehension of the Infinite Good, leading to an upright *will* that tends to the apprehended order of goods. For example, the intellect will always know what is *objectively* good as opposed to apparent goods. Deception concerning apparent goods will no longer occur. Since the will follows the intellect, the *will,* in the beatific vision, will never be drawn to anything objectively evil and will only choose things that are good.

Furthermore, *particular* goods will be seen in perfect relationship to *universal* goodness. And since all weakness in the *will* due to the fall will be perfectly remedied in the beatific vision, the will always chooses goods according to their proper order. It will no longer be able to choose a lower good *in place of* a higher good.

Finally, the intellect's perfect apprehension of the good will preclude it from ever finding a different description under which it can present as a good what it initially judged to be evil. Consequently, it will never be influenced by the will to reconsider an objectively evil action.

This perfection, as Aquinas points out, is the lot of the blessed saints and angels in heaven.

Why not the beatific vision immediately?

Why didn't God create us with the beatific vision to begin with? Why not just create us with perfect intellects and wills so that we always perceive the good and always choose the good?

We had an opportunity in chapter eight to address this question. And one reason that we gave was the dignity of being real causes of our own moral perfection. Another was the dignity of meriting our eternal reward. But I think it's appropriate that we consider here the latter reason in a little more detail and offer another reason to add to the list.

Let's take *the dignity of meriting our eternal reward* first. It is *nobler* to achieve the reward of heaven as a result of something we did in cooperation with God as opposed to God simply giving it to us without our participation. The late George Hayward Joyce states the argument this way:

> God . . . has created the present order such that man should have the glory of meriting his last end . . . . We can see readily enough that in this He has conferred a great privilege upon us. To receive our final beatitude as the fruit of our labors, and as the recompense of a hard-won victory, is an incomparably higher destiny than to receive it without any effort on our part...None can reasonably dispute that an order of things in which beatitude is conferred on man as the reward of personal effort is not merely compatible with the Divine goodness, but exhibits that attribute in an altogether singular degree.[391]

This principle is made manifest in our experience of athletic competition. For example, what is nobler and more rewarding: to be the number one seed because your team is the only team in the league, or to be the number one seed because your team has won the most games against opponents? I think we can agree it's the latter.

Since God has seen fit to create us in such a *noble* condition, it's inevitable that man have the power to sin. The call to merit heaven due to victory necessarily involves the possibility of defeat.

The other possible reason for God creating us without the beatific vision that we can add to the list is that it's more valuable to have a relationship that involves a choice to commit one way or the other.[392]

We value this type of commitment in our own lives. For example, we prefer freely chosen marriages to arranged marriages. Although arranged marriages can be valid and involve authentic love wherein each spouse wills the good of the other and commits to a lifelong relationship, we prefer a situation where people have the *option* of whom they will commit to in a loving relationship for the rest of their lives.

It is also reasonable to value a relationship that involves a choice to commit, because the choice expresses how valuable the other individual is to the one making the choice. Consider how a man's choice to commit to a woman in a non-arranged marriage is also at the same time his choice to *not* commit to other women (the same reasoning applies to the woman's choice). This type of commitment better expresses how *valuable* the woman is to the man. When a man has the option to choose from many women and only chooses one, he is in essence saying, "You are so valuable to me that I want to commit my life to you and no other in this unique way." The woman is saying the same thing with her choice to commit.

So, just as we value the ability to choose whom one will commit one's life to, so too God values this type of committed relationship with human beings.

Why God values commitment

But why would God value this type of committed relationship when he is perfect in himself? Since there is nothing that man's commitment can add to God, this type of relationship must be for man's sake. But what does man gain from it?

One answer is *man gains an awareness of God's greatness.* Recall how the commitment in marriage reveals how valuable one is to the other relative to marital love. Similarly, the requirement for humans to commit to God in a relationship that involves him as the highest priority reveals his value in comparison to the things of the created order. He is most valuable above all things.

This awareness of God's value in turn reveals man's value. If man is called to a relationship with such a valuable being, then man himself is valuable. The committed relationship that God asks of man, to use the words of Pope St. John Paul II, "reveals man to himself."[393]

Another grace man gains from having to commit one way or the other is *a deeper experience of happiness in the beatific vision.*

There is greater glory in receiving our final beatitude as the fruit of our labors—receiving recompense of a hard-won victory.

Consider the following example. Let's say in a championship game a football player plays all four quarters without a break. The game has been a close and long drawn-out battle. It comes down to the last few seconds, and he scores the final touchdown to win the game. I think it's reasonable to conclude that player is going to experience a deeper sense of happiness than the player who sat the bench the whole game.

Similarly, having to put forth effort in making the choice for or against God, the choice to orient one's will away from self and to God, will bring forth a greater depth of happiness in the beatific vision.

The tendency of apologists to appeal to freedom for the possibility of moral evil is understandable. It's the lot we've been given on this side of heaven. But such possibility is not *essential* to freedom. This is good news since we don't want to spend an eternity in heaven knowing that evil could possibly rear its ugly head.

Appendix D

Is God to blame for creating a world with evil?

One line of reasoning that explains the presence of evil in the world (and the suffering it causes) is that evil—whether physical or moral—arises from the *type* of world that God willed to create.

Consider physical evil. Material substances are naturally subject to defect and corruption. Every material thing is composed of what philosophers refer to as *form* and *matter*. For example, a tree is composed of a certain kind of matter—mostly wood—and a certain kind of form—the form of a woody vegetative organism that grows upward with a trunk that produces lateral branches above the ground.

We observe in our experience that material things lose their form. A tree loses its form, for instance, when a fire burns it down or a lumberjack fells it. The human body loses its form (the soul) at death, and the body simply becomes a clump of matter that will eventually take on the new form of dirt.

Furthermore, we notice that material things are *on their way* to losing their forms. For example, the tree outside still retains its *treeness*, but it is on its way to losing its form due to the presence of the aphids that are attacking it. The cancer patient's living body still retains its form, the soul, but is nevertheless on its way to losing that form.

So inasmuch as things are composed of form and matter, which all material beings are, they are subject to losing their form, and are subject to defect even while retaining their form. Therefore, it belongs to the nature of material beings to be subject to defect and corruption, which in certain cases gives rise to suffering.

This allows us to say that physical evil is part and parcel of the material world that God willed to create. The fact that things have a nature subject to defect and corruption is due to God's creative will. How can the presence of defects and corruption that give rise to suffering count against God's existence if he is the one who created such things with these potentials?

Even the *possibility* of moral evil is due to God's creative will. Even though God could have created humans with the capacity to choose only the good (see appendix C), God willed to create humans with a capacity to choose between good and evil. He willed that humans at least have the *possibility* to miss the mark in their choices.

This gives rise to the question, "Is God blameworthy for creating this sort of world?" If he is omnipotent as traditional theism says, then he could have created a better world. Since he didn't, it seems he is blameworthy, and thus not all-good. And if God is not all-good, then he is not the true God as traditionally defined. How do we respond?

No obligation

First, ascribing blame to God presupposes that God has a moral duty or obligation to create a world free from evil. But this is false. God not only has no obligation to create a particular type of world, he has no obligation to create in the first place. In fact, he has no obligation whatsoever. If he did, he would not be God.

Obligation necessarily involves subjection to law, since, as Aquinas says, "a law is imposed on others by way of a rule and measure."[394] Furthermore, obligation to law implies the possibility of change. There exists the potential to be morally good or morally bad depending on whether or not the individual abides by the law. This in turn implies a state of incomplete happiness since there would be some good unrealized. As Aquinas says, "the law must needs regard principally the relationship to happiness."[395]

These aspects of obligation do not apply to God. God is the Supreme Being, and thus has no superior who might impose a duty on him. Because God is pure being itself—that is to say, pure actuality—there is no potentiality within him; hence he is not subject to change. And if he cannot change, then there can be no unrealized good within him.

Furthermore, since God is pure being itself, and being is convertible with goodness,[396] he is pure goodness itself. And if pure goodness, then he possesses the fullness of beatitude, in which case he cannot be ordered toward achieving some unrealized state of happiness as obligation to law implies. Nor can there be any rule or measure outside God by which his actions can be evaluated; otherwise his goodness would be conditioned by conforming to that law, which is not possible since he is Goodness itself.

Moreover, God is not under the moral law because he is the moral law itself. Aquinas puts it succinctly:

> [A]ll that is in things created by God, whether it be contingent or necessary, is subject to the eternal law: while things pertaining to the divine nature or essence are not subject to the eternal law, but *are the eternal law itself.*"[397]

If God cannot be under any obligation, then it follows that he cannot be under an obligation to create a particular type of world, and thus is not subject to blame for creating a world in which evil exists, especially when that evil is ordered to the good of the whole (see chapter 7).

Permission of evil is not evil done

A second response comes from the late Thomistic philosopher Herbert McCabe, who argues that God's permission of evil is not *evil done*, but merely *some good not done*, which doesn't count against his goodness.[398]

He bases his argument on the premise that evil is a privation of a due good. As such, *evil not done* is the same as *good done*. For example, no infidelity in a marriage means fidelity in a marriage. But since good is not a privation of evil, *some good not done* is not necessarily *evil done*. A person doesn't do evil if he chooses not to marry in the first place.

What about sins of omission? Isn't that a case where *some good not done* is evil?

It's true that for us *as creatures* sometimes what we don't will and don't do can be just as wicked as what we will and do. But, as McCabe explains, "this is precisely because we exist in a moral context in which we ought to do this rather than that." [399]

As creatures we are subject to an order of good and evil that God has imprinted into our nature—it's called the natural law. We must live in accord with it in order to achieve human perfection. And inasmuch as God is the source of natural law, we are *obliged* to follow it. So, if we don't will or do the good as spelled out by the natural law (e.g., care for my wife and children), then evil is done, and moral imperfection ensues.

But for God it's different. He has no particular kind of nature that constitutes an order of good and evil for him. This would imply that he could possibly fail to perfectly instantiate that nature, which would reduce him to nothing more than a bigger and better creature than us.

Moreover, as pointed out above, because he is being itself there cannot possibly be a higher being to morally oblige him.

We can go even a little further. Given that God has no potential for the perfection of being because he *is* the perfection of being itself, it's metaphysically impossible for him to be in a state where he would have to *achieve* his perfection or goodness. And since God can't be in potency to actualizing the perfection of his being, or achieving goodness (being and goodness are convertible[400]), he is not *obliged* to *do* anything. There is nothing that he must do in order to be perfect because he's already infinitely perfect.

It follows from this that his *refraining* from *doing* some good, unlike creatures, could not possibly constitute *evil done*. There is no evil done because there is no good that he *ought* to have done.

Hence, his permission of evil in the world (some good not done) is not a sin of omission.

This doesn't mean, however, that God is beyond good and evil. God can't positively will something that is contrary to the order of goodness that he bestowed within our nature—for to do so he would be going against himself, which is absurd. If God were to command us to do something that violates the natural law (order of goodness in our nature), then he would be positively willing that we violate reason, since to act against our nature is a violation of reason.[401]

But God can't command us to act contrary to reason because he can only will in accord with his nature, which is reason itself. Therefore, God can't command us to do anything that will violate the order of goodness that he embeds within our human nature. In short, he can't command us to do evil.

So when God does not wish that *evil not be done*—that is, when he permits evil—he simply does not wish *some good be done*, since *evil not done* and *good done* are synonymous. And since to not wish *some good be done* is not evil, and his not wishing *some good be done* is not a positive command to do evil, God's permission of evil doesn't count against his goodness. As McCabe argues, it doesn't count against God's goodness any more than God's willing to not create more sparrows than he willed counts against his goodness.[402]

No perfect level of goodness

A third way to respond to the "God is to blame" objection is that there is no created world that can have a perfect level of goodness. God can always create a better one. This argument is based on a principle expressed by the late Jesuit Bernard Boedder: "Every finite degree of external glory of God falls infinitely short of an adequate expression of the infinite divine goodness."[403]

Since any created world is a finite expression of divine goodness, it follows that there can always be a world with more goodness. Even if God created a world without evil in it, it would still fall short of adequately expressing God's goodness, and thus in a sense would still be imperfect. Imperfect goodness belongs to the nature of created being. Therefore, there can be no amount of imperfection in a created world that could possibly violate his goodness.

An atheist may not like that God created a world where evil exists, but not liking such a world is not the same as proving such a world undermines God's goodness. If God is infinitely wise, it's reasonable to trust that God has good reason for creating such a world, and thus it's reasonable to continue affirming his all-good nature.

Endnotes

1   In reference to the millions of years of animal suffering and the occasions of innocent children being crushed in earthquakes, atheist philosopher Stephen Law says, "I think these sorts of consideration do establish beyond any reasonable doubt that there is no all-powerful all-good God." Stephen Law, "Atheism a Faith Position?" February 28, 2007, http://stephenlaw.blogspot.com/2007/02/atheism-faith-position.html.

2   See Barna Group, "Six Reasons Why Young Christians Leave Church," September 27, 2011, https://www.barna.com/research/six-reasons-young-christians-leave-church/.

3   Christopher Hitchens, *God is Not Great: How Religion Poisons Everything* (New York: Twelve, 2009), 142.

4   H.L. Mencken, *Treatise on the Gods* (Baltimore: John Hopkins University Press, 2006), 175.

5   Richard Dawkins, "Is Science a Religion?", *The Humanist*, January/February 1997.

6   Steven Morris, "Abortion: Why the Religious Right is Wrong," *Freedom from Religion Foundation*, https://ffrf.org/about/getting-acquainted/item/16916-abortion-why-the-religious-right-is-wrong.

7   See Alex McFarland, "Ten Reasons Millennials are Backing Away from God and Christianity," *Fox News Opinion,* April 30, 2017, http://www.foxnews.com/opinion/2017/04/30/ten-reasons-millennials-are-backing-away-from-god-and-christianity.html#.WQe5gesy-zI.email.

8   Allan Bloom, *The Closing of the American Mind* (New York: Simon and Schuster, 1987), 25.

9   Richard Dawkins and Rowan Williams, "This House Believes Religion Has No Place in the 21st Century," The Cambridge Union Society, January 31, 2013, video debate, https://www.youtube.com/watch?v=-XpEjVlPFrs.

10 Family Policy Institute of Washington, "Exploring Gender Identity: Can a 5'9, White Guy Be a 6'5, Chinese Woman?" online video,

https://www.youtube.com/watch?v=xfO1veFs6Ho.

11 This argument is taken from Edward Feser, "The Absolute Truth About Relativism," September 8, 2015, http://edwardfeser.blogspot.com/2015/09/the-absolute-truth-about-relativism.html.

12 See Siofra Brennan, "I was born in the wrong species: Woman who says she's a CAT trapped in a human body hisses at dogs, hates water and claims she can even see better at night," *Daily Mail,* January 27, 2016, http://www.dailymail.co.uk/femail/article-3419631/Woman-says-s-CAT-trapped-human-body.html.

13 See David Moye, "Chloe Jennings-White Wants Operation To Be Permanently Disabled," *Huffington Post,* July 20, 2013, http://www.huffingtonpost.com/2013/07/19/chloe-jennings-white_n_3625033.html.

14 Peter Kreeft, "A Refutation of Moral Relativism—Transcription," http://www.peterkreeft.com/audio/05_relativism/relativism_transcription.htm.

15 W. Norris Clarke, *The One and the Many: A Contemporary Thomistic Metaphysics* (Indiana: University of Notre Dame Press, 2001), 13.

16 Jesse Prinz, "Morality is a Culturally Conditioned Response," *Philosophy Now* 82, April–May 2017, https://www.google.com/search?client=safari&rls=en&q=Morality+is+a+Culturally+Conditioned+Response&ie=UTF-8&oe=UTF-8.

17 Ibid.

18 Peter Kreeft and Ronald Tacelli, *Handbook of Christian Apologetics: Hundreds of Answers to Crucial Questions* (Downers Grove: InterVarsity Press, 1994), 376.

19 *Fides et Ratio* 27.

20 Tom L. Beauchamp, *Philosophical Ethics: An Introduction to Moral Philosophy* (New York: McGraw-Hill, 1982), 42.

21 "Nothing in the intellect that is not first in the senses." Thomas Aquinas, *De Veritate* 2:3:19. Cf. Aristotle, *De Anima,* Bk. 2.

22 See René Descartes, *Meditations on First Philosophy*, in *Modern Philosophy: An Anthology of Primary Sources*, eds. Roger Ariew and Eric Watkins (Indianapolis: Hackett Publishing Company, 2009), Kindle.

23 D.Q. McInerny, *Epistemology* (Elmhurst: The Priestly Fraternity of St. Peter, 2007), 192.

24 Ralph McInerny, *A First Glance at St. Thomas Aquinas: A Handbook for Peeping Thomists* (Notre Dame: University of Notre Dame Press, 1990), 37.

25 Kenneth Gallagher, *The Philosophy of Knowledge* (New York: Ford-

ham University Press, 1982), 41.

26 Peter Coffey, *Epistemology or the Theory of Knowledge: An Introduction to General Metaphysics,* vol. 1 (New York: Longmans, Green, and Co, 1917), 93.

27 Thomas Aquinas, *Questiones Disputatae de Veritate* q.2, a. 3, arg. 19, trans. Robert W. Mulligan, S.J., http://dhspriory.org/thomas/QD-deVer2.htm#4.

28 Dawkins and Williams, "This House Believes Religion Has No Place in the 21st Century."

29 Ibid.

30 Richard Dawkins argues, "Father Christmas and the Tooth Fairy are part of the charm of childhood. So is God. Some of us grow out of all three." Quoted in *Third Way Magazine* vol. 25, no. 5, June 2003, p. 5.

31 This example is taken from Edward Feser, *Scholastic Metaphysics: A Contemporary Metaphysics* (Neunkirchen-Seelscheid: Editiones Scholasticae, 2014), 22.

32 See Edward Feser, "Blinded by Scientism," *The Public Discourse,* March 9, 2010, http://www.thepublicdiscourse.com/2010/03/1174/.

33 See Paul Davies, *The Accidental Universe* (New York: Cambridge University Press, 1982), 107.

34 For more examples of finely tuned universal constants, see Paul Davies, *The Accidental Universe.*

35 See Roger Penrose, *The Emperor's New Mind* (Oxford: Oxford University Press, 1989), 343.

36 Ibid., 344.

37 See Arvind Borde, Alan H. Guth, and Alexander Vilenkin, "Inflationary spacetimes are not past-complete" *Physical Review Letters* 90 (2003) 151301, https://arxiv.org/abs/gr-qc/0110012.

38 Paul Davies, "Stephen Hawking's Big Bang Gaps," *The Guardian,* September 3, 2010, http:// www.guardian.co.uk/ commentisfree/ belief/ 2010/ sep/ 04/ stephen-hawking-big-bang-gap.

39 Stanley Jaki, *Questions on Science and Religion* (Pinckney: Review Books, 2004), 21.

40 Anyone can understand in his mind the concept of something that which nothing greater can be thought. But for this thing really to be *that than which nothing greater can be thought* it must exist in reality, for what has real existence is greater than what only exists in the mind. Therefore, since *that than which nothing greater can be thought* does exist in our minds, and what exists in reality is greater than what exists

in the mind, *that than which nothing greater can be thought* must exist in reality. This is what we call God.

41   If the universe began to exist, then it would need a cause outside itself. The universe began to exist. Therefore, the universe must have a cause outside itself.

42   See Thomas Aquinas, *Summa Theologiae* I:75:5, ad 4.

43   See also Karlo Broussard, "Testing the Causal Chain," February 19, 2018, www.catholic.com.

44   The question of whether there can be instrumental causes of sheer existence has no bearing on the argument. For a full-length article on this issue, see Karlo Broussard, "Between Existence and Annihilation: Why only God can create *ex nihilo*," *Catholic Answers Magazine,* July–August 2016.

45   See Aquinas, *Summa Theologiae* I:4:2.

46   Another way of looking at this is that wherever essence and existence are distinct but united in a thing, there necessarily needs to be a unifying cause. For an exposition of this argument, see Karlo Broussard, "Testing the Causal Chain," www.catholic.com.

47   For an in-depth defense of the divine attributes traditionally ascribed to God, see Edward Feser's masterpiece, *Five Proofs of the Existence of God* (San Francisco: Ignatius Press, 2017).

48   *Dei Fliius* 2.

49   See Aquinas, *Summa Theologiae* I:2:3.

50   Brian Davies, *The Reality of God and the Problem of Evil* (New York: Continuum, 2006), 176.

51   Ibid.

52   For St. Thomas Aquinas, being and goodness are convertible with one another. See Aquinas, *Summa Theologiae* I:5:1.

53   Kreeft and Tacelli, *Handbook of Christian Apologetics*, 132.

54   The sock example is taken from Herbert McCabe, *God and Evil in the Theology of St. Thomas Aquinas* (New York: Continuum International Publishing Group, 2010), chap. 3, Kindle.

55   See Davies, *The Reality of God and the Problem of Evil,* 177.

56   See Aquinas, *Summa Theologiae* I:8:1.

57   Davies, *The Reality of God and the Problem of Evil,* 178.

58   Ibid.

59   Ibid., 181.

60   Aquinas, *Summa Theologiae* I:49:2.

61   Ibid.

62   See Ibid., I:49:2, ad. 1

63   An objection can be raised here: "What about Ananias and Sapphira
     in Acts 5? It seems that God wills their death (physical evil) without
     the flourishing activity of another substance like in the case of the
     lion eating the gazelle?" Since there is no evidence that God miracu-
     lously willed the flourishing activity of some unknown disease, we
     can presume that their deaths were simply a matter of God willing to
     no longer concur with the operation of their vital processes. Recall
     that nothing can operate for an instant without God imparting causal
     power to it. For a person to die, all God need do is cease imparting his
     causal power. And God's choice to cease imparting his causal power in
     keeping a person alive is nothing more than God's choice to not will
     all the good that he could have caused, since for the person to remain
     alive would be a good. This is analogous to the professor mentioned in
     strategy three of this chapter beginning to draw a circle on the chalk-
     board and ceasing to complete it, only leaving a half-drawn circle. The
     professor wills to not cause all the goodness that he could have caused,
     namely, the completed circle. Is God to blame for not willing all the
     good that he could have caused? The answer is no. I deal with this in
     more detail in Appendix D, but suffice it to say that God not willing all
     the good that he could have caused no more counts against his good-
     ness than God willing to create only four sparrows when he could have
     created six. To not will some good is not the same as willing evil (once
     again, see Appendix D). That God's choice to not will some good
     doesn't count against his goodness becomes even clearer when you
     consider the concomitant good that God does will in the case of Ana-
     nias and Sapphira: punishment and the order of justice. God's decision
     to no longer concur with the vital processes of Ananias and Sapphira
     is an act of punishment for their grave sin of "lying to the Holy Spirit"
     (Acts 5:4). Commenting on this passage, Feser explains that God wills
     the death of Ananias and Saphhira "as part of [the] larger good of se-
     curing retributive justice, as well, perhaps, as part of the realization of
     one of the secondary ends of punishment (deterrence)" (Edward Feser,
     "Davies on Evil Suffered," http://edwardfeser.blogspot.com/2017/05/
     davies-on-evil-suffered.html). This larger good principle parallels the
     above example of the professor. He chooses to not will the good of
     the completed circle for the sake of the larger good of teaching his
     class about the philosophical notion of privation and how it constitutes
     badness, which is parasitic on *goodness*. So, even in the case of evil suf-

fered by Ananias and Sapphira, God cannot be rationally charged with moral fault.

64 See Feser, "Davies on Evil Suffered."

65 Aquinas, *Summa Theologiae* I-II:79:2; emphasis added.

66 See Ibid. I:2:3, ad 1.

67 Pope St. Leo the Great, *Sermon*, 73.4. Quoted in the *Catechism of the Catholic Church* 412.

68 Aquinas, *Summa Theologiae* III:1:3, ad. 3. Quoted in the *Catechism of the Catholic Church* 412.

69 Analogy taken from Edward Feser, "Davies on Evil Suffered," http://edwardfeser.blogspot.com/2017/05/davies-on-evil-suffered.html.

70 Aquinas, *Summa Theologiae* I:22:2, ad. 2.

71 Ibid.

72 George Hayward Joyce, *Principles of Natural Theology* (Veritatis Splendor Publications, 2013), chap. 17, Kindle.

73 An atheist might object that this line of reasoning would preclude the saints in heaven from having the virtue of courage. But this doesn't follow, because the saints in heaven retain the virtue of courage that they developed while on earth. Edward Feser explains, "[W]hile still on Earth the blessed *were* in danger and thereby developed the courage that they retain in Heaven. They don't lose this virtue any more than an eighty-year-old war veteran loses the courage he acquired in battle decades earlier." Edward Feser, *Five Proofs of the Existence of God* (San Francisco: Ignatius Press, 2017), 22.

74 Aquinas, *Summa Theologiae* I:22:2, ad. 2.

75 "The Exsultet: The Proclamation of Easter" in *The Roman Missal*, The International Commission on English in the Liturgy, 3rd typical ed. (Washington D.C.: United States Catholic Conference of Bishops, 2010).

76 Stephen Law, "Atheism a Faith Position?", http://stephenlaw.blogspot.com/2007/02/atheism-faith-position.html.

77 Ernest Rutherford is the individual who discovered the proton by conducting an experiment in which he discovered that the atom must have a concentrated positive center charge that constitutes most of the atom's mass. He named the particle "proton," which comes from the Greek *protos,* meaning "first." See "Proton," *Wikipedia,* accessed online February 7, 2018, https://en.wikipedia.org/wiki/Proton.

78 See Trent Horn, *Answering Atheism: How to Make the Case for God with Logic and Charity* (El Cajon: Catholic Answers Press, 2013), 94.

79   W. Norris Clarke, *The One and the Many: A Contemporary Thomistic Metaphysics* (Notre Dame: University of Notre Dame Press, 2001), 288.

80   Cardinal Mercier, *A Manual of Modern Scholastic Philosophy,* Vol. 2 (St. Louis: B. Herder, 1917), 129.

81   See Edward Feser, "God, Reason, & Reality: Symposium with Ed Feser, Anselm Ramelow, OP & Michael Dodds, OP," online lecture, November 16, 2014, https://www.youtube.com/watch?v=e-KDAXaP_3E.

82   Aquinas, *Summa Theologiae* I:22:3; emphasis added.

83   Aquinas, *Summa Theologiae Suppl.* 72:2, ad.1; emphasis added.

84   See Aquinas, *Summa Theologiae* I:22:1.

85   Aquinas, *Summa Theologiae Suppl.* 72:2, ad. 1.

86   One might object, "What about the blessed in heaven? Having the grace of the Beatific Vision they can't choose evil. Does that mean they don't have the dignity of being a real cause of their moral perfection?" The answer is that they still were able to be a real cause of their own perfection (in cooperation with God's grace) because they made good moral choices while here on earth without the grace of the Beatific Vision. Cf. note 73.

87   Joyce, *Principles of Natural Theology,* chap. 17, Kindle.

88   Peter Kreeft, *Making Sense Out of Suffering* (Cincinnati: Servant Books/St. Anthony Messenger Press, 1986), 144.

89   Thomas Aquinas, *Commentary on Saint Paul's First Letter to the Thessalonians.* Quoted in Eleonore Stump, *Aquinas* (New York: Routledge, 2005), 466.

90   I owe this line of reasoning to my personal correspondence with Fr. Robert J. Spitzer.

91   Quoted in the *Catechism of the Catholic Church* 618.

92   I am grateful to Scott M. Sullivan for pointing this distinction out to me in personal correspondence.

93   This argument is taken from Travis Dumsday, "A Thomistic Response to the Problem of Divine Hiddenness," *American Catholic Philosophical Quarterly* 87, no. 3 (2013): 365–377.

94   St. Thomas Aquinas, *Commentary on the Sentences,* 2:11:1, ad. 6; trans. by Travis Dumsday in "A Thomistic Response to the Problem of Divine Hiddenness" in *American Catholic Philosophical Quarterly* 87, no. 3 (2013).

95   I do not intend to suggest that God's existence can be demonstrated through historical investigation. I only intend to suggest that knowledge of God's existence is a part of God's revelation through his

Son, Jesus. And to believe that God exists based on Jesus' teaching involves historical investigation.

96 See also Second Vatican Council, *Gaudium Et Spes*, 22 and *Catechism of the Catholic Church*, 846–847.

97 *Fides et Ratio* 17.

98 Charles Rice, *50 Questions on the Natural Law: What It Is and Why We Need It* (San Francisco: Ignatius Press, 1999), chap. 2, Kindle.

99 Dan Barker and Doug Wilson, "Does the Triune God Exist," audio debate, 1997, https://www.youtube.com/watch?v=qVL-OoODQhY.

100 Our argument here allows for nature to be a *proximate* ground for moral obligation while acknowledging God as the ultimate ground. Just as God the First Cause brings about certain effects through secondary causes, so too God the supreme lawgiver uses nature to direct us to do good and avoid evil.

101 See Aquinas, *Summa Theologiae* I–II:8:1.

102 Aquinas, *De Veritate* 17.3; emphasis added.

103 See ibid.

104 Aquinas, *Summa Theologiae* I–II:90:4; emphasis added.

105 Ibid., emphasis added.

106 Aquinas, *Summa Theologiae* II–II:60:6.

107 See ibid., II–II:105:2.

108 Thomas Merton, *The Ascent to Truth* (Fort Washington: Harvest Books, 2002), 112.

109 Francis Beckwith and Gregory Koukl, *Relativism: Feet Firmly Planted in Mid-Air* (Grand Rapids: Baker Books, 1998), 169.

110 Aquinas, *Summa Theologiae* I–II:94:2.

111 Pope St. John Paul II, 17th World Youth Day Homily, July 28, 2002, http://w2.vatican.va/content/john-paul-ii/en/homilies/2002/documents/hf_jp-ii_hom_20020728_xvii-wyd.html.

112 See Edward J. Larson and Larry Witham, "Leading Scientists Still Reject God," *Nature* 394, no. 6691 (July 1998): 313.

113 See The PhilPaper Surveys, http://philpapers.org/surveys/metaresults.pl.

114 Daniel C. Dennett, *Breaking the Spell: Religion as a Natural Phenomenon* (New York: Penguin, 2006), 242; emphasis added.

115 Richard Dawkins, *The God Delusion,* 1st ed. (London: Bantam, 2006), 77.

116 See National Academy of Sciences, "Membership," accessed February 13, 2017, http://www.nasonline.org/about-nas/membership/.

117 See National Science Foundation/Division of Science Resources

Statistics, "Table 2: Employed scientists, by broad industry group of employment and detailed occupation: 2001," accessed February 13, 2017, https://wayback.archive-it.org/5902/20150820013514/http://www.nsf.gov/statistics/nsf05313/pdf/tab2.pdf.

118 See David Masci, "Scientists and Belief," *Pew Research Center,* November 5, 2009, http://www.pewforum.org/2009/11/05/scientists-and-belief/.

119 See The PhilPaper Surveys, http://philpapers.org/surveys/results.pl?affil=Target+faculty&areas0=22&areas_max=1&grain=medium.

120 Quentin Smith, "The Metaphilosophy of Naturalism", *Philo* 4, no. 2 (2001): 3–4.

121 Quoted in Varghese, *The Wonder of the World: A Journey from Modern Science to the Mind of God* (Fountain Hills: YR Publishing, 2003), 103.

122 Quoted in Raymond J. Seeger, "Planck, Physicist" in *The Journal of the American Scientific Affiliation* 37 (December 1985): 232–233.

123 Albert Einstein, *Ideas and Opinions,* trans. Sonja Bargmann (New York: Crown Publishers, 1954), 262.

124 Hermann Weyl, *The Open World: Three Lectures on the Metaphysical Implications of Science* (New Haven: Yale University Press, 1986), 28–29.

125 Fred Hoyle, "The Universe: Past and Present Reflections," *Engineering and Science* 45, no.2 (November 1981): 8–12.

126 Robert Jastrow, *God and the Astronomers* (New York: W.W. Norton and Co., 1978), 116.

127 Antony Flew and Roy Abraham Varghese, *There is a God: How the World's Most Notorious Atheist Changed His Mind* (New York: Harper Collins, 2007), 88.

128 Quoted in Varghese, *The Wonder of the World*, 103.

129 Ibid.

130 Ibid.

131 Bruce Gordon, "Inflationary Cosmology and the String Multiverse" in Robert J. Spitzer, *New Proofs for the Existence of God: Contributions of Contemporary Physics and Philosophy* (Grand Rapids: Eerdmans Publishing, 2010), 103.

132 Many of these names and biographical information were taken from Christopher T. Baglow, *Faith, Science, and Reason: Theology on the Cutting Edge*, (Woodridge: Midwest Theological Forum, 2012).

133 Hitchens, *God is Not Great: How Religion Poisons Everything*, 142.

134 Mencken, *Treatise on the Gods*, 175.

135 The A.I.D. acronym is taken from the work of Craig Blomberg and

the arrangement present in this chapter follows the methodology of Scott M. Sullivan in *Christ 101: The Evidence for Christianity Study Manual* (Scott M. Sullivan, 2014), 67.

136 See Eusebius, *Church History* 3:39:15.

137 See Philemon 23–24; Colossians 4:10–11,14; 2 Timothy 4:11;

138 See Brant Pitre, *The Case for Jesus: The Biblical and Historical Evidence for Christ* (New York: Image, 2016), 16.

139 See Irenaeus, *Against Heresies* 3.1.1; Cf. Eusebius, Church History 5:8:2.

140 See Craig Blomberg, "Where Do We Start Studying Jesus?", in *Jesus Under Fire: Modern Scholarship Reinvents the Historical Jesus*, eds. Michael Wilkins and J.P. Moreland (Grand Rapids: Zondervan Publishing, 1995), 29. Cf. Colin J. Hemer, *The Book of Acts in the Setting of Hellenistic History*, ed. Conrad H. Gempf (Tübingen: Mohr, 1989), 365–410.

141 See Jimmy Akin, *Daily Defense: 365 Days (Plus One) To Becoming a Better Apologist* (San Diego: Catholic Answers Press, 2016), 79. Cf. Jack Finegan, *Handbook of Biblical Chronology*, 2nd ed., (Peabody: Hendrickson, 2015) and Andrew Steinmann, *From Abraham to Paul: A Biblical Chronology* (St. Louis: Concordia Publishing, 2011).

142 See William Lane Craig, *On Guard: Defending Your Faith with Reason and Precision,* 1st ed. (Colorado Springs: David C. Cook, 2010), 190. Cf. A. N. Sherwin-White, *Roman Society and Roman Law in the New Testament* (Oxford: Clarendon Press, 1963).

143 See Michael Licona, "Fish Tales: Bart Ehrman's Red Herrings and the Resurrection of Jesus," in *Come Let Us Reason: New Essays in Christian Apologetics*, eds. William Lane Craig and Paul Copan (Nashville: B & H Academic, 2012), chap. 9, Kindle.

144 See Craig S. Keener, "Gospel Truth: The Historical Reliability of the Gospels," in *Come Let Us Reason*, chap. 7, Kindle.

145 See ibid. Cf. Seneca, *Controversia* 1. pref. 2, 19; Philostratus, *Lives of the Sophists* 1.11.495; Pliny, *Epistles* 2.3.3.

146 See ibid.

147 See Blomberg, in *Jesus Under Fire*, chap. 1, Kindle. Cf. Stephenson H. Brooks, *Matthew's Community: The Evidence of His Special Sayings Material* (Sheffield: JSOT, 1987); Stephen C. Farris, *The Hymns of Luke's Infancy Narratives* (Sheffield: JSOT, 1985).

148 See ibid. Cf. Heinz Schürmann, "*Die vorösterliche Anfänge der Logientradition,*" in *Der historische Jesus und der kerygmatische Christus*, eds. Helmut Ristow and Karl Matthiae (Berlin: Evangelische Verlagsanstalt, 1960), 342–70.

149 See ibid.

150 See Pitre, *The Case for Jesus,* 79.

151 See ibid. Cf. Joseph Fitzmyer, *The Gospel According to Luke,* 2 vols., *Anchor Yale Bible* (New Haven: Yale University Press, 1983, 1985), 1.288; Josephus, *Life,* 336; Lucian, *How to Write History,* 55.

152 See Pitre, *The Case for Jesus,* 70–72.

153 See ibid., 73; Cf. Josephus, *Life,* 1; Lucian, *Life of Demonax,* 3.

154 Suetonius, *Life of the Deified Augustus,* 9, trans. in *Suetonius,* trans. John C. Rolfe, 2 vols., *Loeb Classical Library* 31 (Cambridge, MA: Harvard University Press, 1998, 1997), 1.161. Quoted in Pitre, *The Case for Jesus,* 74.

155 Quoted in Eusebius, *Church History,* 3.39.15, trans. Michael W. Holmes, in *The Apostolic Fathers: Greek Texts and English Translations* (Grand Rapids: Baker Academic, 2007).

156 Plutarch, *Life of Alexander,* 1.1, trans. in Plutarch, *Lives,* trans. Bernadotte Perkin, *Loeb Classical Library* 99 (Cambridge, MA: Harvard University Press, 1919), 225. Quoted in Pitre, *The Case for Jesus,* 75.

157 Lucian, *Life of Demonax,* 67, trans. in Lucian, *Volume 1,* trans. A.M. Harmon, *Loeb Classical Library* 14 (Cambridge, MA: Harvard University Press, 1913), 173. Quoted in Pitre, *The Case for Jesus,* 75.

158 See Josephus, *Antiquities* 18.3.3.

159 See Cornelius Tacitus, *Annals* 15.44.

160 See John P. Meier, *A Marginal Jew: Rethinking the History Jesus,* Vol. II *Mentor, Message, and Miracles* (New York: Doubleday, 1994).

161 See Blomberg, in *Jesus Under Fire,* chap. 1, Kindle; Cf. Rainer Riesner, "Archaeology and Geography," in Green, McKnight, and Marshall, *Dictionary of Jesus and the Gospels* (Downers Grove: IVP Academic, 1992), 33–46; E. M. Blaiklock, *The Archaeology of the New Testament* (Nashville: Thomas Nelson, 1984).

162 See ibid. Cf. *Studying the Historical Jesus: Evaluations of the State of Current Research,* eds. Bruce Chilton and Craig Evans (Boston: Brill, 1998), 465.

163 For more details see Craig Evans, "He Laid Him in a Tomb (Mark 15.46): Roman Law and the Burial of Jesus," in *Matthew and Mark Across Perspectives: Essays in Honor of Stephen C. Barton and William R. Telford,* eds. Kristian A. Bendoraitis and Nijay K. Gupta (New York: Bloomsbury T&T Clark, 2016), 61. See also Craig Evans, "Nazareth," in *The Routledge Encyclopedia of the Historical Jesus,* ed. Craig Evans (New York: Routledge, 2008), 423.

164 See Donald Tzvi Ariel and Jean-Philippe Fontanille, *The Coins of*

Herod: A Modern Analysis and Die Classification (Boston: Brill, 2011).

165 See Blomberg, in *Jesus Under Fire*, chap. 1, Kindle; Cf. Markus Bock-muehl, *This Jesus: Martyr, Lord, Messiah*, (Downers Grove: Intervarsity Press, 1996), 70–71.

166 See ibid.

167 See Josephus, *Antiquities* 18.2.

168 See ibid.

169 See ibid.

170 See ibid., 18.5.2.

171 See ibid.

172 Ibid., 20.9.

173 Ibid., 18.3.3.

174 Tacitus, *Annals* 15.44.

175 Richard Bauckham, *Jesus and the Eyewitnesses: The Gospels as Eyewitness Testimony*, 1st ed. (Grand Rapids: Eerdmans Publishing, 2008), 486.

176 This line of reasoning is taken from William Lane Craig, *On Guard*, 186.

177 Tacitus, *Annals* 15.44; emphasis added.

178 Bart D. Ehrman, *The New Testament: A Historical Introduction to Early Christian Writings* (Cambridge: Oxford University Press, 2015), 212.

179 Flavius Josephus, *Antiquities of the Jews* 18.3.3

180 See Luke Timothy Johnson, *The Gospel According to Luke*, in *Sacra Pagina*, Vol. 3, ed. Daniel J. Harrington (Collegeville, MN: Liturgical Press, 1991), 113–114; Cf. Raymond Brown, *An Introduction to New Testament Christology* (New York: Paulist Press, 1994), 373–376; John P. Meier, *A Marginal Jew: Rethinking the Historical Jesus*, Vol. II., 592–593.

181 Josephus, *Antiquities of the Jews* 20.9.1

182 See Robert E. Van Voorst, *Jesus Outside the New Testament: An Introduction to the Ancient Evidence* (Grand Rapids: Eerdmans, 2000), 83.

183 John Dominic Crossan, *Jesus: A Revolutionary Biography* (San Francisco: HarperOne 1995), 145.

184 Bart Ehrman, *Did Jesus Exist? The Historical Argument for Jesus of Nazareth* (San Francisco: HarperOne, 2013), 4.

185 Tacitus, *Annals* 15.44; emphasis added.

186 William Lane Craig, *On Guard: Defending Your Faith with Reason and Precision*, 186.

187 This formulation of the argument is taken from Scott Sullivan, *Christ 101: The Evidence for Christianity: Study Manual* (Scott Sullivan, 2014), 96.

188 See Brant Pitre, *The Case for Jesus*, 143–145.

189 Ibid., 144; emphasis in original.

190 Daniel Boyarin, *The Jewish Gospels: The Story of the Jewish Christ* (New York: The New Press, 2012), 32–33. Quoted in Pitre, *The Case for Jesus,* 144.

191 Kreeft and Tacelli, *Handbook of Christian Apologetics,* 165.

192 Ibid.

193 For a thorough examination of the historicity of Jesus' miracles see John P. Meier, *A Marginal Jew: Rethinking the History Jesus,* Vol. II *Mentor, Message, and Miracles.* For a summary, see Robert J. Spitzer, *God So Loved the World: Clues to Our Transcendent Destiny from the Revelation of Jesus* (San Francisco: Ignatius Press, 2016), chap. 4.

194 C.S. Lewis, *Mere Christianity* (New York: Harper One, 2001), 52.

195 For an in-depth study see John P. Meier, *A Marginal Jew: Rethinking the History Jesus,* Vol. II *Mentor, Message, and Miracles,* chaps. 17–23.

196 With regard to Honi praying to God for rain, see Gary Habermas, "Did Jesus Perform Miracles," in *Jesus Under Fire,* chap. 5, Kindle. Cf. Josephus, *Antiquities of the Jews,* 14: 2, 1, in *Complete Works,* trans. William Whiston (Grand Rapids: Kregel, 1960). Concerning the detail about Honi drawing a circle in which he stood demanding rain from God see Habermas, in *Jesus Under Fire,* chap. 5, Kindle. Cf. *Mishnah,* Taanith 3: 8; C.K. Barrett, ed., *The New Testament Background: Selected Documents* (New York: Harper and Brothers, 1956), 150–51.

197 See Gary Habermas, "Did Jesus Perform Miracles," in *Jesus Under Fire,* chap. 5, Kindle. Cf. Graham H. Twelftree, *Jesus the Exorcist* (Peabody: Hendrickson, 1991); Graham Twelftree, *Jesus the Miracle Worker* (Downers Grove: InterVarsity Press, 1999); Edwin Yamauchi, "Magic or Miracle? Diseases, Demons and Exorcisms" in *Gospel Perspectives,* vol. 6, *The Miracles of Jesus,* eds. David Wenham and Craig Blomberg (Sheffield: JSOT, 1986), 89–183; Barry L. Blackburn, "'Miracle Working ΘΕΙΟΙ ΑΝΔΡΕΣ' in Hellenism (and Hellenistic Judaism)," *The Miracles of Jesus,* 185–218.

198 See Raymond Brown, *An Introduction to New Testament Christology* (New York: Paulist Press, 1994), 63. See also Habermas, in *Jesus Under Fire,* chap. 5, Kindle.

199 These two miracles may seem frivolous on the surface. But when read closely, it becomes clear that they are not frivolous. With regard to the coin in the fish's mouth, Jesus performs the miracle to avoid scandal. Had Jesus and Peter not paid the Temple tax they would have been viewed as impious. But, as Bible scholar A. Jones points out, by

performing the miracle Jesus "yields nothing to the principle ('the children are exempt') because the money does not come from the apostolic purse after all" ("The Gospel of Jesus Christ According to St. Matthew" in *A Catholic Commentary on Holy Scripture*, 883). Concerning the cursing of the fig tree (Mark 11:12-14), scholars suggest that it is to be understood as a "symbolic act or parable in action" (J.A. O'Flynn, "The Gospel of Jesus Christ According to St. Mark" in *A Catholic Commentary on Holy Scripture*, 992). This method of teaching, which often involved giving a warning, was not foreign to the Jews (see Isa. 20:1-6; Jer. 13:1-11; 27:1-11). We know that Jesus intended to perform a symbolic act because Mark tells us "it was not the season for figs" (Mark 14:13). But what was the lesson to be learned? Flynn explains, "The chief lesson of the incident is that those who fail to yield the fruit of good works which Christ seeks will be punished" ("The Gospel of Jesus Christ According to St. Mark" in *A Catholic Commentary on Holy Scripture*, 992). The lesson applied immediately to the Jews of the first-century who rejected Jesus. But it also has application for all time, especially for us as Christians. Flynn also notes that the cursing of the fig tree, and its subsequent withering, was intended to remind the apostles of Jesus' power. Jesus could have "withered" the Jews, but he chose to voluntarily submit himself to be taken to the cross.

200 Q (coming from the German *Quelle*, which means "source") is a hypothetical early written collection of Jesus' sayings translated into Greek. It is believed to have been a common source used by Matthew and Luke, but not Mark.

201 Robert J. Spitzer, *God So Loved the World*, 214.

202 John P. Meier, *A Marginal Jew: Rethinking the Historical Jesus,* Vol. 2 *Mentor, Message, and Miracles*, 969–970.

203 See Bart D. Ehrman, *Jesus, Apocalyptic Prophet of the New Millennium* (Oxford: Oxford University Press, USA, 1999), 160.

204 See Albert Schweitzer, *The Quest of the Historical Jesus*, trans. W. Montgomery (London: Adam and Charles Black, 1910), 239.

205 C.S. Lewis, "The World's Last Night" in *The World's Last Night: And Other Essays* (Fort Washington: Harvest Books, 2002), 98–99.

206 It's possible that Jesus' prophecy has application to his second coming at the end of time as well: "Just as there is a literal Jerusalem, therefore, which is already conquered figuratively, there is also another, spiritual Jerusalem, the church of Christ, which must be tested at the

end of the world and indeed is currently being tested. Therefore the signs of which the Lord spoke must be understood both spiritually and literally. Literally they speak of the destruction of Jerusalem, but spiritually they signify the trial of the church at the consummation of the age. Train your mind on both aspects then, on what occurred before Jerusalem was captured and on what will occur before the final trial of Christ's church" (*Incomplete Work on Matthew*, Homily 48). I am grateful to Jimmy Akin for providing me with this research.

207 For a book-length explanation of this interpretation, see David B. Currie, *What Jesus Really Said About the End of the World* (El Cajon: Catholic Answers Press, 2012).

208 See Eusebius, *Church History* 3.5.3.

209 See Josephus, *War of the Jews* 4.8.1.

210 Ibid., 4.4.5.

211 Ibid., 6.9.2.

212 See Josephus, *Antiquities of the Jews* 20.8.6.

213 See Josephus, *War of the Jews* 5.5.4.

214 See Josephus, *Antiquities of the Jews* 3.6.7.

215 Ibid., 3.7.81.

216 *Commentary on Luke*, Homily 139.

217 Fragment 266.

218 *Commentary on Matthew* 4.24.23–26.

219 C.S. Lewis, *The Great Divorce* (New York: Macmillan, 1971), 90.

220 See Edward Feser, "How to Go to Hell," October 29, 2016, http://edwardfeser.blogspot.com/2016/10/how-to-go-to-hell_29.html.

221 Aquinas, *Summa Theologiae, Suppl.* III:99:1.

222 As the late Jesuit philosopher Bernard Boedder explains, "A willful violation . . . of this right implies a malice which opposes itself to the foundation of all orders." Bernard Boedder, *Natural Theology* (Veritatis Splendor Publications, 2012), Bk. 3, chap. 2, Kindle.

223 Aquinas, *Summa Theologiae* I:104:4.

224 Peter Kreeft and Ronald Tacelli, *Handbook of Christian Apologetics*, 294.

225 Augustine, *The Confessions*, Bk. 1.

226 Pope St. John Paul II, General Audience of Wednesday 28 July 1999, www.vatican.va.

227 Bible scholar James D.G. Dunn's satirical remark embodies this view: "Gosh! So there are still serious scholars who put forward the view that the whole account of Jesus' doings and teachings are a later myth foisted on an unknown, obscure historical figure." James D.G.

Dunn, "Response to Robert M. Price," in *The Historical Jesus: Five Views*, eds. James K. Beilby and Paul Rhodes Eddy (Downers Grove, IL: InterVarsity Press, 2009), 94.

228 Mark Foreman, "Challenging the Zeitgeist Movie" in *Come Let Us Reason*, chap. 11, Kindle.

229 Mary Jo Sharp, "Does the Story of Jesus Mimic Pagan Mystery Stories?" in *Come Let Us Reason,* chap. 10, Kindle.

230 See Franz Cumont, *The Mysteries of Mithra,* trans. by Thomas J. McCormack (Chicago: Open Court), http://sacred-texts.com/cla/mom/index.htm. Accessed January 25, 2017.

231 John R. Hinnells, "Reflections on the Bull-Slaying Scene," in *Mithraic Studies,* vol. 2, 303–304.

232 Manfred Claus, *The Roman Cult of Mithras: The God and His Mysteries* (New York: Routledge, 2001), 7.

233 See Mary Jo Sharp, in *Come Let Us Reason,* chap. 10, Kindle. Cf. Roger Beck, "The Mysteries of Mithras: A New Account of Their Genesis," *Journal of Roman Studies* 88 (1998): 123; Ronald H. Nash, *The Gospel and the Greeks: Did the New Testament Borrow from Pagan Thought?* 2nd ed. (Phillipsburg: P&R Publishing, 2003).

234 See Mary Jo Sharp, in *Come Let Us Reason,* chap. 10, Kindle. Cf. Payam Nabarz, *The Mysteries of Mithras* (Rochester: Inner Traditions, 2005).

235 See Manfred Claus, *The Roman Cult of Mithras,* 62.

236 See Payam Nabarz, *The Mysteries of Mithras,* 19.

237 See ibid.

238 There are various traditions concerning Horus's birth. Plutarch records that Horus was the fruit of sexual intercourse between Osiris and Isis, Osiris's sister, in Osiris's mother's womb (Nut). According to another tradition Isis becomes pregnant with Horus from the golden phallus that she constructed for the dead corpse of Osiris. Osiris was the offspring of an adulterous affair between Nut, the sky-goddess, and Geb, the earth-god. For more details on these traditions, see Mary Jo Sharp, "Does the Story of Jesus Mimic Pagan Mystery Stories?" in *Come Let Us Reason,* chap. 10, Kindle.

239 Henri Frankfort, *Kingship and the Gods: A Study of Ancient Near Eastern Religion as the Integration of Society and Nature* (Chicago: Oriental Institute of the University of Chicago, 1962), 289. Quoted in Mary Jo Sharp, in *Come Let Us Reason,* chap. 10, Kindle.

240 *The Egyptian Book of the Dead,* trans. E. A. Wallis Budge (New York: Barnes & Noble, 2005 [1895]), 74. Quoted in Mary Jo Sharp, in

Come Let Us Reason, chap. 10, Kindle.

241 This list is taken from Mark Foreman, "Challenging the Zeitgeist Movie," in *Come Let Us Reason.*

242 Bart Ehrman, "Did Jesus Exist?" *Huffington Post,* May 20, 2012, https://www.huffingtonpost.com/bart-d-ehrman/did-jesus-exist_b_1349544.html.

243 CCC 643: "Christ's resurrection cannot be interpreted as something outside the physical order, and it is impossible not to acknowledge it as an historical fact."

244 For the quotations, see Gary R. Habermas and Michael R. Licona, *The Case for the Resurrection of Jesus* (Grand Rapids: Kregel Publications, 2004), chap. 3, Kindle.

245 See William Lane Craig, *The Son Rises: The Historical Evidence for the Resurrection of Jesus* (Eugene: Wipf and Stock Publishers, 1981), 47–48.

246 For more evidence on the historicity of the empty tomb see William Lane Craig, *The Son Rises,* chap. 3.

247 For a defense of this argument, see William Lane Craig, *The Son Rises,* 51–52. See also William Lane Craig, "Did Jesus Rise from the Dead" in *Jesus Under Fire: Modern Scholarship Reinvents the Historical Jesus,* chap. 6, Kindle.

248 The term glorious here refers to the unique powers of Jesus' resurrected body, such as freedom from the limitations of space (see John 20:19) and the ability to appear and disappear (see Luke 24:31). For a study on the glorious nature of Jesus' resurrected body, see Robert J. Spitzer, *God So Loved the World: Clues to Our Transcendent Destiny from the Revelation of Jesus* (San Francisco: Ignatius Press, 2016), chap. 4.

249 See Flavius Josephus, *Antiquities of the Jews,* 4.8.15. The atheist activist and historian Richard Carrier, in chapter 11 of his book *Not the Impossible Faith,* objects to this appeal to women. For his arguments and responses to them, see Karlo Broussard, "Why the Resurrection Was Not a Conspiracy," March 30, 2016, www.catholic.com.

250 See N.T. Wright, *The Resurrection of the Son of God* (Minneapolis: Fortress Press, 2003), 205.

251 See ibid.

252 The glorified state of Jesus' resurrected body is evident in his power to appear and disappear at will (John 20:19; Luke 24:31). We can also infer the glorified state of Jesus' resurrected body from St. Paul's teaching that our glorified bodies, which he describes as being imperishable and having glory (1 Cor. 15:42–44), will be similar to

Jesus' glorified body (1 Cor. 15:49).

253 See N.T. Wright, *The Resurrection of the Son of God,* 273.

254 See ibid., 78–82.

255 Sam Harris, "The Temple of Reason: Sam Harris on How Religion Puts the World At Risk," by Bethany Saltman, *The Sun,* September 2006, http://thesunmagazine.org/issues/369/the_temple_of_reason?print=all&url=issues/369/the_temple_of_reason&page=2.

256 Dinesh D'Souza, *What's So Great About Christianity* (Washington, DC: Regnery, 2007), 215.

257 Lactantius, *Divine Institutes*, 5.20, trans. William Fletcher, in Alexander Roberts and James Donaldson, eds., *Ante-Nicene Fathers*, Vol. 7, orig. 1886, online edition copyright (c) 2005 by K. Knight, available at http:// www.newadvent.org.

258 Hilary of Poitiers, "To Constantius," quoted in Lord Acton, "Political Thoughts on the Church," at 24. The edition is *Essays in Religion, Politics, and Morality,* ed. J. Rufus Fears, vol. 3 of *Selected Writings of Lord Acton* (Indianapolis: Liberty Classics, 1988).

259 Isidore of Pelusium, *Epistles*, 3.363, quoted in *Apologist, Saint John Chrysostom,* trans., Margaret A. Schatkin and Paul W. Harkins, vol. 73 of *The Fathers of the Church* (Washington, D.C.: Catholic University of America Press, 1985), 83, note 30.

260 Tertullian, "To Scapula," chap. 2, from *Tertullian: Apologetical Works,* and *Municius Felix: Octavius,* trans., Rudolph Arbesmann, Emily Joseph Daly, and Edwin A. Quain (New York: Fathers of the Church, 1950), 152.

261 John Chrysostom, *Discourse on Blessed Babylas and Against the Greeks,* 13, trans. Margaret A. Schatkin, in Schatkin and Harkins, eds., 83.

262 Athanasius, *History of the Arians*, 4.33, trans. John Henry Parker, in Philip Schaff and Henry Wace, *Nicene and Post-Nicene Fathers,* Second Series, vol. 4, orig. 1892, online edition copyright (c) 2005 by K. Knight, available at http://www.newadvent.org.

263 Alister McGrath, "Challenges from Atheism," in *Beyond Opinion: Living the Faith We Defend,* ed. Ravi Zacharias (Nashville: Thomas Nelson, 2007), 31.

264 Walter Jewell, "The Mark of Holiness," July 1, 1997, www.catholic.com.

265 Pope Benedict uses the word *performative* to describe Christianity's life-changing qualities in his encyclical *Spe Salvi* 2, November 30, 2007.

266 Christopher Kaczor, *The Big Myths About the Catholic Church* (San Francisco: Ignatius Press, 2012), 77–78.

267 See ibid., 77.

268 See Trent Horn, *Hard Sayings: A Catholic Approach to Answering Bible Difficulties* (San Diego: Catholics Answers Press, 2016), 405. Cf. Robert A.J. Gagnon, *The Bible and Homosexual Practice: Texts and Hermeneutics* (Nashville, TN: Abingdon Press, 2001), 368.

269 Henry Chadwick, *The Early Church*, revised. ed. (London: Penguin Books, 1993), 58–59. Quoted in Kaczor, *The Big Myths About the Catholic Church,* 78.

270 See Kaczor, *The Big Myths About the Catholic Church*, 71. Cf. Pope John Paul II, *Letter to Women* 3, June 29, 1995.

271 See ibid., 73. Cf. Pope John Paul II, *Letter to Women* 3, June 29, 1995.

272 See Fides Dossier, "The Roles of the Woman in the Life of the Church," *Catholic Culture*, https://www.catholicculture.org/culture/library/view.cfm?id=8422.

273 See Horn, *Hard Sayings,* 407. Cf. Pope Benedict XVI, General Audience, February 14, 2007, w2.vatican.va/content/benedict-xvi/en/audiences/2007/documents/hf_ben-xvi_aud_20070214.html.

274 See ibid., 407–408. Cf. Jimmy Akin, "Should Women Keep Silence in Church?," *National Catholic Register*, September 9, 2012, www.ncregister.com/blog/jimmy-akin/should-women-keep-silence-in-church#ixzz3UobGd8CH.

275 The question of why women can't be elevated to a clerical status usually arises at this point in the conversation. This topic goes beyond the scope of this chapter and book. For resources on this topic, see Manfred Hauke and David Kipp, *Women in the Priesthood: A Systematic Analysis in the Light of the Order of Creation and Redemption* (San Francisco: Ignatius Press, 1988), and Sara Butler, *The Catholic Priesthood and Women: A Guide to the Teaching of the Church* (Mundelein: Hillenbrand, 2007).

276 See Horn, *Hard Sayings,* 408. Cf. Ben Witherington, *Conflict and Community in Corinth: A Socio-rhetorical Commentary on 1 and 2 Corinthians* (Grand Rapids: Wm. B. Eerdmans, 1995), 276.

277 Witherington, *Conflict and Community in Corinth: A Socio-rhetorical Commentary on 1 and 2 Corinthians*, 276. Quoted in Horn, *Hard Sayings,* 408.

278 Edith Stein, "The Separate Vocations of Man and Woman According to Nature and Grace," in *Essays on Woman (The Collected Works of Edith Stein),* 2nd ed., trans. by Freda Mary Oben, Ph.D. (Washington: ICS Publications, 1996).

279 Richard Dawkins, "Is Science a Religion?", *The Humanist*, Jan–Feb

1997.

280 Julian Baginni, *Atheism: A Very Short Introduction* (New York: Oxford University Press, 2003), 32.

281 See ibid., 33.

282 See John Lennox, *Gunning for God: Why the New Atheists are Missing the Target* (Oxford: Lion Hudson, 2011), 44.

283 Paul Davies, "1995 Templeton Prize Address," https://www.firstthings.com/article/1995/08/003-physics-and-the-mind-of-god-the-templeton-prize-address-24.

284 Pope Emeritus Benedict XVI, General Audience 21 November 2012, https://w2.vatican.va/content/benedict-xvi/en/audiences/2012/documents/hf_ben-xvi_aud_20121121.html.

285 See Christopher Baglow, *Faith, Science and Reason*, 252.

286 Stanley Jaki, *Questions on Science and Religion* (Real View Books, 2004), 48.

287 Ibid., 49.

288 Ibid.

289 Augustine, *The Literal Meaning of Genesis* 15.29. Quoted in Trent Horn, *Hard Sayings,* 45.

290 Augustine, *The City of God* 11:6.

291 Origen, *De Principiis* 4.16.

292 Pope St. John Paul II, General Audience 7 November 1979, https://w2.vatican.va/content/john-paul-ii/en/audiences/1979/documents/hf_jp-ii_aud_19791107.html.

293 Christopher Hitchens, *God is not Great* (New York: Twelve Books, 2007), 110.

294 Bart Ehrman, *The Historical Jesus* (Chantilly: The Teaching Company, 2000), 90.

295 See Josephus, *Antiquities* 18.3.3.

296 See Tacitus, *Annals* 15.44.

297 See ibid.

298 See Michael Licona, *The Resurrection of Jesus: A New Historiographical Approach* (Downer's Grove: InterVarsity Press, 2010), 570. See also Licona, "Fish Tales: Bart Ehrman's Red Herrings and the Resurrection of Jesus," in *Come Let Us Reason,* chap. 9, Kindle. Cf. Suetonius, *Life of Nero* 38.

299 See ibid. Cf. Dio Cassius, *Roman History*, 62.16–17.

300 Trent Horn, *20 Answers: The Bible* (San Diego: Catholic Answers Press, 2016), 45.

301 Suetonius wrote in his biography of Caesar Augustus, "Having given as it were a summary of his life, I shall now take up its various phases one by one, *not in chronological order, but by categories*, to make the account clearer and more intelligible" (*Life of Augustus* 9; emphasis added).

302 Quoted in Eusebius, *Church History* 3.39.15.

303 See Karlo Broussard, "Preaching Forgiveness Versus Actually Forgiving," November 26, 2017, www.catholic.com.

304 See Craig Blomberg, *The Historical Reliability of the Gospels*, 2nd ed. (Downers Grove: Intervarsity Press, 2007), 157. Cf. Pitre, *The Case for Jesus*, 80–83.

305 Thucydides, *The Peloponnesian War*, chap. 1.22.1. Quoted in Brant Pitre, *The Case for Jesus*, 79–81.

306 Jonas Grethlein, *Experience and Teleology in Ancient Historiography: "Futures Past" from Herodotus to Augustine* (Cambridge: Cambridge University Press, 2014), 64.

307 Horn, *Hard Sayings*, 147.

308 See Horn, "Appendix: Has the Bible Been Corrupted?" in *Hard Sayings*, 335.

309 See Eusebius, *Church History* 1:6:7.

310 Craig Blomberg, *The Historical Reliability of the Gospels* (Downers Grove: InterVarsity Press, 1987), 10.

311 See Horn, *Hard Sayings*, 547.

312 See Matthew Ramage, *Dark Passages of the Bible: Engaging Scripture with Benedict XVI and Thomas Aquinas* (Washington, DC: Catholic University of America Press, 2013), chap. 5. See also Mark Giszczak, *Light on the Dark Passages of Scripture* (Huntington: Our Sunday Visitor, 2015), and Horn, *Hard Sayings,* 543.

313 Bible scholar Matthew Ramage writes, "If it seemed clear [to the ancient writer] that God wanted a certain battle won, and the tactics employed therein were successful, then God must have sanctioned or even directly willed these tactics." *Dark Passages of the Bible: Engaging Scripture with Benedict XVI and Thomas Aquinas*, 188. Quoted in Horn, *Hard Sayings,* 544.

314 See Horn, *Hard Sayings*, 544.

315 I do not intend to say here that all natural disasters are due to God's positive will. I only intend to say that it's possible that God can will a natural disaster or plague to bring about death, especially in cases of administering divine justice. Moreover, this doesn't contradict our treatment of physical evil in chapter seven because in such cases God

would not be willing evil as an end in and of itself, but only as a concomitant effect of willing the good of those things that bring about death due to their flourishing.

316 Aquinas, *Summa Theologiae* I–II:94:5, ad. 2; cf. I– II:100:8; II–II:154:2, ad. 2. Aquinas also addresses the subject in a similar manner in *De Malo*, 3:1, ad. 17; 15:1, ad. 8.

317 See Aquinas, *Summa Theologiae* II–II:58:1.

318 See Horn, *Hard Sayings*, chap. 24.

319 Jimmy Akin, "Blunt Commands in the Old Testament," August 2005, http://jimmyakin.com/2005/08/blunt_commands_.html. Quoted in Trent Horn, *Hardy Sayings,* 318.

320 See Jimmy Akin, "Hard Sayings of the Old Testament," February 2007, www.jimmyakin.com. Cf. Trent Horn, *Hard Sayings,* 318–319.

321 This example is taken from Fr. Robert J. Spitzer, "How do I reconcile an all-powerful creator with the God of the Judeo-Christian Bible?" *The Magis Center,* July 19, 2016, https://www.magiscenter.com/creator-god-judeo-christian-bible/.

322 Aquinas, *Summa Theologiae* I:75:5.

323 Jimmy Akin, "Blunt Commands in the Old Testament," www.jimmyakin.com.

324 Mark Giszczak, *Light on the Dark Passages of Scripture* (Huntington: Our Sunday Visitor, 2015), 39.

325 Aquinas, *Summa Theologiae* III:25:6.

326 Jerome, *Ad Riparium*, i, P.L., XXII, 907.

327 St. Jerome, Letter 109:3, http://www.newadvent.org/fathers/3001109.htm.

328 Aquinas, *Summa Theologiae* II–II:85:1.

329 Ibid.

330 G.K. Chesterton, *Heretics* in *The Collected Works of G.K. Chesterton,* vol. 1 (San Francisco: Ignatius Press, 1986), 87.

331 Michelle Arnold, "Rules, Rules, Rules," September 16, 2013, www.catholic.com.

332 The various points found in this strategy were taken from Jimmy Akin's book *A Daily Defense: 365 Days (Plus one) To Becoming a Better Apologist* (El Cajon: Catholic Answers Press, 2016), 87.

333 G.K. Chesterton, *What's Wrong With the World* in *The Collected Works of G.K. Chesterton,* vol. 4 (San Francisco: Ignatius Press, 1987), 166–167.

334 Barna Group, "Six Reasons Why Young Christians Leave Church," www.barna.com.

335 See Aquinas, *Summa Theologiae* I–II:94:2.

336 See Karlo Broussard, "Bringing Sanity to Sex: Part I," February 8, 2017, www.catholic.com.

337 See Karlo Broussard, "Bringing Sanity to Sex: Part II," February 15, 2017, www.catholic.com.

338 St. Augustine, Letter 211:11, http://www.newadvent.org/fathers/1102211.htm.

339 Statement made en route to Portugal. Quoted in "Pope Faults Church in Abuse," *Los Angeles Times,* May 12, 2010, www.pressreader.com/usa/los-angeles-times/20100512/283463547524355.

340 Ibid.

341 Benedict XVI, *Pastoral Letter of the Holy Father Pope Benedict XVI to the Catholics in Ireland,* http://w2.vatican.va/content/benedict-xvi/en/letters/2010/documents/hf_ben-xvi_let_20100319_church-ireland.html.

342 Ibid.

343 United States Conference of Catholic Bishops, "Charter for the Protection of Children and Young People," http://www.usccb.org/issues-and-action/child-and-youth-protection/upload/Charter-for-the-Protection-of-Children-and-Young-People-revised-2011.pdf.

344 See Elisabetta Povoledo and Laurie Goodstein, "Pope Creates Tribunal for Bishop Negligence in Child Sexual Abuse Cases," *The New York Times,* June 10, 2015, www.nytimes.com/2015/06/11/world/europe/pope-creates-tribunal-for-bishop-negligence-in-child-sexual-abuse-cases.html?_r=0.

345 See David Gibson, "10 Years After Catholic Sex Abuse Reforms, What's Changed?," *Washington Post,* June 6, 2012, www.washingtonpost.com/national/on-faith/10-years-after-catholic-sex-abuse-reforms-whats-changed/2012/06/06/gJQAQMjOJV_story.html.

346 See John Jay College of Criminal Justice, "The Nature and Scope of the Problem of Sexual Abuse of Minors by Catholic Priests and Deacons in the United States," www.usccb.org/issues-and-action/child-and-youth-protection/upload/The-Nature-and-Scope-of-Sexual-Abuse-of-Minors-by-Catholic-Priests-and-Deacons-in-the-United-States-1950-2002.pdf.

347 Philip Jenkins, *Pedophiles and Priests* (Oxford: Oxford University Press, 1996), 50–51.

348 See Rachel Sturtz, "Unprotected," www.outsideonline.com. Cf. "The Worst Offenders," www.outsideonline.com.

349 See "Penn State Child Sex Abuse Scandal," en.wikipedia.org.

350 See Jen Kirby, "The sex abuse scandal surrounding USA Gymnastics team doctor Larry Nassar, explained," February 8, 2018, www.vox.com.

351 Pope Emeritus Benedict XVI, Mass Homily on the Solemnity of the Sacred Heart of Jesus 11 June 2010, http://w2.vatican.va/content/benedict-xvi/en/homilies/2010/documents/hf_ben-xvi_hom_20100611_concl-anno-sac.html.

352 Sarah Silverman, "Sell the Vatican, Feed the World," online video, October 10, 2009, https://www.youtube.com/watch?v=3bObItmxAGc.

353 See "Economy of Vatican City," en.wikipedia.org. Cf. *CIA—The World Factbook*, cia.gov, retrieved on August 1, 2017.

354 See "Annual Financials for Starbucks Corp.," https://www.marketwatch.com/investing/stock/sbux/financials.

355 See "The Catholic Church in America: Earthly Concerns," *The Economist*, August 18, 2012, http://www.economist.com/node/21560536.

356 See ibid.

357 See "Company continues to deliver on key strategic priorities," https://news.walmart.com/news-archive/2016/02/18/walmart-reports-q4-adjusted-eps-of-149-fiscal-year-2016-adjusted-eps-of-459.

358 See Michael Tanner, "The American Welfare State: How We Spend Nearly $1 Trillion a Year Fighting Poverty—and Fail," in *Policy Analysis*, no. 694, April 11, 2012, https://object.cato.org/sites/cato.org/files/pubs/pdf/PA694.pdf. Cf. usgovernmentspending.com, https://www.usgovernmentspending.com/welfare_spending

359 See "The 100 Largest U.S. Charities 2017 Ranking," *Forbes*, https://www.forbes.com/top-charities/list/#tab:rank.

360 See William P. Barrett, "The Largest Charities for 2016," *Forbes*, December 14, 2016, https://www.forbes.com/sites/williampbarrett/2016/12/14/the-largest-u-s-charities-for-2016/.

361 See Tony Spence, "Catholic Charities USA makes top 10 in Philanthropy 400," October 31, 2011, https://cnsblog.wordpress.com/2011/10/31/catholic-charities-usa-makes-top-10-in-philanthropy-400/.

362 David Paton, "The World's Biggest Charity," *Catholic Herald*, February 16, 2017, www.catholicherald.co.uk.

363 St. John Chrysostom, *Homilies on the Statues*, Homily 2:15, http://www.newadvent.org/fathers/190102.htm.

364 Steven Morris, "Abortion: Why the Religious Right is Wrong," https://ffrf.org/about/getting-acquainted/item/16916-abortion-why-the-religious-right-is-wrong.

365 Pope John Paul II, Address to the Participants at the Study Confer-

ence on "The Right to Life and Europe", 18 December 1987: *Insegnamenti*, X, 3 (1987), 1446–1447. Quoted in Pope John Paul II, *Evangelium Vitae* 20, www.vatican.va.

366 See Mary Davenport, "Major Study Links Suicide and Other Mental Health Problems to Abortion," September 1, 2011, http://www.americanthinker.com/blog/2011/09/major_study_links_suicide_and_other_mental_health_problems_to_abortion.html. Cf. Priscilla K. Coleman, "Abortion and mental health: quantitative synthesis and analysis of research published 1995–2009," *The British Journal of Psychiatry* 199, no. 3 (August 2011): 180–186.

367 Estimates vary as to how common PAS is. Studies aligned with pro-choice-leaning groups, such as Planned Parenthood, suggest it hardly exists at all, whereas studies from pro-life-leaning groups suggest it's very common. Given how contrary to nature it is to have your biological child killed and evacuated from your womb, it at least stands to reason that for some women it will have negative psychological consequences. Even some pro-choice writers recognize this, such as the feminist icon Naomi Wolf who recommends a period of "grief" after abortion to process its moral gravity. See https://lib.tcu.edu/staff/bellinger/abortion/Wolf-our-bodies.pdf.

368 See Susan Harlap and A. Michael Davies, "Late Sequelae of Induced Abortion: Complications and Outcome of Pregnancy and Labor," *American Journal of Epidemiology* 102 (1975 September 1): 217–224. The abstract of the study, which summarizes the findings, can be found at https://academic.oup.com/aje/article-abstract/102/3/217/168548/LATE-SEQUELAE-OF-INDUCED-ABORTION-COMPLICATIONS?redirectedFrom=fulltext. The study covered 11,057 pregnancies of West Jerusalem mothers who were interviewed during pregnancy. Out of the 11,057, 752 reported having one or more induced abortions in the past. The following is what they discovered about these women during the pregnancy at the time of the interview and subsequent to it: 1) More likely to report bleeding in each of the first three months of the pregnancy of the interview; 2) Subsequently found they were less likely to have a normal delivery; 3) Subsequently found more of them needed manual removal of the placenta or other intervention in the third stage of labor; 4) Early neonatal (first seven days after birth) death was doubled; 5) Late neonatal (7–28 days after birth) deaths had a three to four-fold increase; 6) Significant increase in the frequency of low birth weight com-

pared to births in which there was no history of previous abortion; 7) Increases in major and minor congenital malformations.

369 See Dimitrio Trichopoulos et al, "Induced Abortion & Secondary Infertility," *British Journal of Obstetrics and Gynaecology* 83 (August 1976): 645–650. The study found secondary infertility to be three to four times higher for women who have had an abortion than those who hadn't.

370 See Burkman et al., "Culture and Treatment Results in Endometritis Following Elective Abortion," *American Journal of Obstetrics and Gynecology* 128, no. 5 (1977): 556–559. The study shows that 5.2 percent of women who had an abortion in their first trimester have genital tract infection. It shows 18.5 percent for those performed in the mid-trimester.

371 Studies show that women with a history of one abortion face a 2.3 times higher risk compared to women with no history of an abortion. Women with two or more abortions face a 4.92 relative risk. See "Abortion Risks: A List of Physical Complications Related to Abortion," *Elliot Institute,* www.afterabortion.org. Cf. M-G, Le, et al., "Oral Contraceptive Use and Breast or Cervical Cancer: Preliminary Results of a French Case-Control Study," in *Hormones and Sexual Factors in Human Cancer Etiology,* ed. JP Wolff, et al., (New York: Excerpta Medica, 1984), 139–147; F. Parazzini, et al., "Reproductive Factors and the Risk of Invasive and Intraepithelial Cervical Neoplasia," in *British Journal of Cancer* 59 (1989): 805–809; H.L. Stewart, et al., "Epidemiology of Cancers of the Uterine Cervix and Corpus, Breast and Ovary in Israel and New York City," in *Journal of the National Cancer Institute* 37, no. 1:1–96; I. Fujimoto, et al., "Epidemiologic Study of Carcinoma in Situ of the Cervix," in *Journal of Reproductive Medicine* 30, no. 7 (July 1985): 535; N. Weiss, "Events of Reproductive Life and the Incidence of Epithelial Ovarian Cancer," in *American Journal of Epidemiology* 117, no. 2 (1983): 128–139; V. Beral, et al., "Does Pregnancy Protect Against Ovarian Cancer," in *The Lancet* (20 May 1978): 1083–1087; C. LaVecchia, et al., "Reproductive Factors and the Risk of Hepatocellular Carcinoma in Women," in *International Journal of Cancer* 52 (1992): 351.

372 See Barrett et al., "Induced Abortion, A Risk Factor for Placenta Previa," in *American Journal of Obstetrics and Gynaecology* 141, no. 7 (1 December 1981): 769–772.

373 See Levin, et.al., "Ectopic Pregnancy and Prior Induced Abortion," in *American Journal of Public Health* 72 (1982): 253; Atrash, et.al., "Ectopic Pregnancy in the United States," Center for Disease Control

MMRW 35, no. 29 (1970–1983).

374 St. Teresa of Calcutta, Speech at 1994 National Prayer Breakfast in Washington, transcript available at http://www.priestsforlife.org/brochures/mtspeech.html.

375 Aristotle, *Metaphysics*, IV.3.

376 John Rickaby, *First Principles of Knowledge* (Veritatis Splendor Publications, 2012), chap. 8, Kindle.

377 Quentin Smith, *Theism, Atheism, and Big Bang Cosmology* (Oxford: Clarendon, 1993), 135.

378 From debate between Richard Dawkins and Cardinal George Pell. Available online at https://www.youtube.com/watch?v=tD1QHO_AVZA&feature=youtu.be&t=21m14s.

379 J.L. Mackie, *The Miracle of Theism* (Oxford: Clarendon, 1982), 94.

380 This example is taken from Michael Augros, *Who Designed the Designer? A Rediscovered Path to God's Existence* (San Francisco: Ignatius Press, 2015), Appendix 2.

381 This example is taken from Scott Sullivan, *St. Thomas Aquinas and the Principle of Sufficient Reason* (Conroe: Classical Theist Press, 2015), 217.

382 David Albert, "On the Origin of Everything: 'A Universe from Nothing' by Lawrence Krauss," *The New York Times*, March 23, 2012, http://www.nytimes.com/2012/03/25/books/review/a-universe-from-nothing-by-lawrence-m-krauss.html.

383 I am using "possible being" here different than Thomas Aquinas uses it in his Third Way in the *Summa Theologiae*. It is commonly held by Thomistic scholars that what Aquinas means by possible beings is corruptible beings. My use of possible beings here includes corruptible beings, but also applies to incorruptible beings whose essence and existence are still distinct.

384 Joseph Owens, *An Elementary Christian Metaphysics* (Milwaukee: Bruce Publishing Company, 1963), 71.

385 St. Augustine affirms that the blessed in heaven have free will in his work *The City of God*: "Neither are we to suppose that because sin shall have no power to delight them [i.e., the redeemed], free will must be withdrawn. It will, on the contrary, be all the more truly free, because set free from delight in sinning to take unfailing delight in not sinning. For the first freedom of will which man received when he was created upright consisted in an ability not to sin, but also in an ability to sin; whereas this last freedom of will shall be superior, inasmuch as it shall not be able to sin." Augustine, *City*

of God, ed. Philip Schaff, trans. Marcus Dods (Grand Rapids: Christian Classics Ethereal Library) XXII.30, http://www.ccel.org/ccel/schaff/npnf102.html. Quoted in Timothy Pawl and Kevin Timpe, "Incompatibilism, Sin, and Free Will in Heaven," *Faith and Philosophy* 26, no. 4 (October 2009): 396–417. For other affirmations of this teaching see Thomas Aquinas, *Summa Theologiae*, III:18;4; and Anselm, *On Free Will and De Concordia*, I:6. Both of these latter works can be found in *Anselm of Canterbury: The Major Works*, eds. Brian Davies and Gill Evans (Oxford: Oxford University Press, 1998). It's interesting to note that there doesn't seem to be any ecumenical council that has taught whether the blessed in heaven will be free; hence the language in the text "it is commonly believed." Perhaps we could further support this common belief with Revelation 6:9 where the souls of the martyrs under the altar cry out for God to avenge their blood on their enemies on earth. If they didn't have the exercise of free will, it doesn't seem that they would be able to cry out for God's justice. Moreover, in Revelation 5:8–10 we read how twenty-four presbyters offer to the lamb, Jesus, the prayers of Christians on earth in the form of incense. The total absence of free will in heaven doesn't seem to jibe with the saints engaging in intercessory prayer for us here on earth.

386 Thomas Aquinas, *On Evil*, 16:5.

387 See Aquinas, *Summa Theologiae* I:82:1.

388 See ibid.

389 See ibid., I–II:17:2 and I–II:17:5, ad. 1.

390 Thomas Aquinas, *Disputed Questions on Truth*, 22:6.

391 Joyce, *Principles of Natural Theology*, chap. 17, Kindle.

392 This line of reasoning is taken from Jimmy Akin, "Will We Have Free Will in Heaven?", *National Catholic Register*, January 20, 2013, www.ncregister.com.

393 Pope John Paul II, *Redemptor Hominis* 10.

394 Aquinas, *Summa Theologiae* I–II:90:4.

395 Ibid., I–II:90:2.

396 See ibid., I:5:1.

397 Aquinas, *Summa Theologiae* I–II.93.4; emphasis added.

398 McCabe, *God and Evil in the Theology of St. Thomas Aquinas*, chap. 5, Kindle.

399 Ibid.

400 See Aquinas, *Summa Theologiae* I:5:1.

401 See ibid., I–II;94:3.
402 See McCabe, *God and Evil in the Theology of St. Thomas Aquinas,* chap. 5, Kindle.
403 Bernard Boedder, *Natural Theology*, Bk. 3, chap.2, Kindle.

About the Author

Karlo Broussard is a staff apologist and speaker for Catholic Answers. He travels the country giving talks on apologetics, biblical studies, theology, and philosophy, and is a regular guest on the radio program Catholic Answers Live. You can book Karlo for a speaking event by contacting Catholic Answers at 619-387-7200. You can also view Karlo's videos at KarloBroussard.com. A native of Southern Louisiana, Karlo now resides in Southern California with his wife and five children.

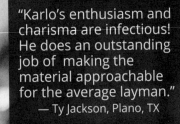